WORD RECOGNITION

WORD RECOGNITION

THE WHY AND THE HOW

By

PATRICK GROFF

Professor of Education
San Diego State University
San Diego, California

and

DOROTHY Z. SEYMOUR

Educational Consultant

CHARLES C THOMAS • PUBLISHER
Springfield • Illinois • U.S.A.

Published and Distributed Throughout the World by

CHARLES C THOMAS • PUBLISHER
2600 South First Street
Springfield, Illinois 62794-9265

© *1987 by* CHARLES C THOMAS • PUBLISHER

ISBN 0-398-05322-7

Library of Congress Catalog Card Number: 86-30171

Printed in the United States of America
SC-R-3

Library of Congress Cataloging-in-Publication Data

Groff, Patrick J.
  Word recognition.

  Bibliography: p.
  Includes index.
  1. Word recognition.   2. Reading (Elementary)—
United States—Phonetic method.   3. English language—
Study and teaching (Elementary)—United States.
I. Seymour, Dorothy Z.   II. Title.
LB15736.G76   1987   372.4'144   86-30171
ISBN 0-398-05322-7

INTRODUCTION

At the beginning of this book on teaching children how to recognize written words, we want to stress that the ability to recognize single, separate, or isolated words is not the ultimate goal of reading instruction. This text does, of course, emphasize the importance of children's acquisition of word recognition skills. These skills are indeed an impressive and fundamental aspect of learning to read. As Perfetti (1985, p. 13) notes: "The ability to decode words consistently — not by chance — is the essential reading process."

Nonetheless, the true "game" of reading is the comprehension of written material. Recognizing individual words is "something like hitting balls over the fence in batting practice" (p. 13). All baseball fans will agree that this accomplishment is far more difficult for players once the real game begins. The same relationship pertains for word recognition and reading comprehension.

If the development of reading comprehension and not word recognition is the main goal of reading instruction, how does word recognition teaching contribute to this objective? First, let us examine what reading comprehension is and the way word recognition fits into it.

Reading Comprehension

The main purposes of reading instruction are to help students to understand, and to recall or remember, written material, or to utilize it by making applications of it or inferences about it. To *understand* a piece of written material a reader must be able to reproduce what its author intended it to mean. A child fails to understand a poem, for instance, if he or she thinks it is funny or about real-life animals when its author intended it to be a serious comment in the form of an allegory.

This illustration demonstrates that readers' understanding of written material depends heavily on their knowledge of its style and form, and on their interest in and knowledge of its subject matter, as well as the purpose for which readers perceive they are reading it. If readers are unfamiliar with the vocabulary an author uses, for example, there can be little chance they will understand the information the author intended to convey. Readers' attitudes toward the material to be read, whether these are negative or positive, also have an effect on their ability to read it. Advice on ways to help children use their background knowledge and experiences (their *schema*) to better understand written materials is now available (Readence, Bean & Baldwin, 1981; Anderson 1984).

While understanding that the meaning of written materials requires that the reader grasp clearly what their authors intended to say, it is observable, however, that "there certainly is no universal agreement as to what exactly comprehension is" (Searfoss & Readence, 1985, p. 236). Even skilled readers of written material will disagree among themselves on what specifically its author intended to say. This disagreement becomes increasingly frequent with the reading of poetry or other forms of literature that use figurative language. The only reasonable definition one can make of what an understanding of written material is, therefore, is that it is what a consensus of mature, intelligent, experienced, and unbiased readers take it to mean.

Reading is also done to *recall or remember information.* Students at all levels of schooling are intimately familiar with this aspect of reading. "Studying is a special form of reading," say Anderson and Armbruster (1984, p. 657). Anyone who has read material in preparation for taking a test on it would agree.

Closely related to understanding and recall of reading are making *applications* of what is read. Giving answers to the questions on a test of the contents of a textbook would be a prime example of the application of understanding and recall.

Applying information we gain through reading is also widespread out of school. Workers at all levels from the professional to the blue collar, constantly apply information they have gained from the material they have read. The success of self-help books on marriage, child-raising, and remodeling the bathroom illustrates the need that society in general has for written information that it can understand and apply to the solution of personal problems.

The final aspect of reading comprehension, *making inferences,* is on the one hand necessary for understanding and yet often goes beyond a simple reproduction of what an author stated in a written passage. The need for a reader to make an inference about written material depends on the material's author. If authors present vast amounts of explicit, factual material in a redundant style, there will be relatively little need for the reader to infer missing information. If, however, authors assume that their audiences have a great deal of stored background knowledge or experience on the subject at hand, they will often write tersely and in an implicit way (e.g. use figurative language).

Even when they process easy-to-read material, readers will infer information that is not explicitly given by an author. For example, in the sentence, *Greg dug a hole near the tree,* the child can infer, probably correctly, many bits of information: Greg used a shovel, he dug during daylight hours, the location of the hole had something to do with the tree, he was old enough to use a shovel, and so on.

Making inferences is also a basic part of what is called *critical reading.* In critical reading one reads, first, to understand what an author intended to say. Then one makes judgements as to logic, truth, thoroughness, utility, recency, and so on, of the material. Critical reading by its very nature is a group effort in that critical readers must first agree among themselves what its author intended the content of a piece of written material to say. If they can not make this communal understanding of its meaning, that is, if they understand it differently they cannot make critical judgements of it. If, for example, a student believes that a written passage is the description of the behavior of real-life animals rather than an allegory, he or she could not read this material critically. Thus, to encourage children to make personal or eccentric decisions as to what an author intended to say denies for them the opportunity of reading critically.

The ability to do critical reading is much affected by readers' ability to think about what they are thinking about (their *metacognition*). Metacognition in reading is the ability to be aware of the way one is thinking or should be thinking when reading, which includes the testing, revising, evaluating, and remediating of one's thinking strategies. Helping children focus on metacognition as they try to comprehend written material "may help teachers improve their teaching of reading comprehension more than anything else" (Ekwall & Shanker, 1985, p. 214). There are now a number of sources that teachers can consult for help in this respect (Ambruster & Brown, 1984; Yaden & Templeton, 1986).

This brief description of the elements of reading indicates that understanding, remembering or recall, and making inferences and applications of written material are all interrelated aspects of reading comprehension. The understanding of what an author intended to say is the basis for reading comprehension. As understanding constitutes the foundation for successful comprehension, so is word recognition the key element for understanding written material. Research indicates clearly that "word recognition is the foundation of the reading process" (Gough, 1984, p. 225). No other factor relates as closely to reading comprehension as does word recognition (Hammill & McNutt, 1981). When we teach word recognition we give children the basis for understanding written materials.

Aspects of Word Recognition

To learn to recognize written words requires that the child develop four supportive skills. First, and foremost, children must learn to *decode* written words. By this we mean that they must learn how to recognize letters and how to convert the letters of a word into speech sounds (*phonemes*). The relationship between the phonemes of a word and the way it is written or spelled is often called *phonics*. In chapters to follow in this book we will describe phonics in a detailed way and explain how it should be taught.

Second, word recognition is facilitated when a reader can break multisyllabic words into separate syllables, and then use phonics skills to decode these word-parts. The contribution that the syllabication of written words makes to word recognition has been a controversial issue in reading instruction (Groff, 1981). A proposal for teaching syllabication for reading instruction that overcomes previous objections to it will be presented in Chapter 5.

Third, the context of the sentence in which a particular word rests aids its recognition. Sometimes the content of a sentence serves this function very effectively, for example, in recognizing the word *lamb* in *Mary had a little lamb*. Sometimes context fails to work well, for example, in recognizing the word *geode* in *Mary had a little geode*. The usefulness and limitations of context cues in word recognition are discussed in Chapter 9.

Fourth, to recognize words efficiently the reader needs to share with an author a common conception of the meanings of the words the author uses. In the beginning stages of reading instruction the common apprehension of the meanings of words by readers and authors is highly likely. The writer of the sentence, *Mary had a little lamb,* for example, is relatively certain that his or her readers will know the meaning of *lamb* as the word is used in this sentence. As reading instruction progresses through the grades of school, however, the problems of word meaning pose a greater and greater handicap to students' recognition of written words. The writer of *Mary had a little geode* would have had to carefully prepare his or her readers for its appearance if the word was to be recognized by them. The development of children's knowledge of special words like *geode* will be treated only briefly in this book, not because words that occur with relatively low frequency in print are insignificant, but because this book emphasizes beginning instruction in word recognition rather than vocabulary building. Limitations in the size and purpose of this book allow for only a minor consideration of ways to develop children's understanding of the meanings of words. There are modern books on this topic that deal with it in detail (Johnson & Pearson, 1978).

Phonics and Word Recognition

We do need to discuss why phonics should be taught because this has been and is a controversial educational issue (Groff, 1986). The emphasis put on phonics over the years has waxed and waned. In the 1930s and 1940s, for instance, experts in reading instruction were advising teachers to use an "incidental" approach to phonics to make use of the knowledge of the relationship between the speech sounds of our language and the manner in which these sounds are written. It was said that if nothing else seems to help a child to learn to read, then the teacher should turn to phonics. During this period reading experts published many erroneous notions about English sounds and their spellings with no fear of rebuke from linguists who were, by and large, uninterested in the question of phonics instruction.

By the middle 1950s this "incidental" phonics methodology was coming under increasingly heavy attack. In his best-selling book, *Why Johnny Can't Read,* Rudolf Flesch (1955) claimed that virtually no phonics was being taught in the elementary school. Although this was an exaggeration, it was true enough for the book to receive widespread acclaim from disgruntled parents and other school critics, though not from the reading experts of the time.

It was not until the late 1960s that a more thorough and scientific study of phonics than Flesch's appeared. In *Learning to Read: The Great Debate,* Jeanne Chall (1967) examined the pertinent research on the effectiveness of "code-emphasis" (phonics) methods as opposed to "meaning-enphasis" methods in teaching children to read. Chall found that phonics methods bring superior results not only in word recognition but in reading comprehension as well. Unlike Flesch's book, which was dismissed as poorly documented, Chall's scholarly work has had a much greater influence. In 1983 Chall reviewed all the pertinent research on this issue up to that date. She found that "the research support seems to be even stronger than it was in 1967" for phonics teaching (p. 43). The following year Chall and Conrad (1984) reported that heavier and more direct phonics emphasis is supported by research. They also observed that basal readers of the 1970s and early 1980s contained stronger phonics programs than did comparable texts of the 1950s and 1960s. Such changes "appear to have resulted in observable improvements in the reading achievement scores of students in the early elementary grades" (p. 212).

Despite Chall's conclusions some reading experts object to teaching phonics of any variety or degree. For example, Smith (1973, p. 186) declares that "there is absolutely no evidence that he [a child] could ever actually use it [phonics] in the process of reading". He maintains that phonics is far too complex and unreliable to be used as a tool for identifying unrecognized words (Smith, 1978). Other opponents of phonics instruction say that it is "the key to all failures in learning to read." Phonics "is a trap, a poisoned apple," Ferreiro and Teberosky (1982, p. 276) contend.

This very short history of phonics and antiphonics shows that conflicts over phonics continue. Despite such controversies, however, there is general acceptance of phonics due to its support from research. Phonics teaching does, in fact, offer the child significant help in learning to read. The research on the teaching of reading makes this clear. As Gibson (1975, p. 298) puts it, "The heart of learning to read would seem to be the process of mapping written words and letters to the spoken language; a process of translating or matching one symbol system to another." Gurren and Hughes' (1965) examination of twenty-two comparisons of various uses of phonics in teaching reading resulted in a clear statement that early and intensive phonics instruction tends to produce superior reading achievement.

Support for Chall's conclusions has come as well from the twenty-seven First Grade Reading Studies (Stauffer 1967). These studies were funded by the United States Department of Education and were designed to test the relative effectiveness of different approaches to first-grade reading instruction. The most significant finding of these studies, in our estimation, was the superior results found for *code-emphasis approaches* (using Chall's terminology). In the great majority of cases when a code-emphasis approach was compared to the traditional basal-reader approach, the former produced significantly better results.

This advantage for code-emphasis learning continued through the second grade. In his review of the results of the second-grade phase of this government-sponsored research, Dykstra concluded: "Early and relatively intensive teaching of sound-symbol [sound-letter] correspondences appears to be highly related to word recognition achievement at the end of second grade" (1968). Not only did these studies show the superiority of the phonics emphasis approaches over that of the traditional basal reader in reading achievement, "all three [phonics emphasis] programs produced significantly superior spellers after two years of instruction" (Dykstra 1968).

Recently two publications of the United States Department of Education commented favorably on the need for phonics teaching. The first of these volumes (Anderson, et al., 1985) asks, "What does research indicate about the effectiveness of phonics instruction? Classroom research shows that, on the average, children who are taught phonics get off to a better start in learning to read than children who are not taught phonics. The advantage is most apparent on tests of word identification, though children in programs in which phonics gets a heavy stress also do better on tests of sentence and story comprehension, particularly in the early grades" (p. 37). Some reading experts have contended that phonics instruction will interfere with the development of children's abilities to comprehend written material. It appears, quite to the contrary, that phonics provides a means for the child when reading to hold individual words in his or her memory until they can be understood. Phonics thus "plays a critical role in the comprehension of printed connected discourse by providing the reader with a strategy for maintaining in memory the wording of, for example, a sentence long enough for that sentence to be comprehended" (Barron, 1978, p. 36).

The second recent government publication (Finn, 1986) agrees that pupils have an advantage in learning to read if they are taught phonics. In this regard Groff (in press) found more than a hundred surveys of the research on phonics that attest to its value to learners of reading. It is reasonable, therefore, to conclude that "the message is clear: if you want to improve word-identification ability, teach phonics" (Johnson & Baumann, 1984, p. 595). As Popp (1975) and Forman (1977) note, publishers of basal reader series had adjusted their reading programs in light of the findings about phonics even before these latest reports on its effectiveness emerged.

The research indicates we cannot merely say that children should learn phonics. To the contrary, the indications are they must learn it if they are to recognize words. A study of the influence of phonics from kindergarten though high school helps make this clear. The findings of this study indicated that the "simple phonological skills are significantly and substantially related to reading and spelling performance through high school. Poor readers have failed to master these skills at the syllable level at all grades" (Calfee, Lindamood, & Lindamood 1973, p. 298) The degree to which children are successful in word recognition thus depends to a large part on their success in learning phonics. Accordingly, the teacher of reading cannot settle for less than a good background of phonics information and an access to many details about ways to conduct phonics lessons.

REFERENCES

Anderson, R.C. (1984). Role of the reader's schema in comprehension, learning, and memory. In R. C. Anderson, J. Osborn and R. J. Tierney (Eds.), *Learning to read in American schools: Basal readers and content texts.* Hillsdale, NJ: Lawrence Erlbaum.

Anderson, R. C., et al. (1985). *Becoming a nation of readers: The report of the Commission on Reading.* Washington, DC: U. S. Department of Education.

Anderson, T. H., & Armbruster, B. B. (1984). Studying. In P. D. Pearson (Ed.), *Handbook of reading research.* New York, NY: Longmans.

Armbruster, B. B., & Brown, A. C. (1984). Learning from reading: The role of metacognition. In R. C. Anderson, J. Osborne and R. J. Tierney (Eds.), *Learning to read in American schools: Basal readers and content texts.* Hillsdale, NJ: Lawrence Erlbaum.

Barron, R. W. (1978). Access to the meanings of printed words: Some implications for reading and for learning to read. In F. B. Murray (Ed.). *The recognition of words.* Newark, DE: International Reading Association.

Calfee, R.C., Lindamood, P. & Lindamood, C. (1973). Acoustic-phonic skills in reading: kindergarten through twelfth grade. *Journal of Educational Psychology,* 64, 293–298.

Chall, J.S. (1967; 1983). *Learning to read: The great debate.* New York, NY: McGraw-Hill.

Chall, J.S., & Conrad, S.S. (1984). Resources and their use for reading instruction. In A.C. Purves & O. Niles (Eds.), *Becoming readers in a complex society. Eighty-third yearbook of the National Society for the Study of Education,* I. Chicago; IL: NSSE.

Dykstra, R. (1968). Summary of the second grade phase of the Cooperative research program in primary reading instruction. *Reading Research Quarterly,* 4, 49–70.

Ekwall, E. E., & Shanker, J. L. (1985). *Teaching reading in the elementary school.* Columbus, OH: Charles E. Merrill.

Ferreiro, E., & Teberosky, A. (1982). *Literacy before schooling.* Exeter, NH: Heinemann.

Finn, C. E. (1986). *What works: Research about teaching and learning.* Washington, DC: U.S. Department of Education.

Flesch, R. (1955). *Why Johnny can't read.* New York, NY: Harper.

Forman, L. A. (1977). *Word attack emphasis in three basal reading systems during the 1930's, 1950's and 1970's in first grade.* Master's thesis, Rutgers University.

Gibson, E. J. (1975). Theory-based research on reading and its implications. In J.B. Carroll & J.S. Chall (Eds.), *Toward a literate society.* New York, NY: McGraw-Hill.

Gough, P. B. (1984). Word recognition. In P. D. Pearson (Ed.), *Handbook of reading research.* New York, NY: Longman.

Groff, P. (1981). Teaching reading by syllables. *Reading Teacher,* 34, 659–664.

Groff, P. (1986). The maturing of phonics instruction. *Reading Teacher,* 39, 919–923.

Groff, P. (In press). *Myths of reading instruction.* Milford, MI: Mott Media.

Gurren, L. & Hughes, A. (1965). Intensive phonics vs. gradual phonics: A review. *Journal of Educational Research,* 58, 339–347.

Hammill, D. D., & McNutt, G. (1981). *Correlates of reading: The consensus of thirty years of correlational research.* Austin, TX: PRO-ED.

Johnson, D. D., & Baumann, J. F. (1984). Word identification. In P. D. Pearson (Ed.), *Handbook of reading research.* New York, NY: Longman.

Johnson, D. D. & Pearson, P. D. (1978). *Teaching reading vocabulary.* New York, NY: Holt, Rinehart and Winston.

Perfetti, C. A. (1985). *Reading ability.* New York, NY: Oxford University Press.

Popp, H.M. (1975) Current practices in the teaching of beginning reading. In J.B. Carroll & J.S. Chall (Eds.), *Toward a literate society.* New York, NY: McGraw-Hill.

Readence, J. E., Bean, T. W., & Baldwin, R. S. (1981). *Content area reading: An integrated approach.* Dubuque, IA: Kendall/Hunt.

Searfoss, L. W., & Readence, J. E. (1985). *Helping children learn to read.* Englewood Cliffs, NJ: Prentice-Hall.

Smith, F. (1973) *Psycholinguistics and reading.* New York, NY: Holt, Rinehart and Winston.

Smith, F. (1978). *Reading without nonsense.* New York, NY: Teachers College Press.

Stauffer, R.G. (Ed.) (1967). *The first grade reading studies.* Newark, DE: International Reading Association.

Yaden, D. B., & Templeton, S. (1986). *Metalinguistic awareness and beginning literacy.* Portsmouth, NH: Heinemann.

LIST OF TABLES

CONTENTS

WORD RECOGNITION

1

A DEFINITION OF PHONICS

What is meant by the term *phonics?* It is obvious from the stem of this word, *phon,* that it is related to the Greek word *phone,* which means *sound.* The words *telephone, megaphone, microphone, euphonious,* and *phonograph* also have something to do with *sound.* Phonics is no exception.

Phonics is related particularly to two other "sound" words, *phonetics* and *phonemics.* (See the Glossary for definitions of these and other technical terms used throughout this book.) As used in this book, the term *phonics* means two things: (1) it is an interpretation of *phonetics, phonemics,* and *graphemics* written for teachers of spelling and reading, and (2) it is a description of the ways information given in phonetics, phonemics, and graphemics may be applied in teaching children to recognize words (decode them) or to spell words (encode them).

We shall examine what it takes to teach children to understand the working of the phonics code or system, that is, the relationship between the way we speak words and the way we read and spell them. Children must learn this relationship if they are to learn to read and to spell. This book describes how the teacher can make it possible for children to understand the relationship between the spoken language and the written language.

Phonetics

The first step in understanding phonics is to learn what is meant by the word *phonetics.* Phonetics is the study of the sounds made in a dissection of the living stream of speech. Just as a specialist in anatomy can divide the human body into its separate parts and can name each of these parts, so can a specialist in phonetics separate the flow of live speech into separate sounds, each of which is given a name.

But phonetics is much more than a guide to the pronunciation of written language. It is a broad field concerned with the symbolic nature

3

of speech: the way in which speech sounds are produced; the physical mechanisms involved in this production; the psychological problems attendant to speech perception; the varieties of usage and style; and the variant pronunciations of speech sounds in different regions of a given part of the world in which a certain language is spoken. It sometimes deals with acoustics, the origin and history of speech sounds, the teaching of speech correction, and the teaching of English as a foreign language.

Most phoneticians purport to only hear speech sounds. Acoustic phoneticians can "see" sounds as these are recorded on machines that print out the wave lengths of sounds. Other phoneticians draw visual diagrams of sounds (Barrutia, 1970). For phoneticians to prove that they can hear separate, distinctly different speech sounds—*phonemes*—they usually use a written symbol for each. These symbols can also be used by others to write down spoken language. But as Liebert rightly puts it:

> To try to write the sounds of a language is a little like trying to describe what it is like to be kissed. Words and symbols are only substitutes. Nevertheless, poets and philosophers have been talking about kissing since the dawn of literature, and linguists have developed a system, known as the *phonetic alphabet,* to make it possible for you and me to discuss speech sounds without hearing each other's voices (1971, p. 71).

Phonemics

Phonemics is a somewhat narrower field of information about speech sounds than phonetics. According to one linguist, "The study of the actual sounds of language is called *phonetics* and the way in which these sounds are used, put together and organized in any one language is called *phonology* (or more usually *phonemics* in America)" (Wallwork, 1969, p. 23). *Phonemics* is that aspect of linguistic study concerned with the identification of the significant sounds of a given language. These significant speech sounds or *phonemes* are sounds in English that make a distinction, or that distinguish, between words *regarding their meanings.* A single phoneme distinguishes the meanings of *till* and *dill* and *fill* and *pill* and *bill.* This is rather obvious. But most of us would probably be surprised to learn that one phonetician has discovered that the first sound in *till* is only one of ten different ways to pronounce /t/, none of which distinguish between words in regard to their meanings (Wise 1957, pp. 75–76). (Notice that in phonemics slant lines, / /, are used to transcribe speech sounds.) The "*t*-sound" is really a family of sounds. *Allophones* is the name given the different sounds of a phoneme.

Graphemics

The teacher of phonics also must rely on the field of *graphemics* for information as to what to teach in phonics. *Graphemics* is the study of writing or spelling systems and of their relationships to phonetics and phonemics. Graphemics deals with the ways we usually transcribe spoken language. In ordinary terms we call this spelling or orthography.

Reading and Phonics

The place phonics has in the teaching of reading depends as well on what one means by reading. The term reading must be determined.

1. Reading is a person's ability to recognize single words in sentences. By *recognize* we mean the act of converting a printed word into spoken language, either spoken aloud or subvocalized. This act is also called *decoding*. The terms *decoding* and *word recognition* cannot be used interchangeably, however, since context cues are also involved in word recognition.

2. Reading also refers to the reader's understanding of what the author of a piece of printed material apparently intended to convey. We do not always know precisely what this meaning is, of course, since we cannot read an author's mind. In poetry, for example, where an author is deliberately ambiguous, we have additional misgivings. As Brown notes, "No one has offered an explicit formulation of the total process of sentence comprehension for either the reading or the hearing case. What we have is a rough general conception and a collection of isolated clues and conceivable heuristics" (1970, p. 186). Being able to understand what a written passage means after it has been read has been called *recoding*.

To recognize a word in a sentence, children use three sources of information: (1) knowledge of phonics, or letter (grapheme)-sound (phoneme) correspondences, (2) understanding of where in the structure of the sentence a given word rests, and (3) awareness of at least one meaning of the word.

A good test of whether children are reading, in the first meaning of the word, therefore, is to listen to them read aloud. As Brengelman notes, a child's progress in learning to read "will be indicated by his supplying suitable patterns of intonation" (1970, p. 108). If children read sentences with what the listener deems to be proper pitch, stress, and juncture they are reading well in one sense of the term. However, if children, after reading sentences aloud in this fashion, cannot satisfactorily answer questions regarding the author's intended meaning, then they are not reading well in the full, complete, higher or second sense of the term.

A problem appears here immediately. It is easy to tell whether children are reading aloud in an unnatural, singsong, "shopping-list" fashion or in a way that impresses one as using natural intonation. Thus a reading test of whether children can recognize a word in a sentence is relatively simple and reliable (that is, it can be administered by several testers with the same results). But this is not true of the second kind of reading. For example, how many of the 172 meanings of *run* given in a large, modern dictionary would children have to indicate they know before a tester says they can "read" *run?* Or should we say that children cannot read *run* until they can show comprehension of *all* 172 meanings? Should we expect children to learn to read *x* number of meanings of *run* per school year? Obviously, these questions about the meaning of reading in its second sense will never be answered.

Some scientific attempts have been made to determine what unique comprehension skills (the second meaning of reading) exist in reading. The ones Davis found to be operative with secondary school students' reading could also be those used by pupils in lower grades. To this extent we agree that the elementary grade teacher should do the following:

1. Make pupils familiar with the meaning of as many words as possible. . . .
2. Encourage pupils to draw inferences from what they read and to do this accurately. . . .
3. Provide supervised practice for pupils in
   a. following the structure of a passage;
   b. finding answers to questions answered explicitly or in paraphrase in the material read;
   c. recognizing an author's attitude, tone, mood, and purpose (Davis, 1968).

The application of phonics is handicapped to an extent by the fact that English spelling is not altogether predictable. In the words *Come home,*

Tom, for example, the letter *o* represents three different vowel sounds. While our spelling obviously is not a simple system, it is systematic to a great extent, however. In fact, the variant spelling system in English presents many cues that aid one in learning to read. For example, seeing the morpheme *bomb* in *bombard* (although it is not pronounced as *bomb* here) indicates to the reader that the latter word has something to do with a bomb. The different spellings of *sitting* and *siting* tell us these have different meanings. The marker *e* on *site* shows this word will have a different sound and meaning from *sit.*

There is serious question, therefore, as to whether our spelling of words is merely a letter-to-sound system riddled with imperfections. It is better viewed as a more complex and more regular relationship wherein phoneme and morpheme share leading roles. The idea "that deviations from a perfect letter-sound relationship are irregularities" is a "purblind attitude", according to Venezky (1967, p. 77). Vallins (1965) agrees that the eccentricities of spelling have been exaggerated. "Looked at in historical perspective, [they] are nothing more than pleasant variations from a reasonably intelligent pattern" (p. 26). Marckwardt (1966, p. 90), taking a historical view, believes that "the language and its writing system are not something indescribable, inscrutable, unexplainable, and uncontrollable, but that in their own highly peculiar way, they do make sense." In a chapter to follow, *Phonemes and Letters*, we describe the degree to which each of our speech sounds is spelled predictably.

REFERENCES

Barrutia, R. (1970). Visual phonetics. *Modern Language Journal,* 54, 482–286.

Brengelman, F. (1970) *The English language.* Englewood Cliffs, NJ: Prentice Hall.

Brown, R. (1970). Psychology and reading: Comentary on chapters 5 to 10. In H. Levin & J.P. Williams (Eds). *Basic studies in reading.* New York, NY: Basic Books.

Davis, F.B. (1968). Research in comprehension in reading. *Reading Research Quarterly,* 3, 499–545.

Liebert, B. (1971). *Linguistics and the new English teacher.* (1971). New York, NY: Macmillan.

Marckwardt, A.A. (1966). *Linguistics and the teaching of English.* Bloomington, IN: Indiana University Press.

Vallins, G.H. (1965) *Spelling.* London: Andre Deutsch.

Venezky, R.L. (1967). English orthography: Its graphical structure and its relations to sounds. *Reading Research Quarterly,* 2, 75–105.

Wallwork, J.F. (1969). *Language and linguistics.* London: Heinemann.

Wise, C.M. (1965). *Applied phonetics.* Englewood Cliffs, NJ: Prentice Hall.

2

THE PHONEMES OF AMERICAN ENGLISH

Phonemes—the speech sounds of our language—are linguistic units that help us determine meaning in language. By linguistic units we mean any part of the spoken language that can be heard as significantly different from any other part. We hear *hat* and *rat* as different words partly because we recognize the differences between the sounds /r/ and /h/. There are different phonemes at the beginnings of *hat* and *rat. Flower* and *flour,* on the other hand, have the same phonemes. When we hear *flower* or *flour,* spoken without support as to their meaning from the sentence they are in (for example, "Which flour/flower is best?"), no differences of sound or meaning are noted. So one difference between *hat* and *rat* is a phonemic difference. Such a phonemic difference exists between the words *flower* and *flour* in the above sentence, although they obviously do not have the same meaning.

By *meaning,* we refer to the communication of ideas between one person and another via oral language. "Watch out! There goes a rat!" evokes a response different from "Watch out! There goes 'er hat." When we hear *phonemic* differences in words, we think immediately of different things. The adult reader understands that it is the speech sounds in words that make the differences in their meanings. For teaching children to read, teachers need to learn ways to separate and identify these speech sounds (phonemes) in ways that can be presented to children for helping them learn.

To describe the nature and limits of the phonemes of English is to ask the question, "How many different sounds are there in our language?" To answer this question we must first examine our phonemic system in more detail. We can prove that a sound is an individual phoneme by showing that it makes a difference in meaning when substituted in a word (substituting /r/ for the /h/ in *hat* gives us *rat*). Phonemes, therefore, determine in part the way we perceive word meanings. But phonemes are also units of sound that can be used interchangeably within words without affecting the meanings of words. For example, in the words *mat,*

9

fat, and *cat,* we hear the same middle and final speech sounds. The regularity of the way we say /at/ in any word indicates why it is possible for us to speak a complicated, extensive language and yet use only a limited number of speech sounds. It is the different *sequence* of phonemes that allows us, while saying the same sounds, to say two different words. This illustrates how we can use the same sounds over and over in different words without confusing our listeners.

In learning to speak as children, we learned to detect and reproduce at will the minor differences in sounds we hear, for example, in *mat, fat,* and *cat.* We also realized at a very young age that these phonemic differences carried differences in meaning. By the time normal children come to school they *comprehend* all of the sounds in their dialect. They also can say or *produce* these sounds.

Phonemes have one other distinctive aspect: *allophones.* Generally we accept the sounds we hear represented by *t* in *teem* and *butter,* for example, (or *ten* or *net*), to be the same. That is, we are aware of no difference in these sounds. We also say that the beginning sounds of *law* and *lit* are the same. And, yet, when *teem* and *butter* are said aloud, one's tongue is not in exactly the same place for both these /t/ sounds. If one's tongue is not in the same place for each of the /t/ sounds, the two sounds cannot be exactly the same. The same test can be made with *law* and *lit.* A difference in the position of one's tongue in saying the two /l/ sounds is again noticeable. These two pairs of sounds, /t-t/ and /l-l/, are acoustically different.

However, if the /t/ sound from *butter* were to be used in *teem,* and vice versa, to a listener the meaning of the two spoken words would not be changed. Thus we can hear, and tolerate, slight differences in the sounds of /t/ and not let these differences affect meaning. And if the two differences in the sounds of /t/ do not affect meaning, we do not consider it important enough to classify them as separate phonemes. "In order to indicate all these facts, one says that the two *t* sounds are different allophones of the phoneme /t/" (Carrell & Tiffany, 1960, p. 19).

For the practical purposes of teaching children to read, this aspect of phonics seems of little importance. Children learning to speak have had much experience in dealing with allophones. By the time they come to school they understand the principle of allophones. They demonstrate this understanding in their ability to infer and reproduce the correct pronunciation of a word after hearing only an approximate pronunciation of it (Groff, 1983). Here is the aspect of allophones that has import for the teaching of phonics: The fact that children can infer a word from sounds that only approach the correct pronunciation helps explain why phonics programs that teach speech sounds in isolation, (for example, /f/-/a/-/t/) have been successful, even though speech sounds made in isolation are always approximations of their true sounds.

To sum up, the following points are the ones we must consider to answer the questions: "What are the different speech sounds?" and "How many of these are there?"

1. Any phoneme, to be a phoneme, must be a speech sound different from any other one. It must also be so *different* from any other that a substitution of it for another phoneme in a word would change the meaning of the word. Therefore slight differences in speech sounds that do not change meaning (allophones) are not counted as separate phonemes. Since the exchange of allophones in words does not change the meaning of words, this aspect of phonemics need not be taught to children.

2. Phonemes are interchangeable speech units. For example, each of the individual syllables in the hundreds of thousands of words in English contains only one of the vowel sounds. Since speech sounds are largely interchangeable, we need to use only a limited number of them to speak our complex language. We do this by using this limited number of sounds over and over again.

3. Some words that have different meanings are made up of identical phonemes, e.g. *flour-flower*. If one is to understand their meanings, therefore, one needs a knowledge of the speech context in which such words are spoken. This illustrates one basic principle of phonemes: no phonemic difference = no meaning difference, unless the meaning difference is shown in the speech context.

4. Some American linguists say they hear more or fewer phonemes than do other linguists. Some include in their list of phonemes all the vowel sounds that are possible in all the dialects in English. Whether or not the *diphthongs* (blends of two vowel sounds that are initiated as one vowel sound, gradually gliding to the sound of the second vowel) are counted as phonemes makes a great difference.

Vowels and Consonants

The phonemes in English are of two general categories. One of these groups of sounds is called *vowels*, the other *consonants*. The distinctions that phoneticians have discovered between these two major kinds of sounds are important for the teacher to understand.

If you open your mouth widely, say "ah," and allow the sound to escape freely, you will produce a *vowel*. If you continue to say "ah" and then move your tongue around so that it touches or very nearly touches the roof of your mouth, or touches your teeth, or if you close your mouth, you will produce a *consonant*. Try this. It is one way to distinguish between what linguists call vowels and consonants.

A *consonant* occurs, then, when one blocks or partly obstructs the breath and causes rubbing noises by forcing one's breath around obstacles or through a gap. To the contrary, when the air stream of speech escapes unrestricted, without rubbing noises, one makes a *vowel* sound.

Another way of distinguishing vowels from consonants is to say that vowels have more *prominence* in syllables than consonants do. That is, they are louder, of longer duration, of higher pitch, and have greater sonority or resonance than do consonants. Vowels, in short, are released with greater energy and pressure than are consonants. When this difference, called prominence, is great, it is relatively easy to hear.

There have been impressionistic notions as to the differences between vowels and consonants. To the poet Robert Duncan (1968, p. 132),

> The vowels are physical
> corridors of the imagination
> emitting passionately
> breaths of flame....

> The consonants are the church of
> hands interlocking, stops
> and measures of fingerings,
> that confine the spirit to
> articulations of space and time....

A more precise way to separate vowels and consonants is to test the initial letter of a word to see whether it begins with a vowel or consonant. Take *bear*, for example, and place before it this pair of words: *a-an*. If the first word of this pair (*a*-an) accommodates itself easily to the succeeding sound, the succeeding sound is a consonant (*a bear*). If the second word, *an*, so accommodates itself, the succeeding sound is a vowel. Say, for example: *a* orange—*an* orange, or *a* dog—*an* dog. Our test shows /ô/ is a vowel and /d/ is a consonant.

Phoneticians say that all vowels but not all consonants are character- ized by *voicing*. Voicing means that sounds "are normally produced with the vocal cords in vibration" (Kantner & West 1960, p. 68). When a person speaks, the vocal cords can be in a wide-open position, in a partly-closed position, in a phonating position (rapid closing and partial opening), and in a closed position. Vowel sounds are also "made with the vocal cords closed to the point of vibration" (Kantner & West 1960, p. 140). Vowels are always voiced and are continuant, or continually flowing, sounds.

Some *consonant* sounds, on the other hand, are voiceless and so are made while the vocal cords are more at rest. Voiced consonants sound as if whispered, while voiceless ones are characterized by hisses and clicks. Pairs of voiced-unvoiced consonants can be noted. These are pairs that are allied or similar in nature and quality, that is pairs that are produced with (1) a similar degree of closure of the sound channel through which the speech breath passes, (2) a similar position of tongue, teeth, and lips, and (3) a similar degree of pressure and release of speech breath. The only difference between the two members of the pair is that one is voiced and the other unvoiced. The conventional pairings of voiceless-voiced consonants are as follows:

Voiceless: /p t k f th (as in *thigh*) s sh ch wh h/
Voiced: /b d g v th (as in *thy*)   z zh j w/

Additional voiced consonants are /l, m, n, ng, y, r/.

You can feel the vibration of the voiced consonant sounds by placing your hand against your throat with the crotch of your thumb and forefin- ger just below the Adam's apple. Say, s-s-s-s-. Then say z-z-z-z-. Which was voiced? Try this with the other pairs given above.

The vowel sounds can be called the "color" of language. The speech one hears, whether it is clipped, drawled, or jerky, depends on the way vowels are said. One can best speed up or retard one's rate of speech by shortening or lengthening vowel sounds.

On the other hand, communication of meaning through language is more dependent on consonant sounds than on vowel sounds. This may be partly due to the fact that although each vowel sound differs from every other, the vowel differences seem smaller to us than those among the consonant sounds. The relative importance of consonant letters over vowel letters in transmitting *written* messages can also be demonstrated by attempting to read sentences with the consonant letters removed as opposed to those with the vowel letters removed. For example, one can read this sentence rather easily: Th_ m_n w_nt t_ t__n. (The men/man went to town.) Now try to read this one: __e_i___oo_ _e_ _o__.[1]

One other difference between consonant and vowel sounds has to do with the places they occupy in words. Consonants can occur at the beginning, middle, and end of words, but this is not true for all vowels. Some vowels can begin a word, as in *add, aid, odd, ode, out, ice*, and so on. Some can end a word, as in *tea, two, say, so, saw, buy, boy, now*. But in our language some vowels never end a word or syllable, such as those heard in the middle of *bit, bet, bat, hut, foot*.

There are several other complexities about consonant and vowel articulation that might be discussed. The only one of great importance to teachers of word recognition is dialect.

Regional and Socioeconomic Variations in Pronunciation

We have shown that the number of phonemes in American English depends on whether the sounds in our language make a difference in the meaning of words. The number of speech sounds in American English is also conditioned by the geographical region in which one learned to speak. For example, *tot* and *taught* are rhyming words on the West Coast. In other sections of America these words are spoken with different vowel sounds. In yet other parts of the country the words *pin* and *pen* are pronounced identically. Many of the readers of this book do not use these pronunciations. They must be careful, however, not to classify them as careless speech (Wolfram & Johnson, 1982). This brings us to what are "right" and "wrong" speech sounds.

A speaker must formulate the sounds in words with sufficient accuracy to make those words easily distinguishable one from the other. A word is, therefore, mispronounced if it has the wrong sounds, or if any of its sounds have been omitted, added, or shifted around.

To decide what a "wrong" sound is, we also must concern ourselves with regional variations in pronunciation. The region of the United States in which one has learned the language as a child influences one's judgment as to the proper pronunciation of words. Linguists who have

---

[1]The girl took her doll.

studied such regional variations in pronunciation say there are three or four great geographical speech regions in the United States. Some classify them as (1) *Eastern American* (New England and New York City), (2) *Southern American* (the old Confederacy and Kentucky, with west and central Texas excluded), and (3) *General American* (the remaining states) (Carrell & Tiffany, 1960). Others call these regions (1) North, (2) South, (3) Midland ("Pennsylvania and adjoining areas to the east, west, and southwest"), and they would add (4) Middle West and Far West (Kurath, 1964, p. 5).

General American Dialect

The phonemes used in this book are taken from what is called *General American* speech. This term applies poorly to some geographical regions, but it does give us a term distinct from "Eastern" and "Southern" although its boundaries touch these areas.

Accordingly, Tables 1 and 2 in Chapter 3 are based on the phonemes used in the *General American/Midland-Middle West/Far West* dialects. The teacher of children from other speech regions than these has the right to ask, "Why so?" Why should this dialect be chosen for the list of phonemes? There are several reasons. *First*, most linguists agree, "GA [General American] comes closest to the common currency of speech in this country. It is accepted anywhere and is spoken far more widely in the United States than are either EA or SA" (Carrell & Tiffany, 1960, p. 7). *Second*, as Wise has said, "America is now suddenly an almost completely mobile country, with nearly everybody traveling nearly everywhere and finding employment in every part; in such a situation, numbers count heavily. What has been called the General American dialect will presumably have the advantage" (Wise, 1957, p. 180). *Third*, among the most important influences on uniform American speech are television, radio, and movies. These mass media tend to use GA dialect. For example, GA dialect is identical to the dialect used on national TV (Crowell, 1965). *Fourth*, with few exceptions dictionaries use GA in their phonemic spelling of words. For all these reasons it seems appropriate to use GA dialect as our guide for the phonemes needed to explain how phonics can be used in teaching reading.

Regional differences do not mean, however, that a New Englander and a Californian cannot understand each other. It is true that "good-quality speech from one linguistic area is rarely unduly conspicuous in another

dialect region" (Carrell & Tiffany 1960, p. 6). "Actually, the really con-
spicuous regional differences among educated speakers from each of
these three areas [EA, SA, GA] are relatively few; most of the more
obvious distinguishing features center around the way the *r* sound is
handled and upon the pronunciation of the *a* vowels" (p. 5). In short, in
the United States there is "no nationally-recognized standard form of
speech" and "little 'real' dialect in the sense of extreme regional differences of the type found in some European countries" (Petyt, 1980, p. 132).

Nonetheless, for the teacher of phonics, these points of difference can
be important. To use a given list of phonemes such as in Chapter 3, the
teacher of children who speak dialects with phonemes that differ from
those found in Chapter 3 will have to make adjustments for those
differences. Teachers should teach phonics in the dialect considered
standard for their speech regions.

As noted, in the United States we do not have a standard form of
pronunciation that is used by educated people in all geographical regions.
As one phonetician says, "The speech of educated Bostonians is no more
'standard' than the educated speech of Tulsa, except in Boston. And the
educated patterns of speech of Chicago or Charleston are not more
accepted than are those of New York. The speech you use in this country,
then, is considered standard *if it reflects the speech patterns of the educated
persons in your community*" (Bronstein, 1960, p. 6).

REFERENCES

Bronstein, A.J. (1960). *The pronunciation of American English.* New York, NY:
    Appleton-Century-Crofts.
Carrell, J. & Tiffany, W.R. (1960) *Phonetics.* New York, NY: McGraw-Hill.
Crowell, T.L. (1964). *NBC Handbook of pronunciation.* New York, NY: Thomas Y.
    Crowell.
Duncan, R. (1968). *Derivations.* London: Fulcrum.
Groff, P. (1983). A test of the utility of phonics rules. *Reading Psychology,* 4, 217–225.
Kantner, C.E. & West, R. (1960). *Phonetics.* New York, NY: Harper & Row.
Kurath, H. (1964). *A phonology and prosody of modern English.* Ann Arbor, MI:
    University of Michigan Press.
Petyt, K.M. (1980). *The study of dialect.* Boulder, CO: Westview.
Wise, D.M. (1957. *Applied phonetics.* Englewood Cliffs, NJ: Prentice-Hall.
Wolfram, W. & Johnson, R. (1982). *Phonological analysis.* San Diego, CA: Harcourt
    Brace Jovanovich.

3

PHONEMES AND LETTERS

Writing is a secondary or derived system for symbolizing language. Giving oral language its rightful precedence over written language does not mean, however, that writing should be considered a crude or misleading picture of speech. English writing may not be the ultimate representation of speech, but it is systematic. Obviously, however, there cannot be a one-to-one match in spelling between the number of phonemes in English—forty-one for the dialect used in this book—and its twenty-six letters. It is partly because of this mismatch that teaching children the various cues to word recognition is so critical.

In its attempts to get out of this problem, English spelling uses combinations of letters to represent speech sounds. There are more than twenty-six functional units in our alphabet: the units *gh, th, ch, ph, rh, sh, oi, oo,* for example, are as functional and basic as *a, b,* or *t.* English does not consistently use one, and only one, letter to stand for each sound, however. There is usually more than one way to represent an English phoneme.

The Grapheme

To help explain this relationship between sound and spelling, we use the idea of a *grapheme.* A grapheme is a letter or combination of letters used to represent a single phoneme. A grapheme can be a single letter like *a* in the word *ask,* or more than one letter like *th* in *the.* Sometimes graphemes are not adjoined letters: the vowel grapheme of *ate* is *a-e.* Some words in English have several letters in a single grapheme. In *though,* a two-phoneme word, *ough* is a four-letter grapheme representing the sound /o/. The following salient points about graphemes will help you to better understand how they work.

1. Graphemes in words are not always the same in number as the letters in those words. A grapheme may consist of one or more letters,

17

sometimes not even contiguous, e.g., the *a-e* in ate. To make up the deficit in English between the forty-one sounds and the twenty-six letters, we add graphemes in two ways: by combining letters, as in *ch, th, sh,* or by using a single letter as a grapheme for different phonemes: note *pan* and *all,* in which the grapheme *a* represents two different phonemes. And we sometimes use more than two letters for a grapheme—for example, *igh* in *high.* In a few cases vowel letters in words represent no vowel sound: note the first *i* in *aspirin.*

2. A single phoneme may be represented by many different graphemes. The phoneme /i/ in *bite,* for example, can be represented by the following graphemes: *i-e (bite), y (my), ye (lye); ai (Cairo), ay (bayou), aye (aye), ei (Eiffel), ie (tie), ui (guise), oy (coyote), uy (buy),* and *y-e (style).*

3. With few exceptions each phoneme is represented by a grapheme. Exceptions are in words like *x-ray,* where the *x* is a grapheme for three sounds, /ekz/ or /eks/; like *extra,* where the *x* represents two sounds, /ks/; like *expect,* where the *x* represents the two sounds /ks/ or /gs/; and *exists,* with /gz/.

4. The sounds /yōō/, which we call a single phoneme, but are actually /y/ plus /ōō/, are generally represented by two graphemes—but not *y* and *oo.* This is also true for /yûr/. To understand these statements, read the word pairs below and listen carefully for the /yōō/ and the /yûr/ sounds.

be*au*ty /yōō/	b*oo*ty /ōō/
m*u*seum /yōō/	m*u*scle /u/
resc*ue* /yōō/	iss*ue* /ōō/
f*ew* /yōō/	fl*ew* /ōō/
rep*u*tation /yōō/	rep*u*blican /u/
gen*ui*ne /yōō/	fr*ui*t /ōō/
f*ue*l /yōō/	cr*ue*l /ōō/
b*u*reau /yûr/	c*u*lture /ûr/
m*u*sic /yōō/	m*u*ster /u/
vol*u*me /yu/	res*u*me /ōō/
p*u*re /yûr/	p*u*rse /ûr/
c*u*rious /yûr/	c*u*rtain /ûr/

From this list it can be seen that (1) *ur* following /ch/ is not pronounced /yûr/ (*culture*), that *ur* following other sounds is pronounced /yûr/, (*bureau, pure, curious*), and (3) that *ue* at the end of words is generally pronounced /yōō/ (*rescue*).

5. We use more different graphemes to represent each vowel phoneme than we use for each consonant phoneme. Malone (1962) has calculated that there are an average of 8.5 different graphemes per vowel sound and an average of 3.6 different graphemes per consonant sound.

6. Although the common marks of punctuation can also properly be called graphemes, we will not deal with them, since the more frequently-used marks are readily picked up by children in an incidental way and therefore pose no great problem.

7. The speech sounds, as they are produced from individual to individual, year to year, and generation to generation, vary more in their production than do the corresponding letters of the alphabet. The reason for this is largely a matter of the relative permanence of the two types of symbols. Of course, auditory symbols—the sound waves—have no permanence. They are gone the instant they are produced. Until the invention of a sound recording apparatus, they could be retained only in memory. The visual symbols, on the other hand, are as permanent as the materials out of which, and on which, they are recorded. This explains in part why "the spoken language has changed so radically since the sixth century that we would be unable to understand the language of that time if we heard it, whereas the alphabet used to record the language, even though changed in many respects, is still essentially the same" (Kantner & West, 1960, p. 6).

HOW PHONEMES ARE WRITTEN

As noted, there are more speech sounds in English than there are letters to represent these sounds, so a given letter or combination of letters must sometimes be used to represent more than one speech sound or phoneme. To avoid any ambiguity when recording speech sounds on paper it is necessary, therefore, to decide on one, and only one way to transcribe each sound. To do this we must first decide how many phonemes there are in English.

The number of phonemes one hears depends on the geographical speech region used as a base. Some speech regions have more or fewer phonemes than others. Tables 1 and 2 identify forty-one phonemes.

Table 1 presents twenty-four consonant sounds and the consonant cluster /hw/ as heard in *what*. (Letters or symbols within slant lines

TABLE 1.
Twenty-Four Consonant Phonemes: Their Spellings and Transcription Symbols

Type of Consonant	Typical Spelling	Percent of Occurrence	Number of Spellings	Linguistic Transcription Symbol	Symbols Used in Dictionary
Plosive	1. *p*at	96	2	/p/	/p/
	2. *t*ap	97	9	/t/	/t/
	3. *ch*ap	55	5	/č/	/ch/
	cul*t*ure	31			
	4. *c*at	73	13	/k/	/k/
	*k*eep	13			
	5. *b*at	97	3	/b/	/b/
	6. *d*ot	98	3	/d/	/d/
	7. *j*et	22	8	/ǰ/	/j/
	*g*em	66			
	8. *g*ot	88	7	/g/	/g/
Fricative	9. *f*at	78	6	/f/	/f/
	10. *th*in	100	1	/θ/	/th/
	11. *s*at	73	10	/s/	/s/
	*c*ent	17			
	12. *sh*ut	26	15	/š/	/sh/
	a*c*tion	53			
	13. *h*it	98	2	/h/	/h/
	14. *v*at	99.5	3	/v/	/v/
	15. *th*e	100	1	/ð/	/th/
	16. *z*ap	23	8	/z/	/z/
	a*s*	64			
	17. u*s*ual	33	5	/ž/	/zh/
	fu*s*ion	49			
Nasals	18. *m*an	94	6	/m/	/m/
	19. *n*ot	97	6	/n/	/n/
	20. si*ng*	59	3	/ŋ/	/ng/
	ba*n*k	41			
Laterals	21. *l*ap	91	4	/l/	/l/
	ab*l*e	95	5		
	22. *r*un	97	4	/r/	/r/
Semivowels	23. *w*et	92	3	/w/	/w/
	24. *y*et	44	3	/j/	/y/
	sen*i*or	55			
Fricative/Semivowel	25. *wh*en	100	1	/hw/	/hw/

indicate the phonemic transcriptions of sounds.) Table 2 presents seventeen vowel sounds.

Column one of Tables 1 and 2 gives some typical spellings for the sounds: for the phoneme /p/, for example, you find the word *pat,* in

TABLE 2.
Seventeen Vowel Phonemes

Type of Vowel	Typical Spelling	Percent of Occurrence	Number of Spellings	Linguistic Transcription Symbol	Symbols Used in Dictionary
Checked	1. it	66	22	/ɪ/	/i/
	myth	23			
	2. at	96	3	/æ/	/a/
	3. foot	31	6	/ʊ/	/o͞o/
	put	54			
	4. up	86	6	/ʌ/	/u/
	5. bed	91	13	/ɛ/	/e/
	vary	29	9		
	care	23			
	hair	21			
	there	15			
Free	6. be	70	16	/i/	/ē/
	eat	10			
	feel	10			
	7. angel	45	16	/e/	/ā/
	ate	35			
	8. find	37	14	/aɪ/	/ī/
	ice	37			
	by	14			
	9. boot	38	16	/u/	/o͞o/
	truth	21			
	who	8			
	rude	8			
	10. both	73	16	/o/	/ō/
	code	14			
	11. cord	unavailable	unavailable	/ɔr/	/ôr/
	12. odd	79	13	/ɔ/	/o/
	arm	89	6		
	13. out	56	5	/aʊ/	/ou/
	how	29			
	14. boil	62	4	/ɔɪ/	/oi/
	boy	32			
	15. union	69	11	/ju/	/yo͞o/
	cute	22			
	16. her	40	14	/ɜr/	/ûr/
	burn	26			
	fir	13			
	after	70	9	/ər/	/ûr/
Free, Less Accented	17. carton	27	22	/ə/	/ə/
	canal	24			
	pencil	22			
	rebel	13			

which the letter *p* represents the sound /p/. Column two of these tables, "Percent of Occurrence," gives the percent of times, in the 17,000 most frequently used words with the given phonemes, that those phonemes are spelled with the indicated letters. The phoneme /p/, for example, when heard in these 17,000 words, is spelled with the letter *p* 96 percent of the time (Hanna, et al., 1966).

Column three of Tables 1 and 2 shows some ways each phoneme can be spelled. The phoneme /p/, for example, can be spelled two ways: *p* and *pp*.

All the percents and numbers in columns two and three of Tables 1 and 2 are based on data from the Hanna, et al., (1966) study of phoneme-grapheme correspondences in the 17,000 most frequently used words. In a few cases the data from Hanna have been combined and recalculated for these tables; this was done when the phonemes used by Hanna did not correspond with the set of 41 phonemes selected for use in this book.

Columns four and five of Tables 1 and 2 show the transcription symbols commonly used by linguists for writing sounds, and the dictionary symbols used for the same purpose. The symbols in column four are taken from Kurath (1964). They are slight variations of the International Phonetic Alphabet.

Tables 1 and 2 show one other aspect of phonemes: the linguistic designations *plosives, fricatives, nasals, laterals,* and *semivowels* for consonants and *checked, free,* and *free, less-accented* for vowels.

The terms used for consonants describe the degree to which we block these sounds or hold them back in the throat, mouth, or nasal cavities when we speak. Plosives are produced by blocking the breath channel and then exploding the breath. Fricatives are formed by narrowing the breath channel and then forcing breath through it. Nasals, laterals, and semivowels escape more freely through the mouth and/or nasal cavities. The ease with which breath escapes when we speak determines the loudness, or sonority, of consonants, so semivowels are the loudest, followed by laterals and nasals. Plosives and fricatives are the least loud of all consonants.

The vowel designations in Table 2—checked, free, and free, less-accented—also have significance for the teacher of phonics. The importance of these distinctions will become clear as we discuss later how they should be taught. You can tell from Table 2 that checked vowels, for example, are found typically in "closed" syllables. Closed syllables are those with vowel-consonant endings, as in *cat.* Free vowels are heard in both closed and open syllables, an open syllable being one that ends in a vowel phoneme, as with *go*. Free vowels can be heard, therefore, in beginning, middle, and ending positions in syllables and in one-vowel words (*oat, goat, go*). Checked vowels do not occur in ending positions.

The terms "long" and "short," usually used by phonics writers to classify vowel sounds, are not useful for sound classification. Such vowel sounds are traditionally said to be heard in these words:

Long	Short
hate	hat
Pete	pet
site	sit
hope	hop
cute	cut

This classification, although visually neat, is inaccurate for sounds, however, since some "short" vowels in the above list are not always shorter in duration than the "long" vowels! This can be shown if we arrange eight of the above words according to how long their vowel sounds last:

hat
hot
hope
Pete
hate
pet
cut
sit.

Notice that some "short" vowels are the longest of all, and that "long" sounds here are actually median-length vowels (Berg & Fletcher 1970, p. 66).

The free, less-accented vowel sound called schwa (and represented by /ə/) is found in less-accented syllables, such as the first syllable in *arise* and the last in *father*. This sound, you will notice, resembles a lightly-accented checked /u/ sound as in *up*.

The Phoneme /r/

The phoneme /r/ is distinct enough from other consonant phonemes to warrant separate discussion. No voiced sound in our language is more variable than /r/: "*r* is a sound, that even more than *t, k,* and *l,* is influenced by neighboring sounds. We will not be far wrong if we think of *r* as being dragged all over the mouth cavity by the various sounds with which it happens to be associated" (Kantner & West 1960, p. 169). The phoneme /r/ is therefore called a glide sound. "Like all other glide sounds, it is characterized by a rapid change of resonance produced by a gliding movement of the organs of articulation involved in its production" (Carrell & Tiffany 1960, p. 213). It is this gliding characteristic that complicates the sound of /r/.

Notice that in Table 2 certain vowel phonemes that precede /r/ are listed for easier identification:

/e/ is heard in *vary, care, hair,* and *there.*
/ô/ is heard in *core.*
/o/ is heard in *arm.*
/ûr/ is heard in *her, burn,* and *fir.*
/i/ is heard in *fear, mere,* and *beer.*
/ər/ is heard in *after* and is considered an allophone of /ûr/.

The complex sound of /r/ should not, however, lead us to assume that it is especially difficult for children to hear and speak. Research has shown that children learn to pronounce correctly all the following sounds *after* they have already learned to pronounce /r/: /s/, /sh/, /ch/, /t/, /th/, /v/, /l/, /th/, /zh/, and /j/ (Templin 1957).

Although all the vowel letter-*r* spellings must be given special care by the teacher, one of these is particularly ticklish. It is the *o* before *r* spelling, as in *more.* Leading phonetic texts generally agree that the vowel sound represented by *o* before *r* is /ô/ or /ō/, depending on one's dialect. To confirm this we also asked phoneticians in forty-three different state universities, representing all the speech regions of the United States, for their views on the problem. A large majority agreed that the vowel sound represented by *o* before *r* was /ô/ or /ō/. They noted that there were other vowel sounds heard here, however, depending on the dialect (Groff n.d.).

Since the vowel sounds in *more* and *rope* are usually different sounds, we use the symbol /ô/ to indicate the vowel sound heard in *more* and /ō/ for the vowel sound in *rope.* Each teacher must decide personally what vowel sound he or she hears in *more,* however, since it varies from dialect to dialect.

Using Tables 1 and 2

The phonemic data presented in Tables 1 and 2 are very important to the teacher. Study carefully the spellings, figures, linguistic symbols, and dictionary symbols given. Read as much as possible of the material aloud to yourself. To hear the "exploding" nature of plosives, for example, say *pat, tap, chap, cat, bat, dot, jet,* and *got.* Listen to yourself saying these sounds. Pay special attention to the formation of your tongue and lips and to breath pressure and its release.

For the sake of readability, we will use the dictionary symbols given in column five as our phonemic transcriptions. Note that some of these symbols are not the ones you might expect to be given the sounds, especially the free vowel phonemes. In *be,* for example, the free vowel is spelled *e* but the dictionary symbol is /ē/.

Do the following exercises to get a more conscious feel for the separate sounds that we make when we speak. As with all the exercises suggested for developing an awareness of phonemes, you must actually engage in these activities in order for them to be effective.

1. Say the words *beet, bit, bait, bet, bat,* and *bought* in this order. Now say *beet-bought.* Hold your hand under your chin as you say them. You will feel your lower jaw drop wider open. You can thus actually feel that different vowel sounds are related to the openness of the jaw. Notice, too, the so-called "long" vowel /ā/ in the midst of the vowel series. This position for /ā/ demonstrates the inaccuracy of the terminology "long" or "short" for vowel sounds.

2. Pronounce the series *beet, Bert, boot.* You will feel your tongue moving progressively backward in your mouth. This exercise should give you a better idea of what phoneticians call front, central, and back vowels.

3. Say the pair of words *see-sue.* Notice that the lips are unround or relaxed for *see* and round or pursed for *sue.* This illustrates the role lips play in producing phonemes. For a similar effect, say *meow* slowly.

4. Say the last sound of *sing* as represented by *ng.* If you hold your nose as you say it, you will find that it can no longer be said. This shows why the phonemes /ng/, /m/, and /n/ are called nasal sounds.

5. Say these pairs of words (some are nonsense words): *sap-zap, fat-vat, pat-bat, tip-dip, chum-jum, shot-zhot, thigh-thy.* The first sound in each pair we recognize as a consonant phoneme, although alert readers will know that no English word begins with the sound /zh/. But if you

say these pair of words several times, you will sense that the second word in each pair feels as if it is said farther back in the mouth or throat. These second sounds are called voiced sounds because they are always accompanied by greater vibrations of the vocal cords. The first sound of each pair is voiceless—that is, said without this vibration.

Tables 3 and 4

Tables 3 and 4 are lists of the common spellings we use for the twenty-four consonant and seventeen vowel sounds found in Tables 1 and 2. For each sound listed in Tables 3 and 4, we present the dictionary symbols and some examples of the ways the sound is spelled in English words. The phoneme /p/, for example, is spelled in two ways, *p* and *pp*, as seen in *pat* and *happy*. Table 3 shows that these two ways are the only ways the phoneme /p/ is spelled.

Tables 3 and 4 do not list all the possible spellings that can be given an English phoneme. The phoneme /t/, for example, has nine possible spellings. Table 3 gives only two of these, *t* and *tt*, as seen in *pat* and *putt*. The other seven spellings of /t/ are omitted because as a group they constitute less than 1 percent of the total possible spellings of /t/. In other words, more than 99 percent of all the words with the phoneme /t/ are spelled with *t* or *tt*. In Tables 3 and 4 no spelling is included if it constitutes less than 1 percent of the total spellings in the 17,000 most frequent English words.

The first spelling in the row of spellings given for each phoneme in Tables 3 and 4 is the most common spelling for that phoneme. From Table 3 you can see that for /p/, /t/, /ch/, and /k/ the most common spellings are *p (pat)*, *t (tap)*, *ch (chart)*, and *c (cab)*. That *c* is the most common spelling for /k/ may seem surprising, and the symbol for *c* might have been a better one for this phoneme than *k*, but convention dictates the use of *k*.

Some Generalities about Sounds and Spellings

Beyond information about predictability of English spellings and pronunciations, the preceding tables suggest certain more general conclusions:

1. Some letters in words appear to represent no sound. Note the "silent" letters in *know* and *comb* (the *k* and the *b*). Some linguists describe this

TABLE 3.
Spellings of Twenty-Four Consonant Phonemes

Plosives

1. /p/ *p*at, ha*pp*y
2. /t/ *t*ap, pu*tt*
3. /ch/ *ch*art, cul*t*ure, wa*tch*, ques*ti*on
4. /k/ *c*ab, *k*ing, ba*ck*, s*ch*ool, e*x*it, o*cc*upy
5. /b/ *b*ad, e*bb*
6. /d/ *d*ad, a*dd*
7. /j/ *g*em, *j*am, bu*dg*et, e*du*cate, a*dj*ust, re*gi*on
8. /g/ *g*o, e*gg*, e*x*act, ro*gue*

Fricatives

9. /f/ *f*arm, *ph*one, o*ff*
10. /th/ e*th*er
11. /s/ *s*it, *c*ent, pa*ss*, *sc*ent
12. /sh/ ac*ti*on, *sh*ip, so*ci*al, mi*ss*ion, pen*si*on, o*ce*an, *ch*ef, nego*ti*ate, *s*ugar
13. /h/ *h*ot, *wh*o
14. /v/ *v*at
15. /ᴛh/ ei*th*er
16. /z/ a*s*, *z*oo, bu*zz*, de*ss*ert, e*x*act
17. /zh/ fu*si*on, mea*s*ure, re*g*ime

Nasals

18. /m/ *m*an, mu*mm*y
19. /n/ *n*ap, i*nn*
20. /ng/ si*ng*, ba*n*k

Laterals

21. /l/ *l*ad, a*ll*, ab*l*e, ease*l*
22. /r/ *r*ap, pu*rr*

Semivowels

23. /w/*w*et, liq*u*id
24. /y/se*ni*or, *y*es

Fricative/Semivowel

/hw/ *wh*at

---

phenomenon by saying that in *comb, m* and *b* together stand for the sound /m/. Letters of this type are less apparent in other words; for example, *g* seems to represent no sound when one says *strong,* but it does in *stronger.*

2. Some phonemes are almost always represented by the same grapheme. It is useful for the teacher to be aware of such predictable graphemes as *th, v,* and *h.*

TABLE 4.
Spellings of Seventeen Vowel Phonemes

Checked

1. /i/ in, give, senate; and before /r/: hero, hear, deer, here, pier, souvenir, fierce, weird
2. /a/ bad, bade
3. /oo/ put, foot, could, woman, sure
4. /u/ up, oven, touch, come, budge
5. /e/ end, head, many, edge; and before /r/: vary, care, hair, there, bear, heir, bolero, millionaire

Free

6. /ē/ senior, feel, eat, eve, elite, ski, chief, ease, baby
7. /ā/ angel, ate, aid, way
8. /ī/ ice, find, by, night, pie, dye
9. /o͞o/ boot, truth, who, rude, you, threw, true, choose, lose, fruit
10. /ō/ both, code, oak, own
11. /ôr/ four, cord, oar, hoarse, horse
12. /o/ odd, all, faucet, dawn, ought, caught, broad, dodge; and before /r/: arm, are, heart
13. /ou/ out, owl, ounce
14. /oi/ oil, boy, voice
15. /yo͞o/ union, use, feud, cue
16. /ûr/ and /ər/* her, burn, fir, word, verse, earn, journey, urge; and in the unstressed syllables of after, honor, altar

Free, Less Accented

17. /ə/ carton, canal, pencil, rebel, pious, medium, science

*These two phonemes are considered the same. The phoneme /ər/ is considered an allophone of /ûr/.

3. Some graphemes appear to be arbitrary spellings of sounds. Notice *eau* and *beauty*, and *igh* in *night*. There are historical reasons for such spellings, however. The influence of foreign languages is apparent in such graphemes as *gu* and *th* from Latin-French, *ou* and *ch* from French, and *ps* from Greek.
4. Homophones like *meet* and *meat* are helpful in reading, since their spellings sometimes make distinctions in the writing system that are unapparent in speech (*right-rite; to-too-two*).
5. Many of the distinctions in writing depend on the marker *e* (as in *hate*). Sound variants in reading are often signalled by this marker *e*, as in the pair *hate-hat*. Here the marker *e* signals that *hate* is to be pronounced with the vowel sound /ā/.

Sometimes, however, *e* on the end of one-syllable words does not have the function it does in *hat-hate*. For example, the *e* on *charge* signals that in this word the letter g stands for the /j/ and not the /g/ sound.

The *e* on *starve* is there because in English no written word ends in *v*. The *e* on *worse* is there so that *worse* will not be mistaken for a plural word.

6. The English spelling system makes extensive use of doubled-letter graphemes, especially in the middle of words (as in bu*tt*er). Sometimes these are useful in reading: *hiss-his, diner-dinner, unnamed-unaimed*. Sometimes they are not: *holy-wholly*. But English phonology does not allow two of the same consonant sounds in a row in words except across morpheme boundaries. (A morpheme is a unit of meaning.) Note how this occurs in *bookcase* and *unknown* (two morphemes— doubled sounds allowed), but not in *butter* or *rubber* (one morpheme— single sound for *tt* and *bb*).

Practical Advice About Phonemes

Here are some hints for your work with phonemes:

1. Individual phonemes cannot be pronounced in isolation without distortion. Distortion is especially true for consonant phonemes. You must be able to isolate phonemes, however, if you are to identify and discriminate them successfully.
2. Learn to listen to the way something is said instead of what is being said. It is our habit as mature listeners to gloss over sounds and to be unaware of deviations in pronunciation, to tolerate them, and yet to get meaning from what we hear. When meaning is not listened for, however, the speech sounds we hear take on added significance. We listen then with a different, more demanding ear.
3. You may need to analyze a word many times before you hear the phoneme you are listening for. Keep on saying the word. The sound you are listening for will eventually emerge out of the word and into your consciousness. The sounds of phonemes can best be studied by listening to them. Simply reading about them is not enough.
4. Instead of thinking of the spellings of words when you hear them, concentrate on an auditory translation of these words into discrete sounds. Then transcribe these sounds with the dictionary symbols in Tables 1 and 2. When you hear the word *palm*, for example, momentarily repress your visual memory of the customary spelling of the word and think /pom/.

5. Because there are different dialects of American English, certain vowel sounds are used, or not used, in different parts of our country. An obvious example of this in Table 2 is the phoneme /o/, where we have described the words *box, calm,* and *fall* as all having the same vowel sounds, even though we know that in certain parts of the country other vowel sounds will be heard in *calm* or *fall.* If your pupils speak a dialect that distinguishes between the vowel sounds in *box, calm,* and *fall,* add the other vowel sounds to their instructional program in phonics. Do not hesitate to make other such substitutions in vowel phonemes.

6. You will notice, by checking column three of Tables 1 and 2, that vowel sounds have many more spellings than do consonant sounds. In fact, the average number of spellings for consonants is 5.4, while the average number for vowel sounds is 13.8—more than 2.5 times that for consonants (Hanna, et al. 1966). This matter is important to the teacher, as we shall see in later chapters.

PRACTICE WITH GRAPHEMES

You can become sensitive to graphemes by practicing their identification in the following words. Identify each grapheme in the following list by putting it in a box or block. Note how *e-e* in *grapheme* is boxed:

$$\boxed{g}\ \boxed{r}\ \boxed{a}\ \boxed{ph}\ \boxed{e}\ \boxed{m}\ \boxed{e}$$

and how *ee* in *feet* is boxed: $\boxed{f}\ \boxed{ee}\ \boxed{t}$

tub	bowl	ideal	fluff	pick
from	coop	noise	valve	length
mad	two	allow	wither	trust
laugh	soot	boat	exit	think
pep	church	weak	fence	angel
fate	better	whirl	beige	angle
mint	cradle	yawl	ration	tenth
feet	basket	huge	hobby	switch
talk	hook	rare	asked	tests
not	able	lark	traded	prolong

Rewrite the following words using the dictionary symbols for each vowel sound given in this box:

a—*at*	i—*it*	u—*up*	ou—*out*
ā—*angel*	ī—*find*	yo͞o—*union*	oi—*oil*
e—*bed, vary*	o—*odd, arm*	o͝o—*foot*	ûr—*her, after*
ē—*be*	ō—*old*	o͞o—*boot*	ə—*carton*
	ôr—*cord*		

does	city	gone	fur	aid	why
loll	hear	veto	anger	waif	know
shaft	creek	stood	bubble	foist	when
says	pause	noon	curling	sour	because
bear	what	broom	soda	brow	toward
locate	soft	hoof	human	quit	fine

Read the following words written in dictionary symbols. Write these words as they are regularly spelled.

wuz	gon	əgrē
laf	dənōt	ād
sed	pətātō	fir
peûr	wo͝olf	oistər
lōcāt	wûri	toun
him	oltər	bōt
krēk	fo͞old	fer
stok	trubəl	fōrən

REFERENCES

Berg, F.S., & Fletcher, S.G. (1970). *The hard of hearing child.* New York, NY: Grune & Stratton.

Carrell, J. & Tiffany, W. (1960). *Phonetics.* New York, NY: McGraw-Hill.

Groff, P. (n.d.). Phoneticians, reading experts, and *more.* Unpublished manuscript.

Hanna, P.R., et al. (1966). *Phoneme-grapheme correspondences as cues to spelling improvement.* Washington, DC: U.S. Office of Education.

Kantner, C.E., & West, R. (1960). *Phonetics.* New York, NY: Harper & Row.

Kurath, H. (1964). *A phonology and prosody of modern English.* Ann Arbor, MI: University of Michigan Press.

Malone, J.R. (1962). The larger aspects of spelling reform. *Elementary English, 36,* 435–445.

Templin, M.C. (1957). *Certain language skills in children.* Minneapolis, MN: University of Minnesota Press.

4

THE STRUCTURE OF SYLLABLES

English words are built not only of phonemes but also of syllables. One of the important ways we can help children analyze new words is to show them how words are constructed of syllables.

Over the years teachers have received frequent and abundant advice from phonics experts about the usefulness of dictionary syllabication. To give proper instruction to children in reading, this advice contends, the teacher should base programs in word-structure analysis on the ways the dictionary syllabicates words. Typical of the kind of advice given on this matter is that of Ekwall and Shanker (1985). They believe that the way the following words are divided illustrates good syllabic principles: (v = vowel letter; c = consonant letter):

1. *hap-pen*	VC–CV	2. *ho-tel*	V–CV	3. *mar-ble*	VC–CV
pen-cil	VC–CV	*ma-rine*	V–CV	*bu-gle*	V–CV
					(the *le* "rule")

These reading experts maintain that the use of these dictionary syllabication rules "may help considerably in attacking an unknown word" (p. 196).

A few reading experts disagree with these statements. As we shall see, so do experts in linguistics who write on this subject. This minority of dissidents insists that the teaching of dictionary rules of syllabication for reading is misleading and futile and, therefore, a waste of children's time in school. One purpose of this chapter is to describe the thinking of those who have rightly objected to the teaching of dictionary syllabication. We shall demonstrate that little said in the defense of dictionary syllabication has any merit. This defense is supported neither by the science of linguistics nor by experimental research. In fact, "most of the rules for syllable division commonly given out in the schools are nothing more than guides to the use of the hyphen; they have no relevance to either rules for spelling or rules for pronunciation" (Brengelman 1970, p. 95).

We will demonstrate, too, the uselessness of some of the so-called rules commonly offered for the teaching of syllabication. One would rightly expect that any such rules must help children decide on the sound to give to the letters in an unrecognized printed word. The usual rules of teaching syllabication fail to do this. If you study the following purportedly important and "most commonly taught syllabication generalizations," you will find that they cannot possibly help children identify a word. Each one depends on knowing in advance whether the first vowel sound is "short" or "long," so in order to apply the rules, children must first be able to read the word. Why, then, would they need to know such rules?

> When a consonant comes between two vowels, the consonant is part of the first syllable if the first vowel is short, e.g., palace.
> When a consonant comes between two vowels, the consonant is part of the second syllable if the first vowel is long, e.g., hotel (Otto, et al. 1974, p. 140).

Linguistics and Dictionary Syllabication

There is no evidence anywhere in linguistics that supports the idea of using dictionary syllabication to analyze words (Groff 1971). This lack of support by scholars in linguistics conflicts sharply with the advice usually given teachers by writers on traditional phonics, who do not seem to realize that dictionary syllabication stems not from accurate descriptions of syllables but from printing conventions.

Linguists who have written about the uses of dictionary syllabication in the teaching of reading have in fact taken a strong stand against this practice. Wardhaugh, for example, flatly rejects it:

> Reading teachers are asked to teach their children to divide words as follows: *but-ter, mon-key, rob-in, ro-bot,* even though, as has been pointed out elsewhere . . . , such rules are often quite circular, have almost nothing to do with the actual sound patterns of English and almost everything to do with line-breaking conventions, and have hardly any possible application beyond the typesetter's domain. They certainly do not make sense as a systematic statement about the syllables of the spoken language, nor are they entirely consistent with one another. . . . if children can use them, they do not really need them, because their use requires that children have the very knowledge the rules are supposed to be teaching (1969, p. 9).

Wardhaugh continues by agreeing with many, however, that "statements about units such as prefixes, roots, and suffixes and for compounding do have some value" (p. 9).

In regard to this last point, Shuy (1969), another linguist, suggests that the boundaries of syllables should be marked (1) between compound words, *ink-well;* (2) to separate affixes, *love-ly;* (3) between certain clusters, for example, *sil-ver,* where morphemes are not involved; (4) to follow rules for open syllables, *ti-ger,* and for closed syllables, *shad-ow;* and (5) to separate syllabic consonants, /l, r, m, n/, as in *pood-le.*

Obviously, these rules generally reject dictionary syllabication.

Research on Teaching Dictionary Syllabication

But should dictionary syllabication be taught anyway, as a matter of expedience? That is, despite the fact that it does not truly describe the English syllable, does the teaching of this kind of syllabication help children learn to read and spell? The answer is a resounding *no.* A thoroughgoing review of the research evidence (Groff, 1981) shows that the use of dictionary syllabication as a means of teaching children to learn to recognize words has no special value.

The disappointing results of teaching dictionary syllabication as an aid to spelling and the negative or inconclusive evidence as to its effect on reading leads us to reject the position of the advocates of dictionary syllabication. Furthermore, the relentless rejection of dictionary syllabication by linguists adds force to our view that the teaching of dictionary syllabication is neither necessary nor useful. Other reviewers of the research on this issue appear to agree (Johnson & Baumann, 1984).

A Revised Approach to Syllabication

The evidence both from linguistics and from research on teaching dictionary syllabication compels us to adopt a new and different set of procedures for teaching word-structure analysis. We recommend a return to the teaching of *word families* or *phonograms.* These are frequently-occurring vowel-consonant patterns, checked and free vowel-consonant combinations. These closed syllables, as they may also be called, are exemplified in *an, en, in, on, un.*

The use of these closed syllables or phonograms for word analysis is the best alternative to dictionary syllabication for several reasons: (1) The phonogram form of syllabication is equally adaptable to any system of reading: the basal reader, language experience or individualized reading, the so-called linguistic approach, programmed readers, and so on. It requires no changes in spelling or any special material for children.

(2) Phonograms act to mark the boundaries of separate syllables in a more linguistically legitimate way than do the divisions ordinarily suggested, such as VC–CV (*but-ter*) and V–CV (*ma-nage*). (3) We have calculated that a high percent of monosyllabic words that are part of high-frequency polysyllabic words can be read with their autonomous pronunciation (as accented syllables) without appreciably distorting the pronunciations of the bigger words (Groff, 1973). For example, a child can read *on* in *demonstrate* as /on/ and then correctly infer the true pronunciation of this word. (4) Closed syllables or phonograms are useful in teaching word analysis because the sounds to give their vowel letters are relatively predictable, so when children see a phonogram anywhere within a word, they can be fairly sure its vowel letter will be pronounced in a consistent fashion.

Research has attempted to indicate the extent of this predictability factor. Emans (1967) found that when a vowel letter is in the middle of a one-syllable word the vowel sound is "short" 73 percent of the time. Jones (1970) investigated the nature of spelling patterns by marking all the vowel-consonant patterns (for example, *on, in, an*) and vowel-consonant-*e* patterns (*ime-ake*) in a large sample of words. These "graph-onemes" served for the syllabication of the words she analyzed. (Jones did not use dictionary syllabication in her study.) Jones found that if all the graphonemes in words were treated as stressed syllables (no schwa sound given to any of them), they would be pronounced with either a "short" vowel or a "long" vowel sound much of the time. In fact, a recalculation of her data shows that almost 80 percent of the closed syllables she identified could be given "short" or "long" vowel sounds ("short" = /a-e-i-o-u/; "long" = /$\bar{a}$-$\bar{e}$-$\bar{i}$-$\bar{o}$-y$\overline{oo}$/).

This compares favorably with the evidence Burmeister (1969) gives from her study of dictionary syllables. Burmeister's data can be calcu-lated to indicate that when all dictionary syllables are spoken as closed syllables, that is when they are all spoken as if they were individual words, they are given the "short" vowel sound from 77 to 87 percent of the time.

Wylie and Durrell (1970) also found that the closed syllables or phono-grams in primary-grade words they studied were "stable," in that they were given either a "long" or "short" sound. They concluded that of the phonograms which appear in primary grade words, 95 percent have stable sounds of vowels. Gibson believes "that the smallest component units in written English are spelling patterns." By a spelling pattern she means "a cluster of graphemes in a given environment which has an invariant pronunciation according to the rules of English." This spelling pattern can be a "unit of one or more letters," its critical feature being that it has a "single, regular pronunciation" (1965, p. 1071). Phonograms fit this definition.

Closed syllables are also useful in that they require no special teaching of vowels or vowel sounds, because vowel sounds can be taught as part of the closed syllables. In teaching phonograms it is also unnecessary to decide which vowels to teach and whether they should be taught before consonants; the teacher simply decides which phonograms to teach, and the decision about vowels comes as a result.

The uncertainty of what sound to give to a vowel letter in a word is also reduced when phonograms are taught. For instance, what pronunciation should be given to the vowel letter *o* when it follows *h* (*ho*) at the beginning of a word? That depends on the word in question, of course. The word could be *hot, hoot, hook, hour, honest, house, hope, honey,* or *hoist.* One must therefore know which letters *follow* the vowel letter if one is to be able to give the vowel letter its appropriate sound. Working with phonograms makes children constantly aware of the fact that in order to identify a vowel sound they must check on the consonant letter that *follows* the vowel letter.

HIGH-FREQUENCY PHONOGRAMS

Which phonograms should be taught? Research provides a good answer. Table 5 presents a list of high-frequency phonograms based on a study of these by Jones (1970). Given here is a ranked distribution of these phonograms as analyzed from a random sample of over 1,400 words taken from a beginning dictionary for children. The 50 phonograms in Table 5 are ranked in the order of frequency of their occurrence in this sample. For example, *er* occurred in 160 phonograms of the total in the sample, so it is ranked number 1. At the other extreme, *ar* as in *car* occurred in only 20 phonograms. It is ranked last, or number 50. Also note that in 19 other phonograms with the *ar* spelling, the vowel sound /r/ heard in *car* did not prevail.

This list of phonograms is important to the teacher since it gives the specific spelling patterns that children are likely to see in the reading materials they use. The list alerts the teacher to those patterns that will occur over and over, the patterns children will be required to read with relatively great frequency, and the patterns that have highly predictable spellings. The implication for the teacher from this data is clear. Make sure your pupils have much practice in the recognition of these high-frequency phonograms so that they will learn to perceive them quickly wherever they appear in a word.

We further analyzed the most frequently-occurring marker-*e* phonograms that appear at the ends of high-frequency words. The teacher can see from Table 6 that the marker-*e* phonograms, with the exception of *ate* and *ure*, occur relatively infrequently. Many of these phonograms have two or more sound-spelling correspondences. Often the correspondence varies between that found for monosyllabic words and for polysyllabic words. This is seen and heard in *late* /lāt/ and *senate* /sen it/. Children must learn to be ready to apply more than one vowel sound to the marker-*e* phonograms in polysyllabic words.

Concluding Advice

Research indicates that the teaching of syllables, *if of the right kind,* may advance children's growth in word recognition (Groff, 1981). The number of research studies that support this teaching stands in contrast to those that advise against it. Although a few reading experts contend that the successful decoding of words is unrelated to syllabication skills, that the syllable is too complex a phenomenon for children to use in word recognition, or that it is impossible for a child to work out the pronunciation of a word through an analysis of the sounds of its syllables, it is difficult to find much research to support such contentions. We therefore recommend that teachers instruct children to isolate syllables in unrecognized written words as a means of word identification. In a later chapter we will describe in detail our revised approach to syllabication.

TABLE 5.
Rank-Order Distribution of Phonograms

Rank*	Times Occurred	Phonogram	Word Example	Number of Exceptions
1	160	er	her	12
2	78	in	win	3
3	75	en	men	3
4	71	or	for	7
5	54	al	pal	3
6	51	an	man	1
7	45	on	on	5
8	39	un	fun	2
9	37	ate	gate	1
10	35	et	set	0
11	37	it	sit	3
12	32	ess	guess	0
13	34	is	his	4
13	30	ing	ring	0
15	28	ent	sent	0
16	33	ic	panic	7
17	27	om	Tom	5
18	23	ab	cab	2
18	22	ap	tap	1
20	28	es	yes	8
21	24	ec	record	5
22	21	im	him	3
22	20	id	hid	2
24	22	ed	red	5
25	16	ex	exit	0
26	18	el	elevator	3
27	17	as	has	3
27	15	if	if	1
27	16	il	civil	2
27	20	ul	ultimate	6
31	16	am	ham	3
31	13	ish	dish	0
31	16	ur	fur	3
34	14	um	hum	2
34	14	us	bus	2
36	11	ant	plant	0
36	11	ill	will	0
36	11	ure	sure	0
39	10	ef	chef	0
39	11	ig	dig	1
39	10	ip	lip	0
39	12	op	top	2

TABLE 5. (Continued)

Rank*	Times Occurred	Phonogram	Word Example	Number of Exceptions
43	17	ac	accent	8
43	13	ad	had	4
43	11	ep	step	2
46	13	ol	olive	7
47	10	ag	bag	5
47	10	os	posing	5
49	33	at	cat	30
50	20	ar	car	19

*Rank is assigned according to number of occurrences minus number of exceptions.

TABLE 6.
Rank-Order Distribution of Marker-*e* Phonograms

Rank	Times Occurred	Phonogram	Word Examples
1	51	*ate*	*late, senate*
2	37	*ure*	*sure*
3	31	*age*	*page, average*
4	30	*ence*	*fence, silence*
5	29	*ine*	*pine, genuine*
6	27	*ance*	*glance, attendance*
6	27	*ive*	*alive, give*
8	17	*ose*	*hose*
8	17	*one*	*one, gone, phone*
10	16	*ite*	*bite*
10	16	*are*	*are, square*
10	16	*ide*	*side*
13	15	*ace*	*face, preface*
13	15	*ake*	*take*
15	14	*ore*	*more*
16	13	*ise*	*rise*
16	13	*ire*	*fire*
16	13	*ere*	*where, severe*
16	13	*ice*	*nice*
20	11	*ame*	*came*
20	11	*ove*	*love, move, drove*
22	10	*ute*	*cute*
23	8	*ale*	*male*
23	8	*ome*	*home, come*
23	8	*ade*	*fade*
23	8	*ile*	*while*
27	7	*ease*	*please, lease*
27	7	*oke*	*woke*
27	7	*ize*	*size*
27	7	*ave*	*have, save*
27	7	*ike*	*like*
32	6	*erve*	*serve*
32	6	*use*	*accuse*
32	6	*ole*	*whole*
32	6	*ote*	*vote*
32	6	*ange*	*range, orange*
32	6	*ime*	*time*
38	5	*ense*	*sense*
38	5	*ume*	*costume*
38	5	*ude*	*rude*
38	5	*ase*	*case*
38	5	*uce*	*reduce*

Adapted from Jones (1970).

REFERENCES

Brengelman, F. (1970). *The English language.* Englewood Cliffs, NJ: Prentice-Hall.

Burmeister, L.E. (1969). The effect of syllabic position and accent on the phonemic behavior of single vowel graphemes. In J.A. Figurel (Ed.), *Reading and realism.* Newark, DE: International Reading Association.

Ekwall, E.E. & Shanker, J.L. (1985). *Teaching reading in the elementary school,* Columbus, OH: Charles E. Merrill.

Emans, R. (1967). Usefulness of phonic generalizations above the primary level. *Reading Teacher,* 20, 419–425.

Gibson, E.J. (1965). Learning to read. *Science,* 148, 1066–1072.

Groff, P. (1971). *The syllable: Its nature and pedagogical usefulness.* Portland, OR: Northwest Regional Educational Laboratory.

Groff, P. (1973). Should youngsters find little words in bigger words? *Reading Improvement,* 10, 12–16.

Groff, P. (1981). Teaching reading by syllables. *Reading Teacher,* 34, 659–664.

Johnson, D.D. & Baumann, J.F. (1984). Word identification. In P.D. Pearson (Ed.), *Handbook of reading research.* New York, NY: Longman.

Jones, V.W. (1970). *Decoding and learning to read.* Portland, OR: Northwest Regional Educational Laboratory.

Otto, W., et al. (1974). *Focused reading instruction.* Reading, MA: Addison-Wesley.

Shuy, R. (1969). Some language and cultural differences in a theory of reading. In K.S. Goodman & J.T. Fleming (Eds.), *Psycholinguistics and the teaching of reading.* Newark, DE: International Reading Association.

Wardhaugh, R. (1969). *Reading: A linguistic perspective.* New York, NY: Harcourt Brace Jovanovich.

Wylie, R.E., & Durrell, D.D. (1970). Teaching vowels through phonograms. *Elementary English,* 47, 787–791.

5

PRINCIPLES OF
WORD RECOGNITION INSTRUCTION

The principles used to guide the teaching of word recognition should be based on two sets of information: (1) the psychology of learning and perception, especially as it pertains to young children *who have not yet learned to read,* and (2) linguistics.

The principles that govern the teaching of word recognition skills can therefore be called *psycholinguistic* principles. They are based on what we know of the psychological nature of children, their learning patterns, their potential, and how they interrelate with the linguistic matters of phonemics and graphemics. The principles of word recognition teaching that follow are stated in such a way that this interrelationship is constantly in view.

To begin, it is important to understand that the principles that guide the learning of word recognition are not the same as those that govern the learning of oral language. In the learning of oral language children proceed best on a *whole-task* basis. They need little or no formal instruction based on a sequencing of component skills. Quite the reverse is true for reading. While learning to speak is a universal and a natural skill, reading is a secondary and contrived one. All societies, however primitive, use spoken language. While the need for written language is not universal to man, speaking is. The need for written language emerges only when a society moves away from what is called its "natural" state of being.

The following principles, which should govern the teaching of word recognition, address common teacher questions like: How much phonics should I teach, and how soon? What about the blending of sounds? Do I need to teach visual discrimination first? Should I begin with "sight words"? Can phonics be taught incidentally? With which words and patterns should I introduce it? What about spelling and writing? Reading aloud? Computer-assisted instruction?

1. **The application of phonics skills is only *one* of the ways children use to**

recognize words. To insist that in all cases the more phonics the better overestimates the value of phonics skills. The ultimate aim of any word recognition program, therefore, is to teach children to eventually displace letter-analysis of words with perception of the larger structures of these words (predictable spellings, closed and open syllables, morphemes, affixes), and with the use of cues from the structure of sentences. Phonics, then, should be taught as much as possible within sentence context. Children need to relate phonics cues to other cues within the reading material.

It is also true that "all that phonics can be expected to do is help children get approximate pronunciations" of unrecognized written words (Anderson, et al., 1985, p. 41). The object of phonics instruction is to teach children (a) to decode written words by assigning speech sounds to the letters of these words, and then (b) to blend these speech sounds together so as to produce a spoken "word," such as *man*. The spoken version of *man*, as gained through decoding, will be an approximate pronunciation of *man*, however. This is so whether or not the child decodes *man* as /m/-/a/-/n/, as /ma/-/n/, or as /m/-/an/. In each of these cases the child will produce an approximate pronunciation of *man*. After hearing this approximate pronunciation young children are able to infer and reproduce its true pronunciation (Groff, 1983). It has been said that being close to the target counts only in horseshoes. We can add phonics to this list.

2. **Research in reading has demonstrated that success in beginning reading cannot be accurately predicted from the chronological age of the pupil.** Authorities disagree as to the minimal mental age necessary for successful reading instruction. Mental age requirements will vary with the instructional procedures used, as Gates demonstrated over 50 years ago (1937).

It is highly unlikely that early instruction in word recognition will have a harmful effect on children. To the contrary, research evidence suggests "that early training is not only unharmful but also may be beneficial" (Mason, 1984, p. 509). There is much evidence, in fact, that young children benefit from early instruction (Anderson, et al, 1985). It is the notion that children will eventually learn to read if they are allowed a longer time to mature that is actually harmful (Mason, 1984).

Teachers (doubtless unwittingly) may contradict themselves in the way they feel about reading success. According to one study (Bridges & Lessler, 1972) only 32 percent of a group of teachers rank "reading skills" as the most important ability to be developed in the first grade. Yet 85 percent of the teachers in the same study cited the lack of reading skills as their most important reason for not promoting children to second grade.

3. **Almost all children when entering first grade have auditory perception adequate to learn word recognition.** The relationship between auditory perception or discrimination and word recognition appears to be just as complex as the relationship between beginning reading and age. Experimental data disagrees as to the relationship. There is little doubt, however, that when normal children first come to school they have highly developed phonological and grammatical systems working for them. They comprehend all the sounds and intonations of the language, and they use almost all the grammatical structures adults do. Ninety percent correctly produce all but seven of the phonemes, /s, sh, z, zh, th, ch, hw/ (Carroll, 1960). By age seven children reach a 90 percent level of correct articulation (Healey, 1963). While it may be that these very young children cannot be expected to have *all* the auditory skills necessary for a successful word recognition program, they have developed *enough* of these skills to make this success likely.

Evidently, few children fail in reading because of faulty auditory perception. In testing more than 700 children on a relationship between the two factors, Dykstra (1966) found the correlation generally to be low. In a related experiment Morency (1968) obtained only a .23 correlation between the auditory discrimination scores of 174 first graders and their later reading scores in the third grade. This suggests only about a 5 percent commonality between the two factors. Children's articulation of sounds, as Wepman (1960) found, is not significantly related to their growth in reading ability in the first grade.

Further evidence of the lack of a close relationship between auditory perception and word recognition comes from a study by Shankweiler and Liberman (1972). They found that the mistakes children make as they repeat a word spoken to them are strikingly different from the errors they make in reading these same words.

Perhaps the most telling evidence that auditory perception ability has little influence on ability to learn word recognition comes from studies of children's improvement, or lack of it, during their school years in the skills of phoneme pronunciation and matching. Templin (1943) found that from grade two through grade six children improve in their ability to correctly match phonemes *by only 3 percent.* Another study shows that when seven-year-olds were asked to say whether initial consonants in spoken words and in nonsense syllables were the same or different, *only 2 percent* of the 432 responses they made were in error. These words and syllables represented "all possible pairings that could occur in English" (Tikofsky and McInish, 1968, pp. 61–62). Similarly, Gray (1963) found that after age 7.0 and through age 8.5 children made no significant gains either in their abilities to say a word correctly after hearing an adult say its phonemes in serial order, as in /k/-/a/-/t/, *cat*, or their abilities to tell the number of sounds heard in a word an adult pronounces in a normal fashion.

Although there is some evidence to the contrary, in balance the research evidence does not seem to support Mason's (1984) view that children's weakness in auditory discrimination is a major correlate of reading disability. Wallach and Wallach (1979) discovered, for example, that it was not auditory discrimination that children lacked, but rather the ability to segment and manipulate phonemes in words. The practice presented in this book will help children gain this ability.

4. **Auditory blending is a necessary part of word recognition instruction.** Auditory blending is usually described as an activity in which the teacher says, in the order they appear in a spoken word, each separate sound of the word. After this, children are asked to say the word in question as it would be normally pronounced. ("Try to guess what word I'm saying") For example, the three sounds in *mail*, /māl/ are isolated and said as /m/-/ā/-/l/, with a pause between each sound. After hearing these sounds, children are expected to say /māl/.

Up to 1977 (Groff, 1977) it could be concluded that research findings as to the value of teaching auditory blending in a word recognition program were highly inconsistent. Since that time, however, the balance of evidence on this issue has tipped in favor of this instruction. It is now fair to say "that there is indeed a relationship between word-identification facility and segmenting/blending skills. It is, furthermore, reasonably well substantiated that both skills must be present if transfer to decoding unknown words is to occur" (Johnson & Baumann, 1984, p. 591). In fact, "it is this last step—blending—that has been shown to be most crucial in the transfer of phonic analysis skills to the reading of unfamiliar words" (p. 595). We therefore recommend instruction that emphasizes the segmentation of words into their phonemes, along with the blending of these speech sounds into words.

The extent to which young children may be able to blend phonemes to produce syllables is suggested by Coleman's (1970) findings. He pronounced two phonemes in isolation, e.g., /a/-/n/, to preschool children who had had no training in phonics. These children were then asked to blend the isolated sounds and say them as a syllable, e.g., /an/. Over 62 percent of these children were successful in this task with combinations of phonemes that began with a consonant, e.g., /n/-/a/. Over 86 percent were successful when these combinations of phonemes began with a vowel, e.g., /a/-/n/.

5. **The so-called visual discrimination skills[1] need not be taught.** They are "discovered by the child for himself by means of perceptual and cognitive skills common to many aspects of visual perception" (Smith 1971, p. 1). As Smith has said, "The main point about the visual aspect of reading is not that a child requires a special kind or degree of acuity to discriminate between two letters; probably any child who can distinguish between two faces at six feet has the ability to do that. The child's problem is to discover the critical differences between the two letters, which is not so much a matter of knowing how to look as knowing what to look for" (p. 1). What a beginning reader must look for are the features of letters and words that actually distinguish them from one another. In this book the letters are arranged for teaching so that these distinguishing features will be made apparent for the beginning reader (see Chapter 7).

A review of the research on the relationships of visual perception and reading reveals, as Waugh and Watson (1971) have reported, that children who receive instruction designed to increase visual perceptual performance demonstrate improvement on perceptual tests but fail to show achievement in reading greater than those not receiving this instruction. Moreover, beyond the first grade level visual perception tests are not predictors of reading achievement and fail to differentiate good from poor readers. Malmquist (1960) obtained on the average the low correlation of .31 between five visual perception test scores of first-grade pupils and their reading achievement. Robinson's study (1972b) also found no such relationship. From her review of the research on visual perceptual training, Robinson (1972) decided that research is inconclusive on the question of the effectiveness of perceptual training designed to improve reading. It is true that the long-term effect of

---

[1]The skills include having children copy or select geometric shapes or forms, to give "eye pursuit" activities, to have them match designs using beads, pegboards, blocks, cutouts, or puzzles, to have them name the parts or details of pictures, and so on.

perceptual training to improve reading is uncertain. In fact, it may be that it is reading instruction that improves scores in visual perception. In any case, we reject the notion that most children need training in visual perception in order to develop word recognition skills.

Pitcher-Baker's (1973) review of the research on perceptual training led her to the same conclusion. She explains that there may well be no one-to-one relationship between perceptual training and reading achievement. It is now apparent that word and letter recognition tasks are better preparation for children's learning to read than are the so-called visual discrimination tasks (Mason, 1984). In summary, it is better simply to try word recognition with children than to wait until they achieve some set score on tests of visual perception. Children's responses to actual word recognition lessons will indicate whether they are ready, and at what pace such lessons should proceed.

6. **In deciding how to teach word recognition the teacher can make only limited use of the descriptions of the ways mature or able readers perceive words.** Smith (1971) makes clear these differences between the beginning and the mature reader. As he correctly notes, not only does the beginner use different means for identifying words than the skilled reader but "the beginning reader has to acquire special skills that will be of very little use to him once he develops reading fluency" (p. 3). It has become increasingly clear that "whatever the definition of reading, the processes involved for the proficient reader and for the beginner do not completely overlap" (Williams, 1970, p. 45). We cannot, therefore, use the act of skilled reading as a model for what should be taught to beginners in word recognition (Johnson & Baumann, 1984; Mason, 1984).

Of consequence here is the fact that most research in word recognition has been done with mature, skilled readers. One must be careful, therefore, when interpreting research findings on this subject to make sure that findings about these able readers are not used as evidence about the reading behavior of young children. Not all the writers on word recognition discipline themselves in this fashion.

7. **At the beginning of their reading instruction children should be taught the letter cues to word recognition rather than a certain number of whole ("sight") words.** As Williams (1970, p. 42) says, "It is most interesting to note the fact that the most widely used reading method over the past thirty years (the look-say or whole word) has stressed identification of words on the basis of overall shape and configuration. But it is adults and not children who sometimes show this strategy in word recognition."

The evidence of research denies the usefulness of teaching sight words before phonics instruction begins. It indicates that "the letter is still the best candidate as the perceptual unit of word recognition" (Gough, 1984, p. 234).

Accordingly, we believe that from the beginning of their instruction children must learn to discriminate graphemes within words. The proposition that children learning to read somehow first recognize "whole" or "sight" words as such has never been substantiated. We, therefore, agree with Gibson (1975, p. 300) that "overall word shape is not sufficiently good differentiator, and children should not use it" because "not only is differentiation [of words] poor without internal analysis, but transfer to new words cannot occur." Desberg and Berdiansky (1970) concluded on the basis of their review of the research that letter cues, especially first and last letters in words, and *not* whole-word shape cues, are the most-used means by which beginning readers recognize words. Both Knafle (1972) and Mason and Woodcock (1973) have found that word shape is an ineffective cue to word recognition. The research shows, then, that training in making grapheme-phoneme associations has more transfer value for beginning readers than does whole-word training.

This fact is underlined when whole-word instruction is compared directly with instruction that emphasizes phonics. "Regarding children's ability to identify unknown words, read orally, and accumulate sight-vocabulary words, there is little doubt that intensive, systematic instruction in phonics results in better performance in all these areas when compared to instruction based on a whole-word methodology" (Johnson & Baumann, 1984, p. 588). Beck and McKeown (1986) agree.

8. **Intensive, systematic, and direct instruction in word recognition is called for.** For the application of word recognition knowledge to work well, children must practice it until it can be done automatically—that is, effortlessly, quickly, and without undue conscious attention to the process. "The notion that automaticity of decoding is needed for efficient reading comprehension is powerful," Beck and McKeown (1986, p. 117) note correctly. Children may never become good readers, therefore, unless they develop fluent word recognition skills. Word recognition that is slow preoccupies the reader with this task and prevents readers from devoting needed mental energy to the comprehension of what is being read (Lesgold & Resnick, 1982).

Intensive, systematic, and direct teaching of word recognition is the best way to develop fluency of word recognition in children (Rosenshine

& Stevens, 1984). Research shows that effective teaching of word recognition is characterized by a systematic sequence of learning activities, clear demonstrations by the teacher as to precisely what is to be learned, close teacher supervision of pupils to ensure that this learning takes place, and much teacher-guided practice by pupils that reinforces and maintains the word recognition skills that have been learned. Research does not support the notion that children best learn to read in essentially the same way that they learned to speak.

9. **Explicit phonics instruction is preferable to implicit phonics instruction.** In *explicit* phonics the phoneme-grapheme correspondences taught children are referred to directly and in isolation. The teacher, for example, tells children that *hat* begins with /h/. Pupils are taught to decode *hat* as /h/-/a/-/t/, and then to blend these sounds together to say /hat/. In *implicit* phonics the phoneme-grapheme correspondences that are taught are examined only within spoken or written words and not as isolated items. To learn the *h*-/h/ correspondence, for example, the teacher using implicit phonics would have children listen to *hit-hat-hot* and then to infer that they all begin with /h/.

Explicit phonics is preferable, *first*, because it does not presuppose what it purports to teach. For children to successfully learn the *h*-/h/ correspondence with *hit-hat-hot*, they have to understand ahead of time that each of these words is made up of discrete phonemes. Implicit phonics presupposes this; explicit phonics teaches it directly.

Second, although we cannot isolate a phoneme as is done in explicit phonics, without distorting its sound, there appears to be no evidence that hearing or producing imprecise speech sounds is an obstacle to children's learning to decode. (Anderson, et al, 1985). In fact, young children readily infer and reproduce the correct pronunciation of words after hearing approximate pronunciations of them (Groff, 1983).

Third, comparisons of the results of explicit and implicit phonics instruction support explicit phonics. "The trend of the [achievement test] data favors explicit phonics" (Anderson, et al., 1985, p. 42). An objection to explicit phonics, that it can "often cause beginning readers confusion as they try to blend the sounds together to form whole words" (Searfoss & Readence, 1985, p. 174) thus seems unsupported by the research.

10. **As nearly as possible, teach children with the words they actually speak.** Along with the relative mastery of the phonological and grammatical system that pupils bring with them as they enter first grade, children

also show that they comprehend and utilize a large number of words. They speak these words in intelligible sentences and respond to them when others say them. Each child because of his or her particular environment out of school has accumulated a vocabulary that reflects these factors.

Since children have shown they understand these words by using them, these words offer a special potential for the teacher. When these words are used in word recognition work, no problems of syntax or word meaning are involved. While the evidence is incomplete, children should learn faster with such words and sentences than with words and sentences from prewritten texts that inevitably involve unfamiliarities of syntax and meaning. It is recommended, therefore, that as nearly as possible the teacher use a child's own words and sentences to teach word recognition. (Make sure, however, that a word chosen is not an exception to a phonics generalization that is being taught at the time.) Research also suggests that words for which children may more easily form mental images (such as *den* vs. *not*) will be easier for them to learn to read. Wolpert (1972) concluded from his study that more high-imagery words were learned by first-grade children than low-imagery words. His findings agree with most other literature dealing with verbal learning.

In this respect it is mandatory that the teacher adapt word recognition instruction to the dialect of his or her pupils. Teachers in any locality must compare the speech sounds of their pupils with the ones used in this book and not hesitate to add, subtract, or exchange the sounds that they hear in their pupils' dialect that differ from the dialect used in this book.

Changing pupils' dialects for the purpose of reading instruction is not recommended. There is no evidence to show that such attempts are successful. Rystrom (1970), for example, found that attempts to change the non-standard dialect of first-grade black children did not significantly increase their reading achievement. In sum, we agree with Wardhaugh that "the task in phonics is one of systematically relating the two systems [phonological and writing] for the child, not trying to change the first system, a doubtful goal, or making it like the second system, an impossible goal" (1971, p. 64).

11. **The teaching of word recognition should adhere to the factual data that one can gather from the science of linguistics.** The usefulness of some of these data is limited when teaching children, however. Whenever this book violates the linguistic data it is done knowingly, with the abilities of

children and teachers to learn or to teach these data clearly in mind. In short, in teaching about language, children's ability to understand linguistic data is more important than is the authenticity of any particular datum itself. When any adjustment of linguistic data is made in this book the reader will be informed of it.

12. **The total number of phonics generalizations to be taught depends on several factors, for example, pupils' needs and abilities and the level of phonics being taught.** In general, nevertheless, we can say that the larger the number of letter-sound relationships children can learn the better. Bliesmer and Yarborough (1965) make this clear from their study, which found 74 percent of comparisons of reading scores to favor programs using deliberate, systematic ("synthetic") phonics over those using nonsystematic or incidental phonics. They conclude that "the order of instruction of letter-sound elements and/or relationships may not be as important in the success of synthetic programs as that the number of letter-sound relationships taught be sufficient to equip pupils with means for independent decoding of words" (p. 504).

It has been held that only the phonics rules that have "utility" should be taught (Clymer, 1963). Clymer, and others who later used his research design, calculated to what extent certain phonics rules "apply" to words. Clymer, for example, tested this phonics rule: When two vowel letters appear side-by-side in a word, the reader should say the "long" sound of the first letter and ignore the second letter. Clymer concluded that this rule "applied" to *need* but not to *head*. This rule should not be taught children learning to decode, Clymer advised, because it supposedly applied to only 34 percent of pertinent spellings.

Clymer never tested this hypothesis with children, however. Groff (1983) did. He found that when children hear an approximate pronunciation of a word, pronounced so as to follow a phonics rule (for example, *head* pronounced as /hēd/), they then can infer and reproduce the correct pronunciation of the word. Groff found that the two-vowel phonics rule may work for the decoding of *head* as well as for *need*. Clymer, and those who later used his research design, were probably wrong, therefore, as to which phonics rules have utility for the child learning to decode words.

It remains for one to say, of course, what a sufficient number of rules is. Since this has not been determined empirically, any decision on the number of rules must be a pragmatic one. The teacher should teach the number of rules sufficient for the particular group of pupils being taught. This text provides a rational sequence of phonics skills. It cannot advise as to the absolute number of these required by any given group of children, however. The individual phonics teacher must make that decision. Unfortunately, at present no reliable, valid, and quick-scoring test of children's knowledge of phonics rules and their ability to apply them is available for teachers to use for this purpose.

13. **The learning of dictionary rules of syllabication (which traditionally has been required of children) is inadvisable both linguistically and psychologically** (Seymour, 1973). Dictionary rules of syllabication violate the notion of a psycholinguistic approach to the teaching of word recognition. The dictionary rules of syllabication do have some usefulness as children later learn to use the dictionary. They can be taught at that time.

14. **A word recognition lesson should be conducted largely with predictably spelled words.** What we know of research in perceptual learning substantiates our belief that as children learn to read they "learn to attend to distinctive features of things, to invariants that lead to perceptual constancy and permanence" (Gibson 1969, p. 445). These invariants help children deduce higher-order structures and rules about reading. This finding implies that unless invariant spellings of sounds are used in the word recognition program, children's natural mode of perception may be thwarted and their later ability to deduce rules may be retarded. A sequence of word analysis that is begun with invariant spellings of words and moves to variant spellings is a critical necessity.

Reviews of the research evidence on this matter support the conclusion that "there is now sufficient experimental evidence to argue that some kind of orthographic regularity facilitates the perception of letter strings." Therefore, "reading instruction must ensure that students acquire an awareness of orthographic regularity" (Venezky & Massaro, 1979, p. 104). See also Juola, et al. (1979) to this effect.

This leaves us with the problem of deciding what an "unpredictably spelled" word is. The propriety of calling some words "regularly spelled" and others "irregularly spelled" has been questioned. These two terms are usually used to mean, for example, that a word like *raft* is "regularly spelled" and a word like *laughed* is not. This decision is generally made by determining the percent of times in a total number of high-frequency words the phonemes in these individual words (*raft-laughed*) are spelled as they are in the individual words. These percents are easily obtained (Hanna, et al. 1966):

/r/ is spelled *r* 97% of the time,

while /l/ is spelled *l* 91% of the time.

/a/ is spelled *a* 97% of the time,

while /a/ is spelled *au* 0.1 of 1% of the time.

/f/ is spelled *f* 78% of the time,

while /f/ is spelled *gh* 0.4 of 1% of the time.

/t/ is spelled *t* 97% of the time,

while /t/ is spelled *ed* 0.4 of 1% of the time.

It is therefore obvious that even in high-frequency words some sound-spelling correspondences occur more frequently than do others.

There still remains the question of deciding what percent of times a certain phoneme-grapheme correspondence must occur before it is called a "regular" one. Should this be 90, 70, or 50 percent? Since there is no way to answer this question, in this book we avoid using the terms "regular spellings" or "irregular spellings." We say, instead, that a predictably spelled word is one the child has been prepared by word recognition instruction to decode successfully. An unpredictably spelled word would therefore be one for which the child has insufficient knowledge to decode.

15. **At the earlier levels of word recognition instruction, only one-syllable words should be used.** The exclusive use of one-syllable words has profound importance. It excludes the need for children to recognize long words, where the number of syllables doubtless acts to inhibit the learning of phonics. A study has calculated the total number of spelling-to-sound correspondence rules necessary to read one-syllable words versus the number needed to read two-syllable words. From this study we found that thirty-eight more rules (for a total of seventy-three) are needed to read the latter words (Berdiansky, Cronnell, & Koehler 1969). Then we calculated from twelve compilations of commonly-used words that, on the average, only 16 percent of these high-frequency words were polysyllabic words. A similar finding came from our survey of the first-grade sections of several prominent standardized reading tests (Groff 1975). Only 20 percent of the words in these sections were found to be polysyllabic. This also seems striking evidence that long words are harder to read than one-syllable words.

There are other matters that suggest the use of one-syllable words in instruction. In one-syllable words children do not have to deal with less-accented syllables, where the schwa sound is found. Moreover, this sound has twenty-two different spellings, by one count (Hanna, et al. 1966). The large majority of one-syllable words that have a one-letter vowel grapheme (such as *cat*) on the other hand, will be spoken with just the checked vowel sounds, plus /o/. The vowel sound-spelling patterns for these one-syllable words are thus more stable than for the /ə/ sound-spelling correspondences. Through the teaching of one-syllable words children also more easily learn the structures of syllables and phonograms, which they then can readily transfer to the analysis of polysyllabic words when they are ready.

The speed with which children can be taught to recognize words is of critical importance. The word recognition program to be described in this book is designed to develop automaticity of word recognition, the ability to recognize words in a seemingly instantaneous way. Henderson (1982) reviewed the research on the relationship between the number of letters in a word and the speed at which it can be recognized. He concludes that the number of letters in a word is "certainly the most prevalent" effect on the speed of word recognition found by researchers (p. 184). He also notes the research to say that the number of syllables in a word has a substantial effect on readers' abilities to decode it, especially when readers are unskilled. Then, studies of the eye movements of readers indicate that stoppages of the eye when reading (fixations) are longer in duration for multisyllabic words than for monosyllabic ones (Perfetti, 1985). These findings are convincing evidence of the need to make careful distinctions between monosyllable and multisyllable words when teaching word recognition.

16. **Spelling-to-sound correspondences do not account for all spelling patterns, such as *nation-national*.** Venezky and Weir (1966), Chomsky (1970), and Chomsky and Halle (1968) are right in noting that another kind or level of correspondences, beyond grapheme to phoneme, is involved here.

Venezky and Weir call this other kind of correspondence "morphophonemic." In *nation* and *national* for example, the position of the first *a* does not tell what sound this letter should be given. Instead, the first *a* in *national* is conditioned by the fact that the morpheme *al* has been added to the morpheme *nation*. In other words, morpheme boundaries must be known in order to predict what certain spelling-sound correspondences will be. Notice how one's knowledge as to whether a word consists of one or two morphemes controls the sounds given to certain words:

One morpheme	Two morphemes
le*tt*er	mi*dd*ay
co*ng*ress	i*ng*rain
s*a*ne	s*a*nity

Venezky and Weir imply that these morphophonemic correspondences should be taught from the beginning of any word recognition program. We do not agree with this advice, however, for two reasons: (1) Many of the morphophonemic correspondences involve only a few high-frequency words. We do not know from Venezky and Weir which of such correspondences involve a relatively high percent of high-frequency words. (2) We are convinced from the research that monosyllabic words are easier for beginners to read and spell than are polysyllabic words and therefore are preferable for early lessons. Most morphophonemic correspondences involve polysyllabic words.

Doubtless, as Brengelman (1970) demonstrates, "the rules for spelling polysyllables are much more complicated" than those for spelling monosyllables. This is due principally to two facts: (1) polysyllables normally contain only one strongly stressed syllable; the others are given a weaker stress, notably the schwa sound /ə/, and (2) most polysyllables are made up of more than one morpheme. The spellings given to morphemes tend to be the same, however, regardless of changes to their sound when they are heard in more weakly stressed syllables of polysyllabic words—for example, *reform-reformation.*

We will in Chapter 8 give examples for teaching the recognition of multisyllabic words that agree with Chomsky's conclusion that "good spellers, children and adults alike, recognize that related words (*president-preside*) are spelled alike even though they are pronounced differently. They seem to rely on an underlying picture of the word that is independent of its varying pronunciation" (1970, p. 303).

17. **Vowel sound-letter correspondences are more variant, and therefore present more teaching problems, than do consonant sound-letter correspondences.** There are many more ways to spell vowels than there are to spell consonants (see Tables 1, 2, 3, and 4). Children thus need more phonics knowledge to decode vowel phoneme-letter correspondences than they do for consonant phoneme-letter matchups. Complicating this matter is the fact that the vowel sound the reader should say for a given vowel letter depends largely on the consonant letter(s) that follow the vowel letter, as in ho-*me*, ho-*nest*, etc. Hence our recommendation for the teaching of the common phonograms (see Chapter 4).

18. **The teaching of word recognition, spelling, and handwriting can proceed hand in hand.** Many of the phonics skills useful for recognizing words are also useful for spelling words, although phonics is decidedly less useful for spelling than for reading. When children learn to spell and handwrite the words they know how to decode, this spelling and handwriting will strengthen their powers of word recognition.

19. **Oral reading is an important part of word recognition instruction, since in learning to recognize words children realize that their speech sounds are represented by letters.** The question arises, nonetheless: Is there any danger to silent reading skills of saying a word aloud? Particularly, should lip movements, whispering of words, or even saying words aloud be discouraged after a certain point in phonics instruction? The evidence on the relationship of subvocalization or implicit speech (as this can be called) and reading says no. Earlier, there were attempts made to teach children to read without saying words aloud (Buswell 1945). This *nonoral* teaching method was based on the theory that a reader can and should go directly from the printed word to comprehension of it without any implicit speech between. We have learned that this is an impossibility — which explains why the children in the early nonoral experiments used as much implicit speech as did children who learned to read by reading aloud. As Gibson (1975, p. 302) rightly concludes, "For a child who is learning, subvocal speech may be essential for getting the message."

Research shows that good readers do use less implicit speech than do poor readers. This should *not* be interpreted to mean, however, that the teacher should try to eliminate beginners' vocalizing as they read. The research indicates that the use or disuse of subvocalization is a developmental matter. Its use proceeds through the stage at which all words are said aloud or whispered to the final stage of silent speech in reading, where implicit speech is hidden (except to an electronic device attached to the reader's throat) (Edfeldt 1960). In sum, research advises us that implicit speech is necessary as a developmental learning reinforcement activity and it should *not* be prematurely eliminated (Davies 1972).

The numerous objections that have been made to the teaching of oral reading in schools can be discredited (Groff, in press). Research on this matter suggests in fact that oral reading practice has the potential to contribute significantly to children's growth in reading ability (Hoffman, 1981). More research is needed on this issue, however (Allington, 1984).

20. **The value of computer-assisted instruction in word recognition is an unsettled issue.** There is evidence that computer assisted instruction (CAI),

when used as a drill-and-practice supplement for ordinary classroom teaching of reading, does develop greater achievement than otherwise would be the case. (Fletcher, 1979). There still remain some handicaps to the utility of CAI, however.

First, although it is judged by some that studies of the effectiveness of CAI have generally yielded favorable results (Otto, Wolf, & Eldridge, 1984), other computer experts disagree. They say that CAI in reading instruction is certainly less effective than traditional methods (Wayth, 1983; Self, 1985). It is important to note that some who declare that "training in rapid word recognition of words can be done better by computer than on the printed page" (Wilkinson, 1983, p. 191) fail to present any experimental evidence as support for this claim. *Second,* the expense of CAI relative to traditional methods has made its cost prohibitive. Geoffrion and Geoffrion (1983) argue to this point that the computer contributes little that is unavailable in printed form at a substantially lower cost. *Third,* CAI is limited for teaching phonics skills in that the computer can neither produce accurate speech (although attempts to improve its production continue) nor assess children's utterances (Geoffrion & Geoffrion, 1983; Clements, 1985). *Fourth,* CAI is useful only for drill and practice of word recognition skills. It is ineffective for the initial teaching of these skills (Lesgold, 1983). *Fifth,* there have been only a relatively few computer programs developed for reading instruction; only about 5 percent of educational software is on the teaching of reading (Williams & Williams, 1985). *Sixth,* the overall quality of computer programs for education is low. Self (1985, p. 146) complains about the "lamentable state of present software." He judges that these programs by and large are poorly programmed, pedagogically inadequate, and lacking in quality, quantity, and variety. Bitter and Gore (1984) found computer programs in reading so poor in quality they could recommend none of them for schools to use in CAI.

Is there a bright future for CAI in word recognition instruction, however? Computer experts like Self (1985) say no. He sees "only a gradual improvement in programming methodology over the past 10 years and no breakthrough . . . foreseeable" (p. 152). Bramble and Mason (1985), on the other hand, contend that the development of CAI is so great that it has outpaced the ability of education to adapt to it. Ekwall and Shanker (1985, p. 56) find the potential of CAI "exciting."

Most recent commentary about CAI in word recognition instruction predicts that CAI will not replace traditional teaching in the near future.

It seems clear that at present CAI is not the final solution to the ills of word recognition instruction. It has been said that if only our schools had the money to buy computers the problems of word recognition teaching would be solved. By most accounts, this is far too optimistic a view of CAI.

REFERENCES

Allington, R. (1984). Oral reading. In P.D. Pearson (Ed.), *Handbook of reading research*. New York, NY: Longman.

Anderson, R.C., et al. (1985). *Becoming a nation of readers: The report of the Commission on Reading*. Washington, DC: U. S. Department of Education.

Beck, I.L., & McKeown, M.G. (1986). *Instructional research in reading: A retrospective*. In J. Orasanu (Ed.), *Reading comprehension: From research to practice*. Hillsdale, NJ: Lawrence Erlbaum.

Berdiansky, B., Cronnell, B., & Koehler, J. (1969). *Spelling-sound relations and primary form-class descriptions for speech-comprehension vocabularies of 6–9 year olds*. Los Alamitos, Calif.: Southwest Regional Laboratory for Educational Research and Development.

Bitter, G.G., & Gore, K. (1984). *The best of educational software for Apple II computers*. Berkeley, CA: Sybex.

Bliesner, E. P., & Yarborough, B. H. (1965). Comparison of ten different beginning reading programs in first grade. *Phi Delta Kappan*, 47, 500–504.

Bramble, W.J., & Mason, E. J. (1985). *Computers in schools*. New York, NY: McGraw-Hill.

Brengelman, F. (1970). *The English language*. Englewood Cliffs, N.J: Prentice-Hall.

Bridges, J. S. & Lessler, K. (1972). Goals of first grade. *Reading Teacher*, 25, 763–767.

Buswell, G. T. (1945). *Non-oral reading: A study of its use in the Chicago public schools*. Supplementary Educational monographs, No. 60. Chicago, IL: University of Chicago Press.

Carroll, J.B. (1960). Language development. In C.W. Harris (Ed.), *Encyclopedia of educational research*. New York, NY: Macmillan.

Chomsky, C. (1970). Reading, writing and phonology. *Harvard Educational Review*, 40, 287–309.

Chomsky, N. & Halle, M. (1968). *The sound pattern of English*. New York, NY: Harper & Row.

Clements, D.H. (1985). *Computers in early and primary education*. Englewood Cliffs, NJ: Prentice-Hall.

Clymer, T. (1963). The utility of phonic generalizations in the primary grades. *Reading Teacher*, 16, 252–258.

Coleman, E.B. (1970). Collecting a data base for a reading technology. *Journal of Educational Psychology Monographs*, 61, 1–23.

Davies, W.C. (1972). Implicit speech — some conclusions drawn from research. In R.C. Aukerman (Ed.), *Some persistent questions on beginning reading*. Newark, DE: International Reading Association.

Desberg, P., & Berdiansky, B. (1970). *Word attack skills: Review of Literature.* Los Alamitos, CA: Southwest Regional Laboratory for Educational Research and Development.

Dykstra, R. (1966). Auditory discrimination abilities and beginning reading achievement. *Reading Research Quarterly,* 1, 5–34.

Edfeldt, A. W. (1960). *Silent speech and silent reading.* Chicago, IL: University of Chicago Press.

Ekwall, E.E., & Shanker, J.L. (1985) *Teaching reading in the elementary school.* Columbus, OH: Charles E. Merrill.

Fletcher, J.T. (1979). Computer-assisted instruction in beginning reading: The Stanford project. In L.B. Resnick & P.A. Weaver (Eds.), *Theory and practice of early reading, vol. 1.* Hillsdale, NJ: Lawrence Erlbaum.

Gates, A. I. (1937). The necessary mental age for beginning reading, *Elementary School Journal,* 37, 497–508.

Geoffrion, L.D., & Geoffrion, O.P. (1983). *Computers and reading instruction.* Reading, MA: Addison-Wesley.

Gibson, E. J. (1969). *Principles of perceptual learning and development.* New York: Appleton-Century-Crofts.

Gibson, E.J. (1975). Theory-based research on reading and its implications for instruction. In J. B. Carroll & J. S. Chall (Eds.), *Toward a literate society.* New York, NY: McGraw-Hill.

Gough, P.B. (1984). Word recognition. In P.D. Pearson (Ed.), *Handbook of reading research.* New York, NY: Longman.

Gray, E. T. (1963). *A study of the vocal phonic ability of children six-to-eight and one-half years,* Ph.D. Dissertation, University of Oklahoma.

Groff, P. (1975). Long versus short words in beginning reading. *Reading World,* 14, 277–289.

Groff, P. (1977). *Phonics: Why and how.* Morristown, NJ: General Learning.

Groff, P. (1983). A test of the utility of phonics rules. *Reading Psychology,* 4, 217–225.

Groff, P. (In press). *Myths of reading instruction.* Milford, MI: Mott Media.

Hanna, P. R., et al. (1966). *Phoneme-grapheme correspondences as cues to spelling improvement.* Washington, D.C.: U.S. Office of Education.

Healey, W. C. (1963). *A study of the articulatory skills of children from six to nine years of age.* Ph.D. Dissertation, University of Missouri.

Henderson, L. (1982). *Orthography and word recognition in reading.* New York, NY: Academic.

Hoffman, J.V. (1981). Is there a legitimate place for oral reading instruction in developmental reading program? *Elementary School Journal,* 81, 305–310.

Johnson, D.D. & Baumann, J.F. (1984). Word identification. In P.D. Pearson (Ed.), *Handbook of reading research.* New York, NY: Longman.

Juola, J.J., et al. (1979). What do children learn when they learn to read? In L.B. Resnick & P.A. Weaver (Eds.), *Theory and practice of early reading, vol. 1.* Hillsdale, NJ: Lawrence Erlbaum.

Knafle, J. D. (1972). Word perception: An experiment with cues in the development of unit-forming principles. *Dissertation Abstracts International,* 32, 4424A.

Lesgold, A.M. (1983). A rationale for computer-based reading instruction. In A. C. Wilkinson (Ed.), *Classroom computers and cognitive science*. New York, NY: Academic.

Lesgold, A.M. & Resnick, L.B. (1982). How reading differences develop: Perspectives from a longitudinal study. In J.P. Das, R. Mulcahy, & A.E. Wall (Eds.), *Theory and research in learning disabilities*. New York, NY: Plenum.

Malmquist, E. (1960). *Factors-related to reading disabilities in the first grade of the elementary school.* Stockholm: Almquist and Wiksell.

Mason, D. E. & Woodcock, C. (1973). First grader's performance on a visual memory for words task. *Elementary English*, 50, 865–870.

Mason, J.M. (1984). Early reading from a developmental perspective. In P.D. Pearson (Ed.), *Handbook of reading research*. New York, NY: Longman.

Morency, A. (1968). Auditory modality—research and practice. In H.K. Smith (Ed.), *Perception and reading*. Newark, DE: International Reading Association.

Otto, W., Wolf, A., & Eldridge, R.G. (1984). Managing instruction. In P.D. Pearson (Ed.). *Handbook of reading research*. New York, NY: Longman.

Perfetti, C.A. (1985). *Reading ability*. New York, NY: Oxford University Press.

Pitcher-Baker, G. (1973). Does perceptual training improve reading? *Academic Therapy*, 9 (1973): 41–45.

Robinson, H.M. (1972a). Perceptual training—does it result in reading improvement? In R.C. Aukerman (Ed.), *Some persistent questions on beginning reading*. Newark, DE: International Reading Association.

Robinson, H.M. (1972b). Visual and auditory modalities related to methods for beginning reading. *Reading Research Quarterly*, 8, 7–39.

Rosenshine, B., & Stevens, R. (1984). Classroom instruction in reading. In P. D. Pearson (Ed.). *Handbook of reading research*. New York, NY: Longman.

Rystrom, R. (1970). Dialect training and reading. *Reading Research Quarterly*, 5, 581–599.

Searfoss, L.W., & Readence, J.E. (1985). *Helping children learn to read*. Englewood Cliffs, NJ: Prentice-Hall.

Self, J. (1985). *Microcomputers in education*. Brighton, Sussex (England): Harvester.

Seymour, D.Z. (1973). Word division for decoding. *Reading Teacher*, 27, 275–283.

Shankweiler, D., & Liberman, I.Y. (1972). Misreading: A search for causes. In J. F. Kavanagh & I. C. Mattingly (Eds.), *Language by ear and by eye*. Cambridge, MA: MIT press.

Smith, R. (1971). *Understanding reading*. New York: Holt, Rinehart and Winston.

Templin, M. (1943). A study of sound discrimination ability of elementary school pupils. *Journal of Speech and Hearing Disorders*, 8, 127–132.

Tikofsky, R.S., and McInish, J.R. (1968). Consonant discrimination by seven-year-olds: A pilot study. *Psychonomic Science*, 10, 61–62.

Venezky, R.L., & Massaro, D.W. (1979). The role of orthographic regularity in word recognition. In L.B. Resnick & P.A. Weaver (Eds.), *Theory and practice of early reading, vol. 1*. Hillsdale, NJ: Lawrence Erlbaum.

Venezky, R.L., & Weir, R.A. (1966). *A study of selected spelling to sound correspondence patterns*. Washington, DC: U.S. Office of Education.

Wallach, M.A. & Wallach, L. (1979). Helping disadvantaged children learn to read by teaching them phoneme identification skills. In L.B. Resnick & P.A.

Weaver (Eds.), *Theory and practice in early reading, vol. 3.* Hillsdale, NJ: Lawrence Erlbaum.

Wardhaugh, R. (1971). A linguist looks at reading. *Elementary English,* 48, 61–66.

Waugh, R. & Watson, Z. (1971). Visual perception and reading. *Education,* 91, 266–269.

Wayth, P.J. (1983). *Using microcomputers in the primary school.* Aldershot, Hants (England): Gower.

Wepman, J.M. (1960). Auditory discrimination, speech, and reading. *Elementary School Journal,* 60, 326–333.

Wilkinson, A.C. (1983). Learning to read in real time. In A. C. Wilkinson (Ed.), *Classroom computers and cognitive science.* New York, NY: Academic.

Williams, J.P. (1970). Reactions to modes of word recognition. In H. Singer & R. Ruddell (Eds.), *Theoretical models and processes in reading.* Newark, DE: International Reading Association.

Williams, F., & Williams, V. (1985). *Success with educational software.* New York, NY: Praeger.

Wolpert, E.M. (1972). Length, imagery values, and word recognition. *Reading Teacher,* 26, 180–186.

6

CLASSROOM PRACTICES IN WORD RECOGNITION TEACHING

The teaching of word recognition is no different in many respects from good teaching in general. Obviously, good teaching calls for a humane, enthusiastic, and well-informed teacher who spends adequate time in preparation for lessons. In this chapter we discuss classroom practices that are especially critical to successful teaching of word recognition.

1. **How much practice, and of what kind, is needed to develop children's word recognition skills?** A logical sequence of activities is likely to result in greater knowledge of word recognition than would random practice. Small-group instruction also is essential if children are to be stimulated to learn at a pace that is commensurate with their abilities and potential. As with other forms of associative learning, word recognition requires, by its very nature, a good amount of practice, exercise, or repetition. There is nothing inherently distasteful about practice or drill, although most of us have experienced bad types of it. Practice, if it takes the forms described in the following chapters, need not be resented by children. In fact, most children seem to take pleasure in perfecting the skill of fluent word recognition. Not only are they conscious of the social implications of such skill, they also derive pleasure from learning to recognize words, since it pleases the adults they admire.

However, word recognition exercises with inattentive pupils are worse than no exercises at all. There are children who are persistently inattentive in lessons, even when their classmates are interested. Forcing such a child to attend generally fails. In our view, the best idea is to excuse this child from group lessons temporarily on the basis that he or she is not emotionally ready for word recognition instruction. An attempt should be made to get a mother, an older pupil, a student teacher, or a teacher's aide to give the child some tutoring, which generally proves more effective at this point. Return this child to the group at a later time.

The nature of word recognition skills makes it important that these skills not only be given in a logical sequence, but that other conditions also prevail:

- Lessons should be relatively short
- Lessons should be frequent—daily, in most cases.
- Lessons should be fast-paced and not linger on any matter, such as a fact that a single pupil in a group seems to misunderstand.
- Lessons should cover only a small segment of information at a time.
- Each lesson should start with an item that children know.
- Pupils should repeat items from lesson to lesson until the teacher feels almost all children in a group can respond correctly.
- No absolute deadline should be set for the amount to be covered in a given time. Only the pupils' responses can determine this.
- The teacher should be constantly on the alert to regroup children on the basis of their growth in word recognition; hence the need for several small groups.
- Some game (see Appendix B) should be played or explained in almost every lesson. The children can be directed to play these games in pairs after they leave the group.
- Keep charts of children's progress in order to reinforce their efforts to learn by knowing they are making progress.
- There should be some individual work.

The pace at which group lessons are conducted is a problem that deserves special comment. The question here is whether the pace of a lesson should be set by the goal of (1) trying to learn with a few errors as possible, or (2) trying to learn as fast as possible. There is evidence that pupils instructed to learn concepts as rapidly as possible do learn concepts faster than pupils instructed to learn concepts with as few errors as possible (Frayer & Klausmeier 1971). This evidence suggests that phonics lessons be conducted at a brisk pace, with more reward given for speed of learning than for errorless responses. Giving positive reinforcement for quick responses in phonics lessons will likely bring out wrong responses that might otherwise be hidden, foster intelligent guessing, and generally act to reduce pupils' reluctance to respond or the tension of the learning situation.

2. **What forms should lessons take?** We have noted above that in some unusual cases children who are restless and inattentive during lessons may truly not be emotionally "ready." However, the large majority of children who exhibit inattentiveness, we feel, do so for other reasons.

The causes of their lack of empathy for the phonics activities probably lie in the form of the lesson itself.

Lessons will frustrate and repel children if they have these four insidious aspects: (1) children must wait long for turns, (2) they do not understand what they are being asked to perceive and how to respond, (3) they are not given immediate "right" or "wrong" feedback for responses, and (4) they are not told by the teacher at all times which words are exceptions to the rules being learned. The *first* of these instructional faults—requiring children to wait for turns—can be avoided easily through the use of *response cards.* These are cards containing the answers the phonics teacher hopes to elicit. Each child is given a few. The teacher asks for a response. *Each child responds each time by raising a card.* The happy result: no child has to wait for a turn. In addition, the teacher learns immediately how many children are catching on.

The *second* major fault of phonics lessons is more difficult to remedy. Part of the problem is solved, nonetheless, by the use of response cards. If children are active at all times, they are more likely to be attentive. And, if they are more attentive, it follows that they will miss less of the lesson, and therefore what is being taught will become more meaningful. It is helpful, too, if the teacher makes quite sure whether a child understands a question *before* assuming the child cannot respond correctly. Unless proved otherwise, the teacher should assume the question is poorly phrased rather than that the child cannot answer. It is remarkable how many times unresponsive children will answer when a question is asked in a different way.

The *third* major fault of lessons—the lack of feedback—is partly overcome by the use of the response cards. The teacher should also be alert at all times to mistakes children make in the lessons and be quick to tell them "right" or "wrong." To be able to respond to children in this way means, of course, that the teacher cannot teach large groups of children. Groups for instruction must be small enough so that the teacher is aware of and can respond to each child.

The need for feedback carries with it a necessary evil. This is the matter of telling children when they are wrong. Unless children are told which of their responses are incorrect, they are unlikely to learn which responses are usable in the future (Frayer & Klausmeier 1971). Some sensitive children who make wrong responses will become anxious in this situation, nonetheless, and rather than run the risk of being punished (in their eyes) for a wrong response, will hazard no responses. Children who develop such anxieties display their fear of the situation by finding other things to do during the lesson, such as talking to or hitting classmates, conveniently losing the place, finding all sorts of objects to play with, daydreaming, talking to themselves, asking irrelevant questions, and so on. With either introverted or extroverted behavior, children signal that they are overwhelmed by the negative feedback received. To help relieve this trauma the teacher must put such children into a group at a lower level of accomplishment where negative feedback for them will be less likely. The confidence these children can build in their ability at this level will condition them for greater tolerance of negative feedback in the future.

Feedback should often take the form of asking, "Did that sound right or make sense?" This helps children develop a strategy for correcting their miscues, especially those that are syntactically acceptable—for example, the substitution of a different noun for the actual noun in a sentence.

Evidence of the danger of erroneous or misinformative feedback by the teacher is now available. A serious hazard to learning is created when children are told by the teacher that their responses are wrong when they are actually correct. Less-well-known (or understood) research findings suggest that misinformative feedback to children on one task may even inhibit their performance on a later task (Frayer & Klausmeier 1971). The clear implication here is that the effective teacher is one who is well informed. Clearly, teachers who "stay one page ahead of the child" in teaching reading are a genuine handicap to the child's learning, since the probability of their providing misinformative feedback is high.

To overcome the *fourth* major fault—words that contain untaught rules—these words must be viewed by pupil and teacher alike as exceptions. A low frequency of such words should be presented, of course. Above all, children must be reminded that it is not their fault if they respond wrongly to exceptional words. Children also should be complimented for their good thinking when they apply a spelling-sound rule to a word to which it happens not to apply.

There are other ways the teacher can shape successful word recognition lessons:

- Utilize children's personal meaning vocabularies. Familiar words imbedded in familiar sentence patterns help pupils understand.
- Consciously endeavor to talk in uncomplicated sentences. Instruc-

tions, directions, or questions given in complex syntax invite misunderstandings.

- Shift or "branch" to something children have previously demonstrated knowledge of when they appear confused.
- Rephrasing directions and questions sometimes helps.
- Giving the activity a game-like format convinces some children that the effort to understand will be worthwhile, that is, it will be rewarded with something that is fun to do.
- Reduce the number of difficult concepts to an absolute minimum and teach these by using examples rather than rules.
- Encourage the children to say aloud the words involved in the lesson. A reinforcement to the written word of its spoken equivalent, even when done in a stage whisper, often makes a relationship clear. Word recognition lessons are not "Be quiet and listen" activities.
- Be persistent and repeat something that was previously misunderstood. Remember, children may be grasping a word recognition concept even though at a given point they cannot produce a proper response.
- Let a child who does understand what is being taught explain it to the others. Somehow, such explanations are often effective when the teacher's are not.
- Practice the general rules of teaching effectiveness. For example, make sure children have settled down before beginning; remove distracting influences; appear enthusiastic and positive about the planned activity; make many rewarding remarks about responses; work off muscular discomfort by having children stand to respond and by alternating activities (board work, response cards, talking); begin by doing something everyone knows how to do; utilize innocuous competition to see who gets a privilege; attach humorous names to difficult concepts (for example, "bossy" *r*); and have children repeat something the teacher says to find how well they understand it.

3. Is small-group instruction the most effective way to teach word recognition? In small-group teaching, the teacher can make it possible for all children in the group to respond regularly to the activities being conducted. The teacher can thus secure the evidence of the different rates at which these children learn so that new, small groups can be continuously formed. Continuing the reformation of these groups is critical to such small-group teaching.

Research on classroom instruction indicates that "teachers who group their students for instruction tend to have more academic-engaged time and higher reading achievement" (Rosenshine & Stevens, 1984, p. 787). Grouping pupils for instruction allows for more teacher-led demonstrations, pupil practice, teacher feedback to pupils, and better management of pupils' behavior.

4.   **What is the optimal kind of writing of letters for word recognition?** It seems a truism that if the material of a lesson is written by a teacher in a legible manner this will facilitate pupils' learning (Groff, 1975). The degree to which the teacher can approximate the models of letters found in handwriting manuals doubtless does help pupils perceive differences in letter forms. While it is more difficult to isolate other factors that affect the readability of letters, there is some relevant evident.

For some time we have known that manuscript handwriting is more readable for pupils and therefore is read by them faster than is cursive handwriting. Turner's finding to this effect in 1930 has been confirmed by several other researchers. Keller's (1974) research also suggests there is no disadvantage to the learner in having to read the teacher's manuscript handwriting rather than printed materials. Zachrisson (1965) has found that both first- and fourth-grade pupils read materials in sans serif print just as well as that in print with serifs. In print with serifs a tiny line is used to finish off a main stroke of a letter, as you can see at the top and bottom of l and x. In sans serif print these letters would appear as l and x). Manuscript letters written by the phonics teacher are sans (without) serif, of course.

Lower-case letters are about as easy for the beginning reader to learn as upper-case (Smythe, et al. 1971), and "several experiments have shown that lower case is more legible than capitals" (Zachrisson 1965, p. 43). It makes sense for the teacher to use lower-case letters as much as possible in instruction.

Length of the most legible line has been investigated, too. Tinker (1963, p. 211) found "a slight and rather consistent tendency for the shorter lines [3.5 inches] to be read faster" by mature readers, and a study by Luckiesh and Moss (1942, p. 203) led them to say that the most readable lines are slightly more than two inches in length. Word recognition worksheets should therefore have lines between two inches and three and a half inches long.

Finally, letters crowded together make a word suffer from an effect called "masking," which makes the middle letters of a word difficult to identify. A study of this effect (Linkz, 1973, p. 164) reveals that a careful separation of the letters reduces the masking effect on middle letters. (Masking probably explains in part why children see the beginning and ending letters of a word more readily than those in the middle.) Teachers writing words for beginning readers should leave generous spaces between the letters. Typewritten material does not allow for generous letter spacing, so children should be able to read well-spaced manuscript handwriting as well as they can typewritten material.

5. **How does one evaluate children's achievement of word recognition?** Generally, the evaluation of children's growth in word recognition should be based on the principles of teaching given in Chapter 5. The teacher should look to several sources of children's reading for such evidence: testing should be done on language the children actually use; the adult model of reading performance should *not* be held as the standard to measure pupil progress; the testing of pupils' skills should first be with one-syllable, predictably spelled words, and so on.

More specifically, a good system of evaluation has the following features:

- An insistence that children read for meaning. With the exception of the use of pseudowords (*glurch*) to test phonics knowledge, children's ability to tell the meaning of what they read should not be overlooked.
- Evidence that evaluation is ongoing with few, if any, formal tests. Each instructional period should allow for a few minutes for the teacher to review what children have learned.
- Teachers' awareness that some children cannot always produce evidence of their comprehension of what is being taught. In these cases, attentiveness is a good sign of learning.
- The testing of children's knowledge of function words within familiar syntax.
- Finding out regularly whether children can apply phonics generalizations they learned at previous levels or times of instruction. Backtracking or recapitulation may be required.
- An emphasis on the analysis of words, and yet the encouragement of reading speed. "How fast can you read this word?" should be a common challenge.
- The absence of requirements that children repeat phonics rules in a verbalized, verbatim fashion. The teacher's basic concern rather should be whether children can actually read, within sentences, certain kinds of words that follow various spelling patterns and structures.

- An awareness that children's use of nonstandard dialect may make it appear they have made a reading error when this is not the case. Children's oral reading may be a translation of the standard English of the written page into the sounds, words, and intonation of their own dialect, which may not be a standard dialect.
- A consideration of whether the mistake children make is similar, grammatically and phonemically, to the words they attempt to read. If the miscue is the *same part of speech* as the word on the page, the child is using sentence structure as an aid to word recognition. If the sounds of the miscue made by children are similar to the sounds the word on the page would have, children are trying to use phonics. The teacher should notice precisely the nature of these attempts to use phonics, and where they went astray, in order to correct the misinterpretation.
- A patient attitude toward children, permitting enough time for them to correct their reading mistakes. Too often teachers correct children at the moment they make errors. It is better, instead, to allow a reasonable amount of time for children to correct themselves. If children return to the word or passage on the page that was involved in the miscue and read it correctly, this should be considered a good sign. These regressions in reading, which traditionally were thought to be a bad practice, are to be seen as normal and can be encouraged.

Standardize tests are yet another means used to evaluate pupils' growth in word recognition. Unfortunately, children have difficulty in following the directions in the standardized diagnostic tests in reading. When such tests are administered to groups of children, it is good to prepare children to do their best on these tests by having them practice completing the types of exercises found in phonics tests. Winkley's analysis (1971) of nine major phonics tests shows that they ask children to:

- Give the names of letters.
- Select a letter from a group of letters so as to mark the one(s) that correspond to a sound heard in a spoken word. This is done at the beginning, middle, and end of words.
- Select a printed word in which a letter appears that stands for a particular phoneme in another word (no spoken word given).
- Select a pseudoword, such as *spiness*, from others after hearing its pronunciation.

- Find and mark the letter representing the sound heard in the name of a pictured object.
- Mark a word for the same purpose. Beginning, middle, and ending errors appear in the words used as foils.
- Recall the grapheme representing a phoneme heard in a word and write it. (Phonics tests have spelling items as well as reading items.)
- Select a word spelled phonetically to match a regular spelling such as *throo-through*.

It is impossible to give specific advice on how to decide at what point children have learned enough of any particular topic in word recognition to move on to the next item. Some argue that a certain criterion, a percent of correct responses like 80 percent, should be set that children would have to meet (Otto, et al. 1974). Some teachers may want to use this rather arbitrary system. Others advise that the teacher have children read aloud selections from graded basal readers at one grade level, then move to the next higher, and so on, until they miss a certain number of words. Some think that scores from standardized tests (given at some indeterminate point) should be used.

Teachers, therefore, might use evidence gathered from all of these methods of evaluation in their efforts to determine when pupils are ready for the next level in word recognition. Overall, the best guide we can offer as to when a teacher should discontinue the teaching of a certain word recognition item or to advance to the one at the next higher level is children's attitudes toward learning the item in question. The teacher must judge when pupil frustration begins to set in, so that a slowing down, a reteaching, or a shift to a new item is called for. Experience with teaching is the best and perhaps the only way to develop such judgments.

6. **What is the difference between teaching word recognition and testing it?** Teachers need to make a clear distinction between the teaching and the testing of word recognition skills. Giving children an assignment that tests their word recognition abilities is not teaching. Having children apply or practice these abilities is not teaching, either. Finding out what children already know, a common practice in schools, is not instruction.

There is evidence that teachers mistakenly believe that seatwork assignments in which children practice skills, or other activities in which children display their skills, is instruction. The likelihood that the classroom time currently given to word recognition tends to be practice and testing rather than teaching is suggested by Durkin (1978–79). She found that less than half of one percent of the time spent on reading instruction in classrooms was devoted to the teaching of reading comprehension skills. It was obvious that the teachers in Durkin's study mistook their testing or drill of students' comprehension with the development of this knowledge through teaching. These teachers confused the overlearning or examination of these skills with their acquisition.

In this book care will be taken to distinguish teaching activity from that which tests or drills children. The teacher, too, is advised to make these distinctions. Knowing the difference between teaching and pupil practice does not mean that this latter activity is insignificant. To the contrary, the overlearning that comes from practice with word recognition information is necessary for children to be able to put this information into their long-term memory. Unless there is overlearning of word recognition skills, children will tend to forget them and thus be unable to apply them when needed.

7. **Should word recognition be taught as a hierarchy of skills?** Research supports LaBerge's (1979, p. 49) view that "Quite probably, the acquisition of word codes proceeds by stages that may be arranged hierarchically." Some reading experts disagree, however, and contend that there is no legitimate hierarchy of reading skills, nor will anyone in the future be able to design one. We have arranged the word recognition skills in this book into a hierarchy partly on the basis of evidence that systematic instruction brings greater reading achievement than does unsystematic instruction (Rosenshine & Stevens, 1984). While the order of these levels of instruction appears logical to us, we have no absolute proof from experimental studies that it is the best for all pupils. Some teachers may note that their pupils find information given at a lower level more difficult to learn than material at a higher level. If so, they should rearrange the levels to suit the abilities of their students.

8. **What are the criteria for effective materials for individual practice (worksheets)?** Osborn (1985) offers some pertinent information in this respect:

- To be effective a worksheet should be closely related to the one that precedes and follows it.
- Occasionally this practice sheet should be a review of previous learning.
- Only the most important aspect of a given lesson should be included in a single worksheet.

- There should be enough items in the worksheet on the aspect to be practiced to make sure pupils master it. Extra worksheets should be available for pupils who need more practice.
- There should be a long enough sequence of worksheets on a single aspect to be learned (massed practice) to make sure a pupil will master it.
- Instructions on the worksheet should be clear and easy to follow. Instructions should use familiar, easy-to-read words in very short sentences.
- The layout or format of the worksheet, including its title, should be stimulating yet explicit and easy to interpret. All art work should be educationally helpful.
- Typographical errors, wrong information, and other faults must be edited out of the worksheet.
- Occasionally the worksheet should be for fun—that is, in the form of a contest, game, or puzzle.
- Pupils should not be asked to use the same mark, e.g., *x*, or —, to indicate whether a word chosen as an answer is the incorrect or correct answer.
- Worksheets should have children write answers, rather than simply mark answers, whenever this is possible.
- The content of worksheets should have educational merit. An undesirable task, for example, would be to have children underline the letter in a sentence that appears most often. Nonfunctional practice like this should be avoided.

REFERENCES

Durkin, D. (1978–79). What classroom observations reveal about reading comprehension instruction. *Reading Research Quarterly,* 14, 481–533.

Frayer, D.A., & Klausmeier, H.J. (1971). *Variables in concept learning: Task variables.* Madison, WI: University of Wisconsin Research and Development Center for Cognitive Learning.

Groff, P. (1975). Can pupils read what teachers write? *Elementary School Journal,* 76, 32–39.

Keller, N.B. (1974). An investigation into the problems of word recognition as affected by different kinds of print. *Dissertation Abstracts International,* 34, 6518A.

LaBerge, D. (1979). The perception of units in beginning reading. In L. B. Resnick & P. A. Weaver (Eds.), *Theory and practice of early reading, volume 3.* Hillsdale, NJ: Lawrence Erlbaum.

Linksz, A. (1973). *On writing, reading and dyslexia.* New York, NY: Grune & Stratton.

Luckiesh, M. & Moss, F.K. (1942). *Reading as a visual task.* New York, NY: D.Van Nostrand.

Osborn, J. (1985). Workbooks: Counting, matching, and judging. In J. Osborn, P.T. Wilson, and R.C. Anderson (Eds.), *Reading education: Foundations for a literate America.* Lexington, MA: Lexington.

Otto, W., et al. (1974). *Focused reading instruction.* Reading, MA: Addison-Wesley.

Rosenshine B., & Stevens, R. (1984). Classroom instruction in reading. In P.D. Pearson (Ed.), *Handbook of reading research.* New York, NY: Longman.

Smythe, P.C., et al. (1971). Developmental factors in elemental skills: Knowledge of upper-case and lowercase letter names. *Journal of Reading Behavior,* 3, 24–33.

Tinker, M. A. (1963). *Legibility of print.* Ames, IA: Iowa State University Press.

Turner, O.G. (1930). The comparative legibility and speed of manuscript and cursive handwriting. *Elementary School Journal,* 30, 780–786.

Winkley, C. (1971). What do diagnostic tests really diagnose? In R. E. Liebert (Ed.), *Diagnostic viewpoints in reading.* Newark, DE: International Reading Association.

Zachrisson, B.L. (1965). *Studies in the legibility of printed text.* Stockholm: Almquist and Wiksell.

7

...NG RECOGNITION OF MONOSYLLABIC WORDS

Because word recognition instruction should begin with aspects that are the easiest for children to learn, we start with teaching children to recognize one-syllable words. They are easier to learn to recognize than are multisyllabic words.

This chapter describes ten different levels of word recognition that children need to master in order to recognize monosyllabic words. These levels are arranged in a hierarchy of difficulty, beginning with material least difficult to learn and advancing gradually to the most difficult. Activities by which children can practice skills taught at each of these levels are in Appendix A.

Level 1. This first phase of word recognition instruction concentrates on the development of children's concept of the word. The purpose of this instruction is to bring to children's conscious awareness the fact that the sentences they speak are made up of separate linguistic units called words. Some children are familiar with the idea of the word when they enter school, but it cannot be taken for granted that children in general understand this concept (Downing & Oliver, 1973–74).

To develop the concept of the word the teacher begins by demonstrating to pupils that spoken language is not a continuous stream of sound but is made up of units called words. The teacher begins this process by reminding children that familiar words can be isolated. The idea that *cat*, for example, is one word is established. This can be done by labeling a picture of a cat with the word *cat*.

It is usually easy at this point for children to realize that *big cat* is two words, that *the big cat* is three, that *the big cat ran* is four and that *the big cat ran away* is five. To successfully participate in this activity children must be able to count objects, one, two, three, and so on. They must also understand the words, *first, second, third,* and so on. When having children identify words in spoken sentences the teacher will often say, "Listen for the first (second, etc.) word in this sentence."

Finally, children should be shown what words look like. To explain that we can write the words we speak, and that they "look like this": (write on the chalkboard the words you have had them listen for, and read them aloud, pointing). Call attention to the spaces between the words; indicate that this is how we know where one word leaves off and another begins. Hold up a favorite storybook and show the separate words in the title, reading them aloud. Ask how many words it has.

Level 2. The second step in word recognition instruction is the development of children's abilities to recognize and name letters. Explain to the children that words we write are made up of letters, and that each letter has a name. Since the 1920s, at least, it has been found that children's abilities to recognize letters is the single best predictor of first-grade reading achievement (Smith 1963). Several research studies reinforce the conclusion that learning letters is of great value to the beginning reader (Speer & Lamb, 1976; Richek, 1977–78). The value to children learning to read of learning the names of letters remains a controversial issue, however (Groff, 1984). There is evidence, on the one hand, that children's knowledge of letter names correlates highly with their success in learning to read. In fact, letter-name knowledge correlates more highly with reading success than does intelligence test scores (Chall, 1983). On the other hand, teaching letter names as isolated information has proved to be of no greater benefit in reading development than other training (Mason, 1984).

It appears now, however, that if letter names are taught simultaneously with phonics the integration of these two factors will significantly affect reading acquisition (Ehri, 1983). Letter-name knowledge seems to act as a mediating help for children as they learn to relate speech sounds to letters (Mason, 1984). One valuable aspect of this interrelationship is that letter-name knowledge facilitates the communication that goes on between pupils and teachers during phonics instruction (Weaver, 1978).

The best method, therefore, is to teach concurrently the letters and their names *plus* the sounds they represent. As Ohnmacht found in her study (n.d.), "initial instruction [for first graders] in letter names and sounds produced significantly greater reading achievement than did instruction in letter names alone." The findings of Nevins (1973) and of Jenkins, Bausell, and Jenkins (1972) agree with those of Ohnmacht. This means that after a couple of letters have been learned the teacher should proceed to activities with words involving these letters. *Repeat this cycle until all the letters are learned.*

We want to stress that the system of letter learning suggested here is not an activity isolated in time from teaching pupils how speech sounds are represented by letters. Pupils should learn very few letters before beginning to learn the relationships of these letters to the sounds they represent. As often as possible words also should be presented to pupils in sentences, *so that children are taught from the beginning to recognize words (1) through the use of phonics cues,* and *(2) from context and semantics cues.* This practice helps keep another all-important principle before pupils— that reading is a meaning-getting activity and not an isolated and formalistic exercise in letter or word identification.

We suggest that the development of children's abilities to recognize and name letters be carried out with the following instructional techniques:

- Have letter cards for each child. By using these response cards the children do not have to wait to take turns. Each can respond at every step of the lesson. When the children hold up their letter cards, the teacher can easily see who has made an incorrect response and can help correct it.
- The use of at least two letters, and therefore two different letter cards, in all lessons has a distinct advantage. It requires that the child make many discriminations that would not be otherwise necessary. When beginning to work with letters, ask children to just say whether the two letters shown them are "the same" or "different." This will be relatively easy for them (Gibson 1963). Then increase the level of difficulty by having the pupils match a given letter with a multiple-choice set of two letters, then three, then four, and so on. After two letters are learned, it is wise in teaching slower learners to introduce only one new letter in the next lesson.
- Use lower-case letters first, since children will need to read these much more often than they will upper-case letters. Lower-case letters are only slightly more difficult to learn to name than are upper-case letters; 84 percent of seven-year-olds can name the former, 86 percent the latter (Smythe et al. 1971).
- The use of colored chalk is recommended as a means of helping children to see isolated letters and letters at the beginnings of one-vowel words. One study (Jones 1965) found that young children did significantly better on matching tests of words and letters when these were in color instead of black and white. In his review of such research Otto saw the implication of these studies to be "that children's

paired-associate learning should be enhanced by the addition of color cues for any or all of the following reasons: aided perception and increased differentiation, the opportunity for cue selection, and greater motivation. Furthermore, there is the possibility that color may serve as a vehicle for mediation" (1967, p. 40). This use of colored chalk seems particularly pertinent for vowel-letter recognition. Each of the vowel letters can be given a different color representing the sound it stands for.

- As children begin reading, they should learn the *allographs* of a grapheme (the different forms of the same letter, such as a-A-*a*). *After* children can distinguish and name the lower-case allograph of a grapheme they should be taught to identify the others (Rystrom 1969). Do not teach different allographs of a grapheme at the same time.

- The letters need not be taught in alphabetical order, since children learning to read have no need for knowledge of this ordering. It is not necessary to use such activities as singing games to learn the alphabet because such ordering has little if anything to do with the central task here, which is learning to make the correct association of letter names and forms.

- The learning of letters depends on learning the distinctive features of the letters to be discriminated, the differences in form that allow children to distinguish one letter from another. While logical to assume, it has also been verified experimentally that it is easier for children to learn highly similar letters (*b-d*) if these are not presented to the child toegether. In fact, the child learns dissimilar letters (*s-b*) better if these are presented together (Williams 1970). Each letter in a pair being taught should differ from the other letter in more than one feature, if possible. As Gibson has explained (1968), a letter that differs in only one feature from another letter is more often confused than one differing in two or more features. Probably the features of letters that are used to recognize them are

curved (*o, c, p*) or straight (*k, l*)
closed (*o, p*) or open (*c, k*)
descending (*g, y*) or ascending (*l, f*)
symmetrical (*v, m*) or nonsymmetrical (*r, f*)
intersected (*t, p*) or nonintersected (*l, c*)
diagonal (*w, z*) or nondiagonal (*g, h*)
vertical (*l, i*) or nonvertical (*e, w*)

horizontal-vertical (*t*) or horizontal-diagonal (*z*)
diagonal-vertical (*k*) or diagonal-horizontal (*z*), and so on.

- A preferred sequence for teaching consonant and vowel letters can be arranged based on the principle that as nearly as possible phonics should be taught with high-frequency monosyllabic words. The following suggested sequence for teaching letters is based on (1) the difficulty of writing and naming these letters, (2) the need to contrast letters with different graphic features, and (3) the frequency with which consonant letters appear initially in high-frequency words (Groff, 1977). On the basis of these considerations the following order for teaching letters should be used (repetitions are indicated with broken lines):

t-s   l-c   f-m   b-r   h-w
\   \   \   \   \
a-t   o-l   e-f   i-b   u-h

p-v   d-n   k-g   j-z   q-x   y-any letter

- As soon as children can identify a letter by name they can be taught to write it. Writing letters reinforces children's recognition of them.

Level 3. At this third stage of word recognition instruction, children learn that spoken words are made up of sounds, which we blend together when we speak. They are taught (*a*) to segment spoken words into their separate phonemes and then (*b*) to blend these individual phonemes together to produce spoken words.

There may be no more important skill in phonics for children learning to read to master than the ability to segment words into phonemes and then to blend these isolated phonemes so that spoken words are produced. The research substantiates the conclusion that being able to manipulate phonemes in words is very important for children learning to read (Weaver 1978). These segmenting-blending skills must be present if a child is to be able to decode an unrecognized written word (Johnson & Baumann, 1984).

If children are to segment words into their phonemes they must recognize first that words are made up of discrete speech sounds. Children at Level 1 learned that sentences are composed of words. Now they are ready to learn that words are made up of speech sounds.

Children at school-entry age normally have an understanding of the concept of *sound.* "What does a train sound like?" and "Can you make the sound a cat makes?" are questions these pupils can ordinarily answer correctly. *Sound* is a concept so central to the teaching of phonics, however, that the teacher should ensure that children at Level 3 understand it fully.

The development of children's awareness that spoken words are made up of separate phonemes may appear at first a difficult task for children to accomplish. It is obviously more difficult to segment words into their phonemes than to segment sentences into their words. The better that children grasp the idea that sentences can be broken down into individual words, and that these words can be said in isolation and then blended together into sentences, the more ready children are to learn to segment words into phonemes. Because of the relative difficulty of teaching children to segment and blend phonemes it is necessary to use some visual aids for this purpose.

Accordingly, it is good to begin Level 3 with blocks or cards of different colors. To start this instruction each child is given these materials. After this, the teacher says: "Listen to this word (/an/; /a/-/n/). Say these two sounds. This green block is for /a/. This white block is for /n/. Let's put a green and a white block together to make /an/. Show me the block you use for /a/. For /n/. Make /an/ on your desk with two blocks. How many sounds are there in /an/? How many blocks are needed to make /an/?" This same procedure would be continued to develop children's abilities to segment the speech sounds out of three-, four-, and five-phoneme words, for example, *man-and; sand; stand.*

As practice to reinforce the ability of pupils to segment spoken words into phonemes it is profitable to use a "total response" technique. Here the teacher displays four colored blocks, for example red, green, white, and blue, and indicates that these represent the speech sounds in *sand.* The teacher now bids the pupils as a group to "Show me the /s/ block, the /a/ block," and so on. This exercise is continued until children can quickly and accurately detect the serial order of phonemes as they appear in spoken words.

At this point in Level 3 the teacher pronounces phonemes in isolation and has pupils say the word that a blend of these phonemes would make. The teacher says, for example, /a/-/n/. The pupils answer /an/. Then children are asked to say in isolation the phonemes they hear in words spoken to them: the teacher says /an/, the pupils /a/-/n/. Another way to test children's abilities to segment words into phonemes is the activity that Heilman (1985) recommends for teaching this ability. If children can listen to words that begin or end with the same phoneme and then volunteer successfully other words that begin or end with this same speech sound, one is fairly sure they have mastered the major goal of Level 3.

A further examination of children's ability to perceive individual phonemes can be made by asking them to speak words from which phonemes have been omitted. For example, the teacher says, "Listen to *man*. Now say *man* without the /m/; without the /n/. Listen to *break*. Now say *break* without the /r/." Continue with *desk* without the /s/, *skin* without the /k/, and with other words.

As noted, there is abundant research evidence to support the conclusion that children's abilities to segment spoken words into phonemes is a critical, if not the most important, prerequisite to their acquisition of reading ability (Ehri, 1979; Liberman & Shankweiler, 1979; Stanovich, 1982). Children who attain this skill quickly and easily ordinarily go on to become good readers. Those who find this accomplishment cumbersome and time-consuming generally fall behind others of their age group in reading growth (Wallach & Wallach, 1979).

When one attempts to say phonemes in isolation one distorts their authentic sounds. This distortion is obviously greater for consonants than vowels, and greater for some consonants than others. When said in isolation the plosive consonant sounds /p, t, ch, k, b, d, j and g/ (see Chapter 3) are the most distorted, because in saying them one has a tendency to add a schwa sound, especially to voiced sounds, and make them sound like *duh, juh,* and so on. The teacher should try to avoid adding vowel sounds to consonants and avoid voicing unvoiced sounds.

Should the ease of saying a phoneme in isolation be taken into consideration when teaching children to segment spoken words into their phonemes? Coleman (1970) and Marsh & Mineo (1977) say yes. It does appear logical that children will be better able to segment and blend sounds from words like *man* (nasal consonants) than from words like *pick* (plosive consonants). As Anderson, et al. (1985, p. 41) say, however, "this problem may be more hypothetical than real, since there does not appear to be evidence that hearing or producing imprecise speech sounds is an actual obstacle to figuring out words."

Level 4. In this fourth period of monosyllabic word recognition instruction children are taught to recognize (1) the correspondences between single consonants and vowel letters and the speech sounds these spellings represent, and (2) the correspondences between consonant clusters and the speech sounds they represent. Children thus are taught to recognize correspondences between phonemes and graphemes. Children will have been prepared for this task by having previously been taught the concepts of *words, letters,* and *speech sounds* (phonemes). At Level 4 these three aspects of knowledge are brought together for the purpose of teaching children to decode monosyllabic words.

Instruction at Level 4 proceeds in the following manner. Teachers have children segment the phonemes out of a monosyllabic word spoken to them, such as *man.* The pupils note that this word has three different sounds, /m/-/a/-/n/. The teacher then demonstrates that *man* is written with three letters. The pupils are asked to write and then say the names of these three letters. The teacher now says, in serial order, the phonemes that each of the letters in *man* represent. The pupils are directed to repeat the teacher's expression of these three phonemes, and to say the word they produce. This cycle is repeated for other monosyllabic words, including ones with initial and ending consonant clusters, such as *shot* and *hand.* A preferred order of instruction for monosyllabic words with consonant clusters (Groff, 1977) is displayed in Tables 7 and 8. The orderings in these tables are based on the readability of words with such clusters, on the frequency of occurrence of these words, on the total number of these words, and on their spelling difficulty.

TABLE 7.
A Recommended Sequence for Initial Clusters

1. sh	6. sp	11. th (*thing*)	16. fl	21. thr
2. st	7. pl	12. dr	17. pr	21. sw
3. gr	8. tr	12. wh (*when*)	17. cr	23. gl
4. cl	9. ch	14. bl	19. str	24. qu
5. th (*the*)	10. br	15. fr	20. sl	25. sk

TABLE 8.
A Recommended Sequence for Ending Clusters

1. ll	6. nt	11. nk	16. sh	21. sk	26. ct
2. nd	6. ch	12. ss	17. rn	22. lt	27. pt
3. st	8. th	13. rm	18. mp	23. lk	28. mb
4. ng	9. ld	14. rk	19. ft	24. ff	29. rl
5. ck	10. rt	15. rd	19. gh	25. lf	30. lm

The teaching of consonant-letter clusters can follow two patterns. These clusters can be taught in the recommended sequence as entities. For this purpose children can be given cards on which the separate clusters *sh, st, gr,* and so on, are printed. The children hold up the *sh* card if, in a word said by the teacher, they hear the sound *sh* stands for. They can also play bingo and other games involving this cluster. (See Appendix B.) They can write *sh* as they hear it in words and can add it to given phonograms.

A second useful activity is to lead children to realize that they can build or recognize many new unfamiliar words by changing a single letter in a consonant-letter cluster. For this purpose a list of words (for example, *lack, lame, lank, last*) to which single letters can be added (in this case, *b*) to make words with clusters (*black, blame, blank, blast*) should be used. Here is an example of how such an activity can be conducted.

Write *top* on the chalkboard. Tell the pupils that they are now going to create a different word by adding another sound and letter before *top.* Ask them—

- to listen to the word *stop* as you pronounce it;
- to say *stop* and listen to the word as they say it;
- to tell what sound was added to *top* to make *stop,* and what letter stands for that sound.

Write *s* before the word *top* on the chalkboard and ask the class to say *top* and *stop* and listen to the difference between the two words. Discuss this difference with the class. Remind the pupils that while the cluster /st/ seems to be almost one sound, it is really two separate sounds and must be written with two separate letters (Hanna, Hodges & Hanna, 1971, p. 138).

Level 5. In Level 5 children are taught to recognize the sound-spellings of closed syllables, or phonograms. These are one-vowel phonograms that use single-letter vowel graphemes. They are found in words

- spelled with beginning single consonants, as in *c*at;
- spelled with beginning consonant clusters, as in *st*op;
- spelled with ending consonant clusters, as in da*sh,* ta*ll,* ha*nd;* and
- spelled with both beginning and ending consonant clusters, as in *crash.*

Level 5 presents an additional way to teach children the relationships between vowel phonemes and the ways they are spelled. At this level children strengthen their understanding of vowel phonemes and the letters that represent them by seeing these correspondences in phonograms. See Chapter 5 for lists of these phonograms.

Phonograms whose vowels are represented by single-letter graphemes are taught at this early level principally because these phonograms represent certain predictable sound-spelling correspondences. We found in our analysis of high-frequency monosyllabic words (Groff 1972) that the graphemes *a, e, i, o, u* represented the sounds /a, e, i, o, u/ in 86 percent of the phonograms in these words.

There seems little doubt that phonics helps the child develop a system for determining which of the sixteen vowel phonemes to give to a vowel grapheme. Whatever graphemes *follow the vowel grapheme in a word* generally act as signals to the pronunciation of that vowel grapheme. In learning to read phonograms, therefore, pupils learn to look beyond the vowel letter. That is, to determine the sound of the vowel letter in the phonogram, they must recognize the consonant letters that follow it. These consonants signal the sound the vowel letter represents. For example, we cannot read the *co* of *co_____* until we see the consonant letters that fit the slot (*co-b, co-ld, co-rd, co-me*).

To provide for individual differences, it is wise to teach children both methods of recognition: attending to vowel graphemes as isolated word parts, and recognizing the vowel grapheme along with the following consonant. Sullivan, Okada, and Niedermeyer (1971) and Neuman (1981) found that some pupils learn word recognition better with isolated vowel graphemes, while others learned better by seeing them in phonograms.

Using phonograms as an approach to reading vowel letters eliminates the questions of whether instruction should begin with letters that represent free vowel sounds or checked vowel sounds. Since a very high percent of closed syllables (V–C clusters) have either a checked vowel or /o/, it is reasonable to begin with phonograms that have checked vowels and move to those with free vowels.

Develop the phonogram approach in two main stages: (1) Writing and expanding on phonograms and (2) identifying longer words by first recognizing their phonograms.

(1) Writing phonograms is not difficult. As soon as pupils can write the vowel letters and a few consonant letters, they can write phonograms. For example, when pupils can write the five vowel letters and two consonant letters (*t-n*), they can write the following ten phonograms: (t)*an*, (t)*en*, (t)*in*, *on*, (n)*un*, *at*, (n)*et*, *it*, (n)*ot*, (n)*ut*. When pupils have learned three more consonant letters, they can write the words *ben, bin, ban, bun; can;*

den, din, dan, don, dun; fin, fan, fun. Have them write the words here that are in their listening vocabularies. Most experienced teachers agree that teaching children to write these few letters takes only a relatively short time. Moreover, with the exception of *ot* and *ut*, these phonograms occur in the top five percent of the most frequently seen phonograms in common words (Jones 1970).

It is relatively easy to show the pupil how a short phonogram can be extended. For example, (c)*ar* can be extended to *art*, (c)*art;* arm to (h)*arm;* (f)*or* to (f)*ort*, (f)*ord*, (f)*orm*. This is another application of the rule: Find the phonogram by going past the vowel letter until the consonant letters stop, unless you see a suffix.

(2) Recognizing phonograms is a vital aid to identifying longer words. The phonogram approach adapts itself to the linguistic controls on its identification—that is, as pupils mature in their ability to use phonograms, they notice that their search for them is conditioned by additional instruction given for analyzing multisyllabic words. For details on how this works, see Chapter 8.

Level 6. In this level children are taught to recognize another kind of closed syllable, or phonogram: the one-vowel letter phonogram that ends with the marker letter *e*. This *e* serves as a sign that tells the reader which sound the vowel letter just before it represents, e.g., m*a*ke.

At this level children learn to say a different vowel sound for a vowel letter than they have at previous levels. Earlier, they learned to give one-vowel letter phonograms the sounds /a, e, i, o, u/. At Level 6 they are moved to phonograms that use free vowel sounds and that end in the marker *e*.

In *cake*, for example, the marker *e* signals that the previous *a* represents /ā/. At Level 6 children are taught to recognize phonograms that end in the marker *e* (often inaccurately called "silent e") both in words with single consonant letters, as in *cake, home, nice, cute,* and in words with beginning and/or ending consonant clusters as in *tribe, paste.* The single vowel letters for the above spellings in (1) and (2) represent the vowel sounds /ā, ē, ī, ō, yōō/.

Our suggested instruction for marker-*e* words is based on our analysis of high-frequency monosyllabic words with the marker *e* (Groff, 1972), which revealed that:

- Fifty-eight percent had the spelling CVC*e*, as in *bake*. The vowel sounds /ā, ē, ī, ō, yōō/ occurred in these words 91 percent of the time.

- Thirty-one percent had the spelling CCVC*e*, as in *blame.* The vowel sounds /ā, ē, ī, ō, yōō/ occurred in these words 97 percent of the time.
- Four percent had the spellings CVCC*e* or CCVCC*e*, as in *waste, change.* The vowel sounds /ā, ē, ī, ō, yōō/ occurred in them 100 percent of the time.
- Seven percent had the spellings CVCC*e* or CCVCC*e*, as in *judge, bridge.* The vowel sounds /a, e, i, o, u/ occurred in them 88 percent of the time.

The goal of Level 6, accordingly, is to lead children to realize that a very high percent of single vowel letter marker-*e* phonograms represent the vowel sounds /ā, ē, ī, ō, yōō/.

Level 7. At Level 7 the child is introduced to what we call *vowel-cluster* graphemes, often called vowel digraphs, as in f**oo**t, s**ee**n, p**ea**ch. At this level children are taught to recognize these in closed syllables (phonograms) in the following kinds of words:

- Those spelled with vowel-letter clusters and single consonant letters (*seat, boat, fail/raise, seen*)
- Those spelled with other vowel-letter clusters and single consonant letters (*boil/voice, foot, boot, loud/down*)
- Those spelled with vowel-letter clusters plus beginning and/or ending consonant-letter clusters (*steal, peach, beast*)
- Those spelled with other vowel-letter clusters and consonant-letter clusters (*spoil, shook, cloud/house, clown, round, ground, smooth/groove*)

Words taught at Level 7 raise the issue of *diphthongs.* A diphthong is a gliding complex of sounds that involves a change of resonance and that begins with one vowel sound but ends with another. While each diphthong "is separable phonetically into two units, the diphthongs are single units phonemically" (Wise 1957, p. 63). A diphthong, which always occurs within one syllable, for purposes of meaning functions like a single vowel sound. We consider it appropriate in teaching phonics to view it as a single vowel. Thus, when we refer to one-vowel words, we mean one-syllable words with single vowel sounds and/or diphthongs. The avoidance of the term *diphthong* when teaching children is another example of how to abstain from the use of complex linguistic information, when it is unnecessary for children, in order for them to apply phonics in reading. The complexity of this matter is noted by linguists who say that a large number of diphthongs could be listed, since "nearly all the vowels are diphthongized to some extent, and these resonance changes are necessary for accurate pronunciation" (Carrell and Tiffany 1960, p. 121). The idea of the diphthong is best avoided when teaching word recognition.

In Level 7 we move to word spellings that are sometimes said to have "silent" vowel letters. The second vowel letter in *seat*, for example, could be said to represent no sound, and therefore to have no usefulness. The *a* in *seat* is not, however, a so-called "silent" letter in the sense of serving no function. The *a* in *seat* does have utility. It acts as a visual marker for the sound that one should give the letter *e* in seat, signalling that this letter is given the /ē/ sound. The twenty-six letters of English orthography are not enough to make possible the optimum rule of one letter-one sound. The *a* in *seat* serves, then, to signal the reader to read the word *seat* not as /set/, but as /sēt/.

The predictability with which the second vowel letter in *seat* performs this service is impressive. The data presented in Table 9 indicates this. Here it is shown that when the spelling *ea*, for example, is found in monosyllabic words it represents the /ē/ sound 77 percent of the time.

TABLE 9.
Predictability of Selected Vowel-Letter Clusters in Monosyllabic Words

Vowel Clusters	Percent	Example
oa as /ō/	94%	*coat*
ee, ee–e as /ē/	98%	*beef, cheese*
ae as /ē/	77%	*bead*
ai, ai–e as /ā/	97%	*fail, raise*
ei as /ā/	78%	*vein*
ie, ie–e as /ē/	89%	*brief, niece*
oi as /oi/	100%	*oil*
ou as /ou/	59%	*out*
ow as /ow/	59%	*how*

In Level 7 /o͞o/ and /o͝o/ are taught as parts of phonograms. We thus avoid a problem that traditional phonics brought on itself, which was trying to "explain" these sounds. "Explaining the sounds of *oo* is much more complicated than actually learning to pronounce the frequently used words which contain this letter combination" (Heilman 1964, p. 69).

Instead of trying to "explain" to pupils the phonemic differences between these sounds, the child should be led to realize that the phonogram in which the spelling *oo* is a part will be a dependable signal for the pronunciation of *oo*, whether this be read /o͞o/ or /o͝o/. Notice how the final consonant letter of the phonograms in these words signal to the reader which of the two sounds the *oo* spelling represents:

Column 1	Column 2
/o͞o/	/o͝o/
poo*l*	
roo*m*	boo*k*
foo*d*	woo*d*
moo*n*	
hoo*p*	
boo*t*	
too*th*	
proo*f*	

With the exception of the single consonant letter *d* (*food-wood*), this system works quite well. Therefore, within a short time, the child should come to realize the value of these spelling signals. The teacher should first teach the phonograms in the first column above, of course. Then, the exceptions *ood* and *ook* can be given.

There are dialect complications, of course: In some parts of the country *root* and *roof* are spoken with /o͝o/. The teacher needs to be alert to such variations.

Level 8 In Level 8 children are taught to recognize phonograms in which the vowel grapheme precedes *r*. These are phonograms in which the letter *r* follows:

- the free vowel /o/ as in *arm, part, park, carve;*
- the checked vowel /e/ as in *care, scarce, hair, there, bear, their;*
- the free vowel /ô/ as in *cord, door, score, four, war;*
- the free vowel /ī/ as in *fire;* and
- /ûr/ as in *her, burn, nurse, fir, bird, worm, were, nerve, worse.*

Level 8 is concerned with "*r*-colored" vowel sounds and spellings. These are words with vowel sounds followed by /r/, in which /r/ is affected by the preceding vowel sound—although it may appear to us to be the other way around. As Kantner and West put it, because /r/ is associated with various vowel sounds, "different sounds that we recognize as *r* are sometimes produced by fundamentally different movements" (1960) p. 169). This helps explain why linguists call *r* sounds *glides*. A glide sound is one in which the speech mechanism moves without interruption from the position of one sound to that of another. For example, the tongue moves all the time a vowel /r/ sound is being made.

In examining the peculiarities of the sound-spelling correspondences of the vowel sound followed by an /r/ sound in high-frequency monosyllabic words (Groff 1972), we found nine different vowel-*r* sounds. Five of them accounted for 95 percent of these words: /ôr/, /ûr/, /or/, /er/, and /ir/.

The most frequently occurring spellings and the degree to which they predictably represent the indicated sounds in monosyllabic words (Percent of Occurrence) is shown in Table 10.

TABLE 10.
Predictability of Sound–Spelling Correspondences of Vowel-*r* Words

Spelling	Sound	As in	Percent of Occurrence	Exceptions
ar	/or/	barn	89	*quart, war, warm, warn*
or	/ôr/	born	82	*word, world, worm, worth*
ir	/ûr/	bird	100	
ar–e	/er/	care	71	*charge*, large*, starve***
ear	/ir/	dear	50	*heard, learn, bear, heart*
or–e	/ôr/	more	91	*worse†*

*e signals that /j/ and not /g/ sound should be given.
**e is added because in English a word cannot end in *v*.
†*e* is added so *worse* will not be mistaken for a plural word.

Table 10 indicates which of the "r-colored" vowel sound-spellings should be taught. We suggest that the order in which these be taught correspond with the frequency with which these sounds occur in high-frequency words and the predictability of their spellings. This is difficult to do for the "*r*-colored" vowel sound-spellings.

This order is the best that can be determined:

1. /ûr/ as in *her, bird*
2. /ôr/ as in *born*
3. /or/ as in *barn*
4. /ôr/ as in *more*
5. /er/ as in *care, hair*
6. /ir/ as in *dear, here*

Level 9. In Level 9 children are taught to recognize monosyllabic words as *open syllables.* Open syllables are one-vowel words that end in free-vowel phonemes. Monosyllabic words that are open syllables, such as *go*, are relatively scarce. We found that only 8 percent of words that occur with high frequency were open-syllable words, yet they are often found in the early books of children's reading programs.

In the first stage of Level 9, six open syllables are taught. Given below are the spellings for the open syllables that occur most frequently in monosyllabic words. These represent, with 100 percent predictability, single vowel sounds (*ow* represents /ou/ 72 percent of the time). These spelling-sound correspondences are as follows:

1. *aw* for /o/, as in s*aw*
2. *ay* for /ā/, as in pl*ay*
3. *e* and *ee* for /ē/, as in b*e* and b*ee*
4. *ew-ue* for /o͞o/, as in bl*ew* and bl*ue*
5. *o* for /ō/, as in g*o*
6. *y* for /ī/, as in m*y*.

At the second stage of Level 9, open-syllable spelling-sound correspondences that occur with high predictability but with relatively infrequent occurrence are taught. The following spelling-sound correspondences occur with 100 percent predictability in high-frequency, open-syllable monosyllabic words. For example, all words like *ma* and *pa* have the *a*-/o/ correspondence; all ending in *ie* are spoken with the /ī/ sound.

1. *a* pronounced /o/, as in h*a*
2. *ea* and *i* pronounced /ē/, as in s*ea* and sk*i*
3. *ie*, *igh*, and *uy* pronounced /ī/, as in d*ie*, h*igh*, and b*uy*
4. *oe*, *oh*, and *owe* pronounced /ō/, as in t*oe*, *oh*, and *owe*
5. *oo*, *ou*, *u*, and *wo* pronounced /o͞o/, as in t*oo*, y*ou*, fl*u*, and t*wo*.

Teaching open-syllable words raises some new issues for the teacher. Up to this point, pupils have been accustomed to working with words that ended in consonant letters or consonant-letter clusters (pa*t* or pa*th*), or consonant letter plus marker *e* (ca*ke*). They have been taught to see the vowel letters (*a*, *e*, *i*, *o*, *u*) as the first parts of phonograms, and then marker *e* as a signal letter.

Now pupils are presented with new tasks:

- To hear and see that vowel sounds and letters can be at the ends of words (*go*, *he*).
- To realize that *y* and *w* at the ends of words (d*ay*, s*aw*) do not represent

the consonant sounds that they represent at the beginnings of words. They are instead part of the vowel representation (*ay, aw*).

- To note that vowel letters can represent different vowel sounds than they have previously learned they represent (*pot-go*).
- To understand that vowel-letter clusters can occur at the ends of words (*see*).
- To sense the difference between marker *e* (at*e*) and the final letter *e* (h*e*).

In short, Level 9 reminds pupils that they must be versatile in the application of vowel sound-spelling rules. From this point to the conclusion of their word recognition program, pupils will increasingly become aware that the spelling system is not as simple as the preceding levels taught to them have indicated it to be. Children probably are aware of this, to some extent, since by this time they doubtless have learned to recognize some words that are not spelled according to the patterns given in the previous levels.

Level 10. In Level 10 children are taught to recognize certain closed syllables (phonograms) that occur infrequently. These phonograms are read as follows:

1. /ō/ before *l* as in *cold, colt.*
2. /ī/ before *gh* as in *night.*
3. /ī/ before *nd* as in *find.*
4. /o/ before *ll* and *l* as in *all, salt.*

Also taught at this level are words in which the marker *e* does *not* signal free vowels as in *edge, prince, chance, fence, budge* (exception: *solve*); and words in which /ōō/ is represented by *u* as in *pull, put.*

The teaching of these words is delayed until Level 10 for two reasons: (1) words with these sound-spelling correspondences occur relatively infrequently, and (2) we want to introduce the single-vowel letter grapheme with these sounds at a time distant enough from the same graphemes with /a, e, i, o, u/ sounds so that children at Level 5 will not be presented with the contradictory material offered by the Level 10 sound-spelling correspondences. We want children to have the correspondences of other levels firmly fixed in their minds before being given those of the present level. We contend that success in word recognition depends on movement from the main body of correspondences to the correspondences that occur less frequently and are in conflict with rules taught previously.

It can be seen that the postvowel consonant-letter clusters in the words in Table 11 signal the free vowel sounds /ō, o, and ɪ/. They indicate where the *o* is read as /ō/, *a* as /o/, and *i* as /ɪ/.

TABLE 11.
Sound–Spelling Correspondences in High-Frequency Monosyllabic Words

Correspondence	As in	Percent of Occurrence
/ɪ/ before *ght*	*tight*	100
/ɪ/ before *ld–nd*	*child, bind*	100
/ō/ before *ld–lt–ll*	*cold, bolt, roll*	100
/ō/ before *st*	*host*	100
/o/ before *ll–lt*	*ball, salt*	100

SUMMARY

The description of Levels 1 through 10 for teaching the recognition of monosyllabic words presents the information about phoneme-grapheme correspondences (phonics) that the child needs to know in order to decode such words. This description has not commented on *context cues,* the other important means children use to recognize words. Beyond phonics knowledge, children depend on the sentence or passage in which a given word occurs as a cue to its recognition. Since this system of context cues applies to both monosyllabic and multisyllabic words, we will discuss it in detail in Chapter 9.

The final aspect of monosyllabic word recognition, the child's knowledge of the meanings of individual words, plays an insignificant role in word recognition for beginning readers because of our careful utilization of word frequency, which "has earned a reputation as the single most important variable in word recognition" (Gough, 1984, p. 240). The teaching done at Levels 1–10 is done with words that occur with high frequency. This practice significantly lessens the difficulty that children have in learning to recognize written words, since high-frequency words are ones whose meanings are already familiar to children. Three additional facts make these high frequency words even more powerful as learning tools: Of the 500 most frequently occurring words, only about 40 percent have multimeanings (Johnson & Pearson, 1978); only 29 percent of these words have more than one syllable (Carroll, Davies &

Richman, 1971), and they constitute between 75 and 80 percent of all the words the child will see in print (Ekwall & Shanker, 1985).

EXCEPTIONAL MONOSYLLABIC WORDS

We have previously noted that an unpredictably spelled word is one that children have not been prepared to decode. As children learn more and more rules for decoding words, the number of unpredictably spelled words they encounter decreases steadily. A word that will appear to children to be unpredictably spelled at one level of the word recognition program will not be so viewed at a later level.

In the course of learning to read, children will doubtless come into contact with words that they find they have not yet been prepared by their teachers to decode. A standard procedure for handling these unpredictably spelled words should be established. When such a word occurs in the material given children to read, *the teacher may supply it,* along with the promise that "We will learn how to read this word later" (perhaps "tomorrow," "next week"). Children should not be blamed for being unable to decode such words. Pupils are thus reassured that they will not be expected to perform in certain ways unless they have been prepared to do so. Again: *be prepared to supply for children the written words they have not so far been taught to decode.*

The wise teacher will see to it that the need to make such explanations about unrecognized words is infrequent. In short, reading programs should have controls on the selection of words used in materials provided for children's use. By and large, the words selected for children to read at any given point in the reading program should be those they have been prepared to decode. Reading material that is heavily interlarded with unpredictably spelled words inevitably creates frustrations and a sense of failure for the child attempting to read them. Since a positive attitude in children is important to their success as readers, care must be taken not to overwhelm pupils with unpredictably spelled words.

As children learn sound-spelling correspondences at the different levels of this program, however, they will normally observe that there are words to which phonics generalizations do not apply. This is especially the case for vowel sound-spelling correspondences. We call such words "exceptional words." How serious a problem for systematic word recognition instruction is the occurrence of exceptional words?

To answer this question we turn to some statistics about the frequency of word occurrence. It has been found that the 100 most frequently occurring words constitute 60–65 percent of all the words a child will ever read (Ekwall & Shanker, 1985). An inspection of a reputable tally of the frequency of the occurrence of words (Carroll, Davies, & Richman, 1971) indicates that about 25 percent of these 100 words could be called unpredictably-spelled. These words are: **of**, *to*, **was**, *are*, *they*, **have**, *one*, **what**, *were*, **there**, their, said, **do**, some, *would*, two, *could*, **first**, **been**, *who*, *find*, **words**, *where*, *most*, and *know*. Note that some of these words are boldfaced; you will find out why in a few moments.

This list is considerably shorter, however, than it first appears to be. We found (Groff, 1983) that when children hear the approximate pronunciations of words, they generally can infer and reproduce their correct pronunciations. For example, when second-graders heard *have* pronounced as /hāv/ (so as to follow the phonics rule that the marker *e* on the end of a word indicates that the previous vowel letter should be given its "long" sound), 98 percent of these pupils could infer and reproduce the correct pronunciation of *have*.

The boldfaced words in the above list, if pronounced according to phonics rules, would not be given their correct pronunciations. But on the basis of our study (Groff, 1983) we predict that if children can reach approximate pronunciations these boldfaced words, in a sentence context, they will be able to then infer and reproduce their correct pronunciations.

The problem of exceptional words in monosyllabic word recognition instruction thus is not as imposing as it first appears to be. It is fortunate to be able to report, too, that the percentage of unpredictably spelled monosyllabic words found in the second 100 most frequently occurring set of words decreases sharply. This decrease is also seen in the successive (third, fourth, and so on) sets of 100 words.

Nonetheless, there are monosyllabic words, such as *are*, whose vowel sounds are spelled so unpredictably that a useful approximation of their true pronunciations cannot be gained by the application of phonics rules. (By "useful approximation" we mean a pronunciation of a word close enough to its true pronunciation that its correct pronunciation can be inferred.) It is often said that in the case of *are*, children must be versatile in their decoding of its vowel letters. That is, they must be able to choose from a range of vowel sounds for this purpose so as to finally select /o/. In this book we say that there are 17 different vowel sounds. Is it practical, then, to direct children to search through this list of vowel phonemes to find the one needed to decode *are*? The letter *a* does not frequently represent all seventeen vowel sounds, but it can stand for enough vowel phonemes to make the search time-consuming. We say no.

We suggest that for *are* there is a faster and more effective approach. This should be to have the child simply remember that the string of letters *a-r-e* is equal to the pronunciation /or/—remembering it by its spelling. For what are the alternatives? Attempts to use context cues or phonics cues to decode are less practical than this spelling approach. So in the current absence of experimental evidence as to the best way to decode words like *are* we recommend the spelling approach. It can be used for any short words that are spelled highly unpredictably.

For the foreseeable future teachers will have to decide which words are "exceptional" ones for their pupils. They will then have to determine whether these children can gain useful approximations of the pronunciations of these words by the application of phonics rules. If this system does not help children decode exceptional words, the spellings of these words can be used as cues to their recognition, as with *are*.

REFERENCES

Anderson, R.C., et al. (1985). *Becoming a nation of readers: the report of the Commission on Reading.* Washington, DC: U. S. Department of Education.

Carrell, J. & Tiffany, W. (1960). *Phonetics,* New York, NY: McGraw-Hill.

Carroll, J.B., Davies, P., & Richman, B. (1971). *The American heritage word frequency book.* Boston, MA: Houghton Mifflin.

Chall, J.S. (1983). *Learning to read: The great debate,* NY: McGraw-Hill.

Coleman, E.B. (1970). Data base for a reading technology. *Journal of Educational Psychology Monograph,* 61, 1–23.

Downing, J., & Oliver, P. (1973–1974). The child's conception of "a word." *Reading Research Quarterly,* 9, 568–582.

Ehri, L.C. (1979). Linguistic insight: Threshold of reading acquisition. In T.G. Waller & G.E. Mackinnon (Eds.), *Reading research: Advances in theory and practice, Volume 1.* New York, NY: Academic.

Ehri, L.C. (1983). A critique of five studies related to letter-name knowledge and learning to read. In L.M. Gentile, M.L. Kamil, & J.S. Blanchard (Eds.), *Reading research revisited.* Columbus, OH: Charles E. Merrill.

Ekwall, E.E., & Shanker, J.L. (1985) *Teaching reading in the elementary school.* Columbus, OH: Charles E. Merrill.

Gibson, E.J. (1963). An analysis of critical features of letters, tested by a confusion matrix. In H. Levin (Ed.), *A basic research program in reading.* Ithaca, NY: Cornell University Press.

Gibson, E.J. (1968). Perceptual learning in educational situations. In R.M. Gagne & W.J. Gephart (Eds.), *Learning research and school subjects.* Itaska, IL: F. E. Peacock.

Gough, P.D. (1984). Word recognition. In P.D. Pearson (Ed.), *Handbook of reading research.* New York, NY: Longman.

Groff, P. (1972). A phonemic analysis of monosyllabic words. *Reading World,* 12, 94–103.

Groff, P. (1977). *Phonics: Why and how.* Morristown, NJ: General Learning.

Groff, P. (1984). Resolving the letter name controversy. *Reading Teacher,* 37, 384–388.

Hanna, P.R., Hodges, R.E., & Hanna, J.S. (1971). *Spelling: Structure and strategies.* Boston, MA: Houghton Mifflin.

Heilman, A.W. (1964). *Phonics in proper perspective.* Columbus, OH: Charles E. Merrill.

Heilman, A.W. (1985). *Phonics in proper perspective.* Columbus, OH: Charles E. Merrill.

Jenkins, J.R., Bausell, R.B., & Jenkins, L. (1972). Comparison of letter name and letter sound training as transfer variables. *American Educational Research Journal,* 9, 75–86.

Johnson, D.D., & Baumann, J.F. (1984). Word identification. In P.D. Pearson (Ed.). *Handbook of reading research.* New York, NY: Longman.

Johnson, D.D. & Pearson, P.D. (1978). *Teaching reading vocabulary.* New York, NY: Holt, Rinehart and Winston.

Jones, K.J. (1965). Colour as an aid to visual perception in early reading. *British Journal of Educational Psychology,* 35, 21–27.

Jones, V.W. (1970). *Decoding and learning to read.* Portland, OR: Northwest Regional Educational Laboratory.

Kantner, C.E., & West R. (1960). *Phonetics.* New York, NY: Harper & Row.

Liberman, I.Y. & Shankweiler, D. (1979). Speech, the alphabet, and teaching to read. In L.B. Resnick & P.A. Weaver (Eds.), *Theory and practice of early reading, Volume 2.* Hillsdale, NJ: Lawrence Erlbaum.

Marsh, G., & Mineo, R.J. (1977). Training preschool children to recognize phonemes in words. *Journal of Educational Psychology,* 69, 748–753.

Mason, J.A. (1984). Early reading from a developmental perspective. In P. D. Pearson (Ed.). *Handbook of reading research.* New York, NY: Longman.

Neuman, S.B. (1981). A comparison of two methods of teaching vowel knowledge. *Reading Improvement,* 18, 265–269.

Nevins, R.J. (1973). The effect of training on letter names, letter sounds, and letter names and sounds on the acquisition of word recognition ability. *Dissertation Abstracts International,* 34, 1490A.

Ohnmacht, D.C. (undated). Effects of instruction in letter knowledge on achievement in reading in first grade. Columbia, Mo: University of Missouri.

Otto, W. (1967). Color cues as an aid to good and poor readers' paired-associate learning. In H. K. Smith (Ed.), *Perception and reading.* Newark, DE: International Reading Association.

Richek, M.A. (1977–78). Readiness skills that predict initial word learning using two different methods of instruction. *Reading Research Quarterly,* 13, 200–222.

Rystrom, R. (1969). Evaluating letter discrimination problems in the primary grades. *Journal of Reading Behavior,* 1, 38–48.

Smith, N.B. (1963). *Reading instruction for today's children.* Englewood Cliffs, NJ: Prentice-Hall.

Smythe, P.D., et al. (1971). Developmental patterns in elemental skills: Knowledge of upper-case and lower-case letter names. *Journal of Reading Behavior,* 3, 24–33.

Speer, O.B., & Lamb, G.S. (1976). First grade reading ability and fluency in naming verbal symbols. *Reading Teacher,* 29, 572–576.

Stanovich, K.E. (1982). Word recognition skill and reading ability. In M.H. Singer (Ed.), *Competent reader, disabled reader: Research and application.* Hillsdale, NJ: Lawrence Erlbaum.

Wallach, M.A., & Wallach, L. (1979). Helping disadvantaged children learn to read by teaching them phoneme identification skills. In L.B. Resnick & P.A. Weaver (Eds.), *Theory and practice of early reading, volume 3.* Hillsdale, NJ: Lawrence Erlbaum.

Weaver, P. (1978). *Research within reach: A research-guided response to concerns of reading educators.* Washington, DC: U.S. Department of Education.

Williams, J.P. (1970). Reactions to modes of word recognition. In H. Singer & R. B. Ruddell (Eds.), *Theoretical models and processes of reading.* Newark, DE: International Reading Association.

Wise, C.M. (1957). *Applied phonetics.* Englewood Cliffs, NJ: Prentice-Hall.

8

TEACHING RECOGNITION OF
MULTISYLLABIC WORDS

So far we have dealt exclusively with one-syllable words. For the reasons given earlier, for a period of time a child's learning of word recognition is better accomplished with monosyllabic words than with both monosyllabic and multisyllabic words. How should children be taught to recognize multisyllabic words? To support our approach we begin by presenting the particular problems the pupil faces in learning to recognize words of more than one syllable and, in general, how the teacher can deal effectively with these difficulties.

We separate multisyllabic words from monosyllabic words for a fundamental reason: multisyllabic words are harder to read and to spell. A survey of the pertinent evidence and comment on this matter (Groff 1975) convinces us, as it did Gates and Boeker (1923) more than sixty years ago, that "the length of a word" is a factor that "demonstrably influences the difficulty of learning" a beginning reader faces with it.

Other evidence of the relative difficulty of multisyllabic words comes from a study by Berdiansky, Cronnell, and Koehler (1969) which found that many more spelling "rules" are needed to read two-syllable, high-frequency words than are needed to read one-syllable words. Thirty-five rules can be said to be necessary to read all the single-vowel letters in one-syllable words. To read these same single-vowel letters in two-syllable words, an additional thirty-eight rules are required. Only a very small number of additional rules are needed, however, to read single-consonant letters and consonant clusters in two-syllable words than in one-syllable words.

Hodges's data (1968) also help confirm our reasoning that monosyllabic words are easier for young children to learn than multisyllabic ones. Hodges found that these shorter words are more predictable in their phoneme-grapheme correspondences than are the total 17,000 most-used words. For monosyllabic words he found simple phoneme-grapheme correspondences to occur 81 percent of the time. This seems to us one probable reason why, with beginning readers, as the length of words increases the number of those recognized decreases (Richard 1935; Gates & Boeker 1923).

It is worth repeating that up to this point the teacher supplies for children written words that they have not been prepared to decode. Hold children responsible at all times *only* for what they have been taught to do.

The /ə/ in Multisyllabic Words

One major cause of the additional rules needed to read two-syllable words versus one-syllable words is the schwa sound, represented by the symbol /ə/. It has been shown that the schwa sound can be spelled twenty-two different ways (Hanna et al., 1966). Since the sound /ə/ appears in almost all multisyllabic words, it poses a constant problem for the child learning to recognize longer written words.

Information about this "demon" phoneme need not be taught to children, however. Knowledge about /ə/, which is applied when reading syllables in multisyllabic words, can be inferred by pupils—*if they are well-rooted in all the other aspects of phonics used to read one-syllable words.*

In learning to read one-syllable words, children have learned all the other major vowel sound-spelling relationships. At this point rather than teaching them that they will no longer be able to depend on their hard-earned knowledge of vowel sound-spelling relationships, another stratagem is employed.

This tactic is to encourage children to use their single-syllable vowel phonics knowledge to infer (to make intelligent linguistic guesses) about unknown words. For example, suppose pupils face the unrecognized word *juvenile*. Their knowledge of predictable single-syllable phonics rules would tell them this is probably pronounced /juvenīl/. Research (Groff, 1983) suggests that from this approximate pronunciation of *juvenile* children will be able to infer the correct pronunciation of this word.

Syllabication

In order to decode *juvenile*, first as /juvenīl/ and finally as /jūvenīl/, the child needs some means of separating it into parts in order to identify its syllables. Because *juvenile* is a far more daunting visual challenge for the child learning to read than is *juv en ile*, a reduction of *juvenile* to three single-syllable components, *juv en ile,* reduces the task of word recognition. This reduction allows children to put into effect the information about word recognition they have acquired previously. This conversion of *juvenile* to *juv en ile* thus provides pupils with the opportunity to transfer to a new reading demand the information about word recognition they already know.

The question remains; What kind of syllabication of unrecognized written words is most likely to facilitate this transfer of knowledge? The advice to teach children the dictionary rules of syllabication for this purpose must be rejected. These "rules" often require that an unrecognized written word be decoded *before* the rules can be applied, so one must be able to pronounce the word in question in order to syllabicate it. There also are many words that are exceptions to these rules, which were devised by typesetters in the early days of printing for the purpose of end-of-the line division. These rules are thus not linguistically sound (Seymour, 1973). Finally, the teaching of these rules has not resulted in greater reading achievement than otherwise would be the case.

The *phonogram approach* to syllabication is a preferred method for breaking up long words into manageable parts. It teaches the child to locate and identify known phonograms in long words and to apply the appropriate speech sounds to these phonograms. By watching in words for vowel-consonant combinations they know, children recognize them and say them in sequence, along with the related consonant sounds for single consonant letters. They thus arrive at a pronunciation that approximates that of a word they have heard. At this point they can usually infer the correct pronunciation of this word.

The process works like this:

Assume, for example, that pupils have learned to recognize the phonograms *in* and *ish* in the words *pin* and *fish.* They can now apply these to read *finish:*

Known: p*in*   f*ish*

Unknown: f*in* *ish*

Essentially the same process is used with scores of other multisyllabic words:

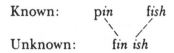

Known: f*un*   h*er*   r*ock*   p*et*   g*un*   h*er*   h*and*

Unknown: *un* d*er*   r*ock* *et*   *un* d*er*   st*and*

The same sort of analysis is called for with words in which the final *y* is changed to *i* before a suffix is added:

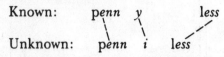

Known: p*enn*   *y*   *less*

Unknown: p*enn*   *i*   *less*

Here, of course, the child has learned the recognition of *y* as an open syllable. Other words involve somewhat more complicated analyses:

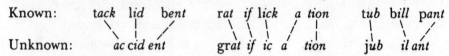

Known: *tack* l*id* b*ent*   *rat* *if* l*ick* *a* t*ion*   *tub* b*ill* p*ant*

Unknown: *ac cid ent*   *grat if ic a' tion*   *jub il ant*

With *accident, gratification,* and *jubilant,* correspondences between the phonograms in the shorter words and those in the longer words are inexact. Nonetheless, *ac* is not too distant in spelling from *ack,* or *ick* from *ic,* for pupils to extrapolate one from the other. Note that *tion* is recognized as a unit, an affix, without extension from a monosyllabic word.

Of the three words, *jubilant* presents the most difficult task of transposition of known phonograms. According to phonogram teaching, this word would be pronounced /jub-il-ant/. It is at this point that a test is made of whether instruction in phonogram recognition has developed in pupils the notion of a versatile use of vowel sounds. If it has, they will automatically shift the sound given to the first syllable to /ōō/ or /yōō/, and give the word the pronunciation /jyōōb-il-ant/, which should be close enough to /jyōōb-əl-ənt/ for them to recognize the word if they have it in their memories.

The phonogram approach to syllabication illustrates that "All that is needed for decoding multisyllabic words is an extension of the principles on which English monosyllables are built" (Seymour, 1973, p. 283). It avoids the learning of complicated new rules and is the easiest system to apply that we have discovered.

Should the Meaning of Affixes Be Taught?

It is readily apparent to mature readers that affixes (prefixes and suffixes) occur often in multisyllabic words. Because of this pupils should be taught to identify affixes, as such, in words. This knowledge will enable them to speed up and improve the accuracy of their syllabication of multisyllabic words.

A pertinent question regarding the teaching of affixes as a means of breaking multisyllabic words into their separate syllables, however, is whether it is worthwhile to teach children the *meaning* of affixes. For example, should the phonics teacher instruct children in the fact that these affixes have the meanings listed below?

	Prefixes		**Suffixes**
a-:	Against, without, of, to	*-er:*	one who
ab-:	from, away	*-or:*	doer
com-:	together	*-ent:*	state of
pre-:	before	*-tion:*	state of
pro-:	forward	*-able:*	able, like
re-:	backward, again	*-less:*	without

We surveyed the writings of over forty leading experts in reading and spelling as to their opinions on this matter (Groff, 1972). The majority of these authorities endorsed the notion of teaching the meanings of affixes. They believe that such knowledge helps elementary school children (at least from the third grade upwards) to recognize words, to spell better, to develop larger vocabularies, or to be more critical readers. Moreover, some of these experts said the study of these meanings was intriguing fun for children.

The opponents of the idea either had no comment on the matter (damning it by no praise), or objected to it on logical or empirical grounds. The logical objection is typified by the remarks of Schell:

> The obvious problem is that these prefixes have meaning to an elementary school child only when there is a known base word. Even though in Latin these prefixes were attached to base words, over the years these bases have lost their independent standing and the prefixes have become known as "absorbed prefixes." In such words, knowledge of the meaning of the prefix is virtually worthless.
>
> Suffixes present difficulties in two ways. Many suffixes have multiple meanings; e.g., *-ment* may mean act, condition, or concrete instance. To use the suffix to help derive the word's meaning, the reader must (1) recall these three meanings, (2) choose the appropriate one, and (3) apply this meaning to the base form—a prodigious task for most elementary school pupils. Surely, there must be a *more efficient* procedure (1967, pp. 133–134).

While there continues to be favorable opinion as to the value of teaching the meanings of affixes (Swaby, 1984), and elaborate programs have even been designed for this purpose (Dale, O'Rourke, & Bamman, 1971), there is no relevant empirical data to support the notion. There appear to be better aspects of word recognition to teach, therefore, than knowledge about the meaning of affixes.

The main reason analyzing and learning the meaning of affixes in words is not a useful practice for the child learning to read is that affixes are *bound* morphemes. They cannot stand alone as words and appear only when attached (bound) to other morphemes (*free* morphemes). Because of this condition an affix often has no standard meaning in all words in which it is found. It may even have no discernible meaning, as in *protest*, or a meaning that has been lost over the ages. The study of these meanings thus has very limited usefulness for word recognition purposes.

Should the Accent in Words Be Taught?

We know that the separate syllables in multisyllabic words are given differing degrees of accent (vocal loudness and pitch). One of the syllables in a multisyllabic word "always has stronger stress than any other" (Kurath, 1964, p. 140). The degree of stress that an individual syllable in a word receives is even affected by the sentence context in which the word is located.

Does teaching children about these linguistic phenomena improve their ability to recognize multisyllabic words better than would an equal amount of some other kind of instruction? Some reading experts say yes. Stoodt (1981), for example, would have children sound out familiar words, experimenting with stress on different syllables. Other reading authorities advise that children learn generalizations they believe are helpful in determining what syllables to stress (McNeil, Donant, & Atkins, 1980). Some want children to learn "how changes in stress can change grapheme-phoneme correspondences" (Ives, Bursuk, & Ives, 1980, p. 162).

We know of no objective evidence, however, that supports taking time away from other instruction in the word recognition program to teach about accent in words. No advocate of this teaching has offered any substantiation that this instruction is of special benefit to children learning to read. The principal objection to teaching children about accent is that the child must be able to recognize a word in order to assign accent to it. How, then, could knowledge about accent assist the child in word recognition? Finally, it is observable that when children gain the approximate pronunciation of a word by decoding it they then can infer and reproduce its correct pronunciation. In this reproduction the child automatically gives the word its proper syllabic stress. For these reasons we do not recommend the teaching of accent.

Morphemic Analysis and Word Recognition

Parts of multisyllabic words will often trigger a cue system of word recognition that we have yet to describe. This cue system relies on the morphemes found in words. Recall that a morpheme is a unit of meaning. The word *jobber*, for example, has two morphemes, *job* and *er*. The former morpheme has an exclusive meaning; it stands alone. The latter can be affixed to other words. A child who does not know the meaning of *jobber* is likely to infer, nevertheless, that this word has something to do with *job* or *work*. From the sentence context of *jobber*, he or she might also infer that this *work* involves selling something. In this way the morpheme *job* has acted as an effective cue to the word *jobber*.

This examination of *jobber* is called *morphemic analysis*, the process by which children determine the meaning of an unfamiliar word by analyzing each of its parts that have a separate meaning. They may, for instance, recognize that *nation* and *nationality* are not different words in the sense that *nation* and *notion* are. A reader may at some point sense that *nationality* is a variant form of *nation*. Accordingly, in a sentence like *What is that man's nationality?* the reader may not have to read all the parts of *nationality* to get the meaning because *What is that man's nation?* communicates almost the same degree of meaning. Many similar examples can be worked out, for example *The parents were anxious about the sick child* as compared with *The parents had anxiety about the sick child.*

Therefore, in order to teach the suffix *ion/tion*, the teacher should use not only such words as *notion, motion, nation, ration, cushion,* and *pension,* but also such groupings as *apply, applies, applied, applying, applicant, application, applicable, applicator, applique, appliance, applicative, applicatory.* The point here is that although children may not be able to attach a single peculiar meaning to each of these above derivations of *apply* as they see them in print, being able to recognize *apply* teaches them that all the other eleven forms are connected to the meaning of *apply.*

To learn to read *application*, for example, children should be taught to note the "apply" part of *application*, and react to the slot in the sentence it fits (for the sake of meaning). Notice how this works:

1. He will   *apply*   for a job.
2. He will *make an application* for a job.

If children read the second sentence as *He will make an apply for a job*, they have essentially gained the meaning of the sentence.

Levels of Multisyllabic Word Recognition

As with teaching the recognition of monosyllabic words, instruction for multisyllabic word recognition should start with aspects that are the easiest for children to acquire and proceed to those that are more difficult. This chapter describes seven levels of multisyllabic word recognition. Activities by which children can practice skills taught at each of these levels are in Appendix C.

Level 1. Before any instruction is given for the different kinds of multisyllabic words, the teacher should make sure children are consciously aware of the concept of the *syllable*. In learning to speak pupils have gained an implicit understanding that multisyllabic words are composed of syllables, and that one phoneme in each syllable (its vowel) is louder, longer in duration, higher pitched and more resonant than are any other phonemes in the syllable. It thus is not difficult to teach children that multisyllabic spoken words can be divided into parts (Groff, 1981). In fact, it is easier for children to segment spoken words into their syllables than it is to teach them to segment words into their phonemes. (Mason, 1984).

Technically, a syllable is a spoken word part, a combination of speech sounds, not a combination of letters. When we speak of written syllables, we mean the visual word parts that stand for a word's oral syllables.

Because children have an implicit understanding of the syllabic nature of words, learning to count the number of syllables in a spoken word usually proceeds quickly. To begin this process the teacher says *cow*, for instance, and establishes that it is one word. The same is done for *boy*. Then the teacher says *cowboy* as a single word. At this point children usually find it easy to answer the questions, "How many words do you hear in *cowboy?*" or "How many parts does *cowboy* have?" The term *parts* is exchanged at this juncture for *syllables*. Children can respond to such queries by holding up two fingers, by saying "two," by placing two cards or blocks on their desks, by tapping twice, and so on.

A further examination of children's abilities to detect the number of syllables in words can be made by having them pronounce words with missing syllables. For example, the teacher says, "Listen to *cowboy*. Now say *cowboy* without the *boy*. Listen to *location*. Now say *location* without the *ca*."

After demonstrating the number of syllables in compound words like *cowboy*, the teacher moves on to multisyllabic words like *running*, *unlike*, *farmer*, and *deeply*. Finally, polysyllabic words are so examined. Both classroom practice and experimental surveys reveal that these learning activities normally proceed swiftly and smoothly.

Level 2. The second step in multisyllabic word recognition teaching is to instruct children to recognize, as syllables, familiar monosyllabic words within multisyllabic *written* words. For example, in monosyllabic word recognition instruction children learn to recognize *in*, *to*, *down*, *hill*, *grand*, and *pa*. At Level 2 they will be directed to find these words in the compound words *into*, *downhill*, and *grandpa*.

With compound words like *pigpen* children should be taught to look for two words within the larger word. Paying attention to familiar words within words is much like the phonogram approach to word recognition previously learned.

Some compounds useful for teaching word recognition are:

offside	steamboat	sawdust	horsehair
baseball	shoelace	hairpin	airport
bedroom	fireplace	doormat	catfish
armchair	bedtime	schoolbus	wishbone
boxcar	cartwheel	popcorn	sunshine
grandstand	pancake	starfish	towtruck
pigpen	sandbox	postcard	cowhide
campfire	mailbox	horseback	dishpan
tiptoe	sidewalk	sunburn	pigtail
eardrum	locksmith	mudslide	bluebird

The practice of finding "little words in big words," in words other than compound words, is also useful. We analyzed high-frequency words to find the extent to which monosyllabic words, such as *pen*, could be spoken in bigger words, such as *penny*, without distorting the sound of the bigger word. We concluded that this is possible 65 percent of the time (Groff, 1973).

Level 3. The third stage of multisyllabic written word recognition is taken up with teaching children to syllabicate certain inflected written words and to recognize their syllabicated parts. For this purpose children are taught to identify not only words they have previously learned to recognize, like *walk*, but phonograms as well, like *ing*. Inflected words like *walking, dipped, running, ladies, judges, greatest,* and *higher* are taught at *Level 3.*

When monosyllabic words like *walk* are inflected to produce *walking,* they become multisyllabic. To read such words the beginning reader recognizes the familiar word *walk* and the familiar phonogram *ing*, and then says the two as one word. The same holds true for inflected forms like *faster* and *fastest.* But for words that have the past-tense inflection, like *walked,* if the pupils apply the same principle they will expect to pronounce *walked* with two syllables, /wok-ed/—unless the teacher quickly teaches the exception to the rule.

The generalization for pronouncing past-tense words as disyllables does not, unfortunately, hold true for the majority of high-frequency verbs. In fact, about 70 percent of these verbs, when given the past-tense inflection, do not become disyllabic. Changing *bake* into the past tense (*baked*) merely adds the consonant sound /t/.

This seems to complicate the matter of teaching children to recognize the majority of tense-inflected verbs. However, if children are taught to use one principle of this inflectional system, the problem can be resolved: When a monosyllabic word ends in either the sound /t/ or the sound /d/, it will, when the inflection *ed* is added, become a disyllabic word. When it does not, it will not be disyllabic. This rule is strengthened by the fact that 96 and 93 percent, respectively, of the syllables that end in /d/ and /t/ are spelled *d* and *t* (*had, pat*) (Hanna, et al. 1966). Our analysis of high-frequency monosyllabic verbs reveals that 100 percent of these verbs have the correspondences /d/-*d* and /t/-*d*.

Moreover, children's knowledge of their language aids them here, and usually prevents them from mispronouncing past-tense words.

Another problem regarding the past-tense inflection of monosyllabic verbs comes when the final consonant letter is doubled, as in *patted*. We have seen that the sound at the end of a verb will determine whether one pronounces it as a disyllable when the verb is given the past-tense inflection. This rule does not extend to the verbs whose final consonant letters are doubled when their inflected forms are spelled with *ed*. For example, in *pitted* and *pinned* we note that the first inflected word is pronounced /pit-əd/ and the second word /pind/. These pronunciations are signalled by the final consonant sound in *pit* and *pin*.

Notice, however, that the final *t* and *n* in verbs are doubled before *ed* is added. The doubling of the final consonant letters in verbs works, in certain cases, to aid the reader in the recognition of these words. We can see that different spellings for different words can help for this purpose:

bared—barred	moped—mopped	taped—tapped
bated—batted	pined—pinned	tubed—tubbed
hoped—hopped	raped—rapped	waded—wadded
mated—matted	robed—robbed	waged—wagged

Children should also be given practice in seeing how the *y* at the end of certain multisyllabic words is changed to *i* before these words are given a plural inflection, a past-tense inflection, or other changes.

To spell these verbs children must be taught to recognize that the *y* is changed to *i*, for example, when the following are added:

es—abilit*i*es	*ment*—merr*i*ment	*ful*—piti*ful*
ance—compl*i*ance	*ness*—read*i*ness	*less*—penn*i*less
ous—injur*i*ous	*er*—empt*i*er	*est*—hungr*i*est
ed—bur*i*ed		

They must also realize that with some additions the change is *y* to *a*, as in occup*a*tion, memor*a*ble. Sometimes the addition is longer: *cation*—appli*cation; zation*—coloni*zation*.

Level 4. The written words that children are taught to recognize at Level 4 are those that have common closed-syllable suffixes, as in bank*er*, arm*or*, differ*ent*, descrip*tion*, discus*sion*, form*al*, enjoy*able*, develop*ment*, tight*ness*, light*en*, care*less*, care*ful*, desir*ous*, differ*ence*, ignor*ance*, fortun*ate*, and defect*ive*.

The child should experience few problems in recognizing common closed-syllable suffixes. According to Thorndike (1941), the twenty most common closed-syllable suffixes are

-able	-ate	-ic	-less
-age	-ance, -ence	-ical	-ment
-al	-ent	-tion, -sion	-ness
-an, -ian	-er	-ish	-or
-ant	-ful	-ive	-ous

Most of these by now should be familiar as phonograms: *er, or, ent, ment, ful, ence, ance, ate, ness, less, en.* It will be necessary for the teacher to make special efforts for the child to identify -*tion* and -*sion*, however, since these are unpredictably spelled suffixes.

Level 5. In Level 5 the common open-syllable suffixes, as in deep*ly*, deliver*y*, and honest*y*, are taught with written words. Common open-syllable suffixes will be relatively easy for the child to learn to read: they all end in *y*. The single task for the child here is to remember that this *y* (as in hap*py*) represents the sound /ē/,

Level 6. The multisyllabic written words taught in Level 6 have common closed-syllable prefixes, as in *ab*sent, *ad*vise, *com*pel, *dis*patch, *en*tire, *ex*cite, *in*cline, *sub*mit and *un*like. It will not be difficult for children to syllabicate words that have these prefixes. All they need to do is recall the manner in which they syllabicated words at previous levels. This means they will search for phonograms and/or for familiar words. In this way, *absent*, for example, is syllabicated either *ab-sent* or *abs-ent*. The pronunciation of either *ab-sent* or *abs-ent* by children will be close enough to the correct pronunciation of *absent* that they then will be able to infer its correct pronunciation.

It is helpful here to recall the fact that a relatively few prefixes make up the great majority of those used. Stauffer found that 15 prefixes account for 82 percent of all the prefixes to be found in a list of the most frequently used 20,000 words (1942). These prefixes, in the order of their frequency, are as follows:

1. com-	4. un-	7. dis-	10. en-	13. sub-
2. re-	5. in-(into)	8. ex-	11. pro-	14. be-
3. ad-	6. in-(not)	9. de-	12. pre-	15. ab-

Of the 20,000 words studied by Stauffer, 24 percent had prefixes.

Level 7. In this final level the common open-syllable prefixes in written words are taught. These prefixes are *be, de, pre, pro,* and *re.*

The difficulty for children in identifying these prefixes stems partly from the fact they are open syllables. Open syllables are more troublesome for children to decode than are closed syllables because they are spelled less predictably—that is, letters in open syllables represent a greater variety of speech sounds. Besides, there are no familiar phonograms among open-syllable prefixes. The child inclined to search for such phonograms thus may read *reform*, for example, as /ref-ôrm/. Is there a handicap to the child in this practice? We would say no. Children can infer the correct pronunciation of *reform* as easily from /ref-ôrm/ as they can from /rē-fôrm/.

SUMMARY

Reading multisyllabic words depends on the knowledge children have gained in reading monosyllabic words, along with additional principles that modify that knowledge. They discover that applying what they know about phonograms must be conditioned by such circumstances as:

- whether the word has a prefix. If so, they identify parts of *mischance* as *mis-chance,* not *misch-ance.*
- whether the word has a suffix. If so, they identify the parts of *apartment* as *ap-art-ment,* not *ap-artm-ent.*
- whether there is a group of letters that does not form a standard English cluster. If so, they identify the parts of *convent* as *con-vent,* not *conv-ent.*
- whether the word is a compound word (has little words in it). If so, they identify the parts of *dollhouse* as *doll-house,* not *dollh-ouse.*
- whether a cluster in the word is made up of two of the same consonant letters (a digraph). Digraphs should not be divided. If so, they identify the parts of *dollar* as *doll-ar,* not *dol-lar.* Being ready to analyze a word for these various circumstances is a sign of mature knowledge of word recognition practices.

Exceptional Multisyllabic Words

We have noted that as children learn to decode monosyllabic words they will on occasion see words that they have not been prepared to decode (See Chapter 7). These unpredictably spelled words, "exceptional words," as we call them, also occur as children learn to recognize multisyllabic words.

How serious a problem for systematic instruction in multisyllabic word recognition is the occurrence of exceptional words? Again, we turn for an answer to this question to statistics of the frequency of word occurrence. The 500 most frequently occurring words make up from about 75 to 80 percent of all the words the child will ever read (Ekwall & Shanker, 1985). An inspection of a reputable tally of the frequency of occurrence of words (Carroll, Davies, & Richman, 1971), indicates that of these 500 words only 44, or less than 9 percent, are spelled unpredictably. Examples of such words are: *finally, everyone, sometimes,* and *began.*

This list of exceptional words is considerably shorter, however, than it appears at first glance. We know that when children reach the approximate pronunciations of words, they then can infer and reproduce their correct pronunciations (Groff, 1983). For example, it was found that when second-graders heard *secret* pronounced as /sekret/ (so as to follow the phonics rule that single vowel letters in closed syllables are given their "short" sound), 98 percent of these pupils could infer and reproduce the correct pronunciation of *secret.*

On the basis of these research findings we predict that most of the 44 multisyllabic words referred to above would be decoded by pupils. For example, it is highly predictable that if pupils gained the pronunciation /sōmtīm/ after applying phonics rules to *sometime*, they would be able to infer and reproduce the correct pronunciation of this word. We would say, as well, that this conclusion is true for the following multisyllabic words found among the 500 most frequently occurring words: *money, coming, already, animal, mountains, beginning, another, again, below, something, together, began, mother, story, second, many, father, other, against,* and *only.* In addition, children likely could gain useful approximate pronunciations of the following multisyllabic words, found in the first 500, if they isolated the smaller word found within each larger word: *toward, today, later, wanted, taken, carefully, moved,* and *everyone.* (By "useful approximate. pronunciations" we mean those close enough to true pronunciations that children can infer the true pronunciations.)

In sum, exceptional words pose much less of a problem for the recognition of multisyllabic words than for single-syllable ones—*if instruction in the recognition of monosyllabic words has been successful.* This conclusion underscores the importance of making sure that children can recognize monosyllabic words readily before they are expected to recognize multisyllabic ones. The hierarchy of skill development in this aspect of word recognition is quite apparent.

In the event that a multisyllabic word cannot be decoded by the use of rules previously taught for that purpose the teacher should supply its name for children. If the word recognition program described in this book is taught successfully, however, the number of such words would be very small. Thus the best explanation of why children cannot decode words is they have not learned to do so, and not that these words are exceptional ones.

REFERENCES

Berdiansky, B., Cronnell, B., & Koehler, J. (1969). *Spelling-sound relations and primary form-class descriptions for speech-comprehension vocabularies of 6-9 year olds.* Inglewood, CA: Southwest Regional Laboratory for Educational Research and Development.

Carroll, J.B., Davies, P., & Richman, B. (1971). *The American heritage word frequency book.* Boston, MA: Houghton Mifflin.

Dale, E., O'Rourke, J., & Bamman, H.A. (1971). *Techniques of teaching vocabulary.* Palo Alto, CA: Field Educational Publications.

Ekwall, E.E. & Shanker, J.L. (1985). *Teaching reading in the elementary school.* Columbus, OH: Charles E. Merrill.

Gates, A.I., & Boeker, E. (1923). Study of initial stages in reading by pre-school children. *Teachers College Record,* 24, 469–477.

Groff, P. (1972). Teaching affixes for reading improvement. *Reading Improvement,* 9, 28–30.

Groff, P. (1973). Should youngsters find little words in bigger words? *Reading Improvement,* 10, 12–16.

Groff, P. (1975). Long versus short words in beginning reading. *Reading World,* 14, 277–289.

Groff, P. (1981). Teaching reading by syllables. *Reading Teacher,* 34, 659–664.

Groff, P. (1983). A test of the utility of phonics rules. *Reading Psychology,* 4, 217–225.

Hanna, Paul R., et al. (1966). *Phoneme-grapheme correspondences as cues to spelling improvement.* Washington, DC: U.S. Office of Education.

Hodges, R.W. (1968). Phoneme-grapheme correspondences in monosyllabic words. In J.A. Figurel (Ed.). *Forging ahead in reading.* Newark, DE: International Reading Association

Ives, J.P., Bursuk, L.Z., & Ives, S.A. (1979). *Word identification techniques.* Chicago, IL: Rand McNally.

Kurath, H. (1964). *A phonology and prosody of modern English.* Ann Arbor, MI: University of Michigan Press.

Mason, J.M. Early reading from a developmental perspective. In P.D. Pearson (Ed.), *Handbook of reading research,* New York, NY: Longman.

McNeil, J.D., Donant, L., & Alkin, M.C. (1980). *How to teach reading successfully.* Boston, MA: Little, Brown.

Richard, G.E. (1935). The recognition vocabulary of primary pupils. *Journal of Educational Research,* 29, 281–291.

Schell, L.M. (1967). Teaching structural analysis. *Reading Teacher,* 21, 133–137.

Seymour, D.Z. (1973). Word division for decoding. *Reading Teacher,* 27, 275–283.

Stauffer, R.G. (1942). A study of prefixes in the Thorndike List to establish a list of prefixes that should be taught in the elementary school. *Journal of Educational Research,* 35, 453–458.

Stoodt, B.D. (1981). *Reading instruction.* Boston, MA: Houghton Mifflin.

Swaby, B.E.R. (1984). *Teaching and learning reading.* Boston, MA: Little, Brown.

Thorndike, E.L. (1941). *The teaching of English suffixes.* New York, NY: Columbia University Press.

9

TEACHING THE USE OF CONTEXT CUES

Recognizing a word when it is presented in isolation depends on at least three factors: (1) children's abilities to recall the speech sound correspondences of the graphemes they see in a word, (2) their memory of the various combinations of letters that are used to spell English words, "sequential redundancy," as Smith (1971) calls it, and (3) the ability to find phonograms and smaller words and morphemes within the word that is being decoded.

But most reading, even for beginners, presents words not in isolation but in sentence context. And word meaning depends in large part on this context. Just as the normal environment of the phoneme is the syllable, so the natural setting for a word is the sentence. It is the sentence that lends to a word its authentic meaning and forms its unique connotation. How does context aid the beginning reader?

The Role of Context Cues

Gough (1984, p. 244) expresses the general agreement among reading experts as to the usefulness of context when he maintains that "no theory of reading can deny the importance of context in *reading*." Johnson and Baumann (1984, p. 602) agree that "there is little doubt that contextual clues are potentially powerful aids in identifying unknown words." Their review of the research on this matter revealed for them that "there is a reasonably firm psychological base for a reader's use of contextual aids and the subsequent teaching of these skills in word-identification instruction" (p. 599).

The precise extent to which children's use of context cues helps them decode words remains a controversial issue, however. The degree to which context helps children in grades one, two, and three to recognize words has been studied by Goodman (1965). He found that when reading words in a story rather than reading words in a list, "average first graders could read almost two out of three words in the story which they missed on the list. The average second grader missed only one-fourth of the words in the story which he failed to recognize on the list. Third graders were able to get, in the stories, all but 18 percent of the words which they did not know in the list" (p. 641).

The accuracy of Goodman's data is suspect, however. The findings from Singer, et al. (1973–74), Chester (1972), Pearson (1978), and from Groff (1979) do not confirm Goodman's. Nicholson and Hill (1985) found, in fact, that by the time they are third-graders children do *not* make significantly fewer errors when reading full story context than they make when reading words in isolation. In these researchers' judgment, "to avoid the decoding problem, by relying on context, is to avoid becoming a fluent reader" (p. 196). In this regard, Gough (1983) had good readers read the first eight words in various easy-to-read sentences. He found that only 10 percent of the time could they guess correctly the noun, verb, adjective, or adverb that followed.

Stanovich (1980), in contradiction to Goodman, finds the research to say that the usefulness of context cues diminishes as the reading ability of children advances. He believes the research suggests that context cues are most useful at the stage of reading development when children still have difficulty in recognizing individual words. This means that children with poor word recognition skills use context cues as a crutch to compensate for their word recognition deficiencies. It does seem clear that the research on word recognition "suggests that the poor [beginning] reader may have to go through an obligatory letter-by-letter sequence, regardless of the context in which the words are presented" (Samuels & Kamil, 1984, p. 203). Telling children that "guessing words is a desirable way to figure them out" (Richek, List & Lerner, 1983, p. 239) thus may be misleading advice.

To discuss the role and the value of context cues, it is important to separate out the various potential uses of context. Children may try to use context:

(a) to arrive at the approximate pronunciation of an unrecognized word, so that they can then infer its exact pronunciation;

(b) to arrive at the particular meaning of a word, the meaning that the author intended;

(c) to make critical judgments about a word — to decide whether the author's intended meaning is appropriate, relevant, up-to-date, comprehensive, a figure of speech, and so on;

(d) to infer other information unprovided, for example, to infer, after reading *Bill dug a hole near the tree*, that Bill used a shovel.

These four aspects of context cue usage appear to involve different thought processes, ones of a hierarchical order. That is, unless children are able first to reach the correct pronunciation of a word (aspect *a* above), it is hardly likely they will be able to decide on aspects *b*, *c*, and *d*. The modern research on context cues we have reviewed appears to say that the use of context cues has greater significance in the attainment of aspect *b* above, however, than for aspects *a*, *c*, and *d*. The child who is confused about the particular meaning of a written word that its author intended for it doubtless can find help for the resolution of this confusion from context cues in the sentence in which the word in question is imbedded. Context cues offer less help for children, it appears, in decoding words, in evaluating the merits of the author's judgment in selecting them, and in inferring information that the author did not specifically provide.

To prove the proposition that context cues have a special value in word recognition, the proposition would have to pass an important test: studies would have to show that there is a greater difference between good and poor readers' abilities to recognize words in sentence contexts than in isolation. This does not appear to be the case, however. There have been several studies that have compared good and poor readers in this way (Stanovich 1980). In every such study, good readers have been found to recognize words both in context and in isolation significantly better than poor readers. The difference in the ability of these two groups to recognize words in sentence contexts is no larger, however, than the difference between their abilities to recognize words in isolation. In short, the addition of context fails to increase the difference between the reading abilities of good and poor readers. In fact, some studies show that there is less difference between good and poor readers' abilities to recognize words in context than there is between their abilities to recognize words in isolation. It seems clear, therefore, that "the most conspicuous difference between good and poor readers is found in the swift and accurate recognition of individual words" (Gough, 1981, p. 95).

So much so, concludes Henderson (1982, p. 345), from his review of the research, that there are "good grounds for disputing whether any facilitatory effect of sentence context obtains if the task closely resembles normal reading." "There is no doubt that in word recognition, context matters," he goes on, but the effects of context cues "while potentially important, are at present very unclear" (p. 287). For skilled readers Gough (1984, p. 245) interprets the research to say that "it remains an open (and important) question whether the average context has any effect at all" on their reading comprehension. After a child can recognize words automatically, therefore, context cues lose much of their function. For these children, any effect that context cues might have on comprehension may take place *after* word recognition has been accomplished. Automatic recognition of words is rarely attained completely, however. There will always be some need for context cues to compensate for deficiencies in children's word recognition skill.

It seems accurate to say, therefore, that the degree to which context cues aid children in word recognition depends to a great extent on children's reading skill (Samuels & Kamil, 1984). Beginning readers have few word recognition skills, so they must depend more on context cues in order to identify written words. At the same time if the teacher does not soon wean pupils away from their dependence on context cues and instruct them in the use of other word recognition skills, their early reading growth will be handicapped (Biemiller, 1970). This weaning away is necessary, since the closer children come to the goal of automatic word recognition the less need they appear to have for context cues.

Teaching children to use context cues too soon may create in them a dependence on this mode of word recognition that can hinder their overall reading growth. The data from Biemiller's study of the effects of too early a dependence on context cues shows

> ... that the child's first task in learning to read is mastery of the use of graphic information [roughly, phonics], and possibly, of the notion that one specific spoken word corresponds to one written word. The child's early use of contextual information does not appear to greatly facilitate progress in acquiring reading skill. The longer he stays in the early, context-emphasizing phase without showing an increase in the use of graphic information the poorer a reader he is at the end of the year. Thus, the teacher should do a considerable proportion of early reading training in situations providing no context at all, in order to compel children to use graphic information as much as possible. As they show evidence of doing so (through accurate reading out of context) they would be given contextual material to read (1970, p. 95).

That good readers have less need than beginners for context as a word recognition technique, is also suggested by the fact that skilled readers hardly have time to make much use of context cues, anyway. They normally fixate their eyes on three or four different words per second (Perfetti, 1985). If words can be recognized so quickly and accurately, why would a reader need to spend time guessing at their identify from the context? In this case, using sound-letter relationships to recognize a word is easier and quicker than guessing it from context. Skilled readers may very well use context only to confirm the evidence gained from word recognition. Furthermore, written words that are hard to decode usually are also hard to guess. Guessing gives little if any help here.

As Gough (1984) says, at the point of automatic word recognition the usefulness of context cues for children may be narrowed down to helping them decide which of the various meanings of a word they have recognized best fits the sentence being read. This is a thought process quite distinct from the application of phonics rules or finding phonemes in words.

Determining the precise meaning an author intended for a word is an important function, of course. Understanding what an author intended to say is basic to reading comprehension. This description of the role of context cues does put their usefulness into proper perspective, however. Furthermore, it questions the assumption made by some reading experts (Smith & Robinson, 1980) that word recognition instruction should start with teaching the use of context cues and only then proceed to other word recognition strategies. This view seems in error, since the immature reader normally depends too much on the use of context cues. Early reading instruction thus should put emphasis on the development of other cues to word recognition; it should not stress the cue that contributes the least to mature reading ability.

It is important, therefore, to be skeptical of the assumption that smooth, fast oral reading is largely the result of greater and greater use of context cues. It is clear that for a period, children read orally in a "shopping list" fashion: haltingly, dwelling on one word at a time. To get a feel of the clumsy manner in which beginning readers necessarily operate read this list of words: *it, in, toys, the, on, up, check, to, box, the, into, looked, Bill.* Now reverse the order of these words; read the list backwards. Your first reading was the typical "shopping list," word-by-word, singsong manner of beginning readers who have yet to develop fluent word recognition. This immature oral reading ability is not likely the result of lack of instruction in the use of context cues, however. More probably, what causes this poor reading is a lack of emphatic and systematic attention by the teacher to other word recognition skills (Lesgold & Resnick, 1982). It is wise to remember in this respect, says Perfetti (1985), that the most con-spicuous characteristic of reading ability is context-free word recognition.

Other Limitations of Context Cues

Several other reasons make context cues inadequate for use in word recognition. Nearly a dozen of these can be mentioned.

One is that the different words that could fit into grammatical slots in sentences often have very similar shapes (as in *doll* and *ball*). An author's intended meaning in a sentence would be lost to readers not attending to the letter differences in *doll* and *ball.* Beginning readers are well served by advice to check the letter forms of all the words they attempt to read and not depend on grammar plus general word shape.

Two, it is true that, for an unknown word, a reader can often think of a likely substitute in order to give some sense to a sentence. But there are limits to intelligent guessing, and the word used as a substitute may not contribute the sense intended by the author. Recourse to letter percep-tion is necessary for the author's exact sense to be apprehended.

Three, written language that is unnatural, that is not normally heard or spoken by the child, such as poetic language, may reduce the reader's ability to utilize context cues. Such abnormal sentence patterns work against the use of context cues because they sound strange and artificial to the child.

Four, the more complex the sentence the more unlikely it is that one can use context cues. It is doubtless easier to use such cues in the sentence *Sally saw the dog* than in *Just before Sally walked into the school yard, she saw a large, black dog that was lying in the roadway gasping for air, as if he were sick or had been run over by a car.* The clausal structure of the latter sentence may prevent children from applying context cues.

Five, children may be handicapped in their use of context cues when certain parts of speech take on functions they do not usually fulfill. For example, a word ordinarily known to a child as a noun, such as *bike,* may appear as an adjective, as in *He is a bike rider.* Such usage puts a limit on the child's ability to use sentence context.

Six, if children read the sentence *Bill saw the dog* as *Bill was the dog,* it will do them little good to check the context to see if *was* would fit the sentence slot. Both *was* and *saw* will fit, because either sentence is grammatical. It becomes necessary for the reader at such a juncture to check the serial order of the letters in the word *saw* to see if it is *w-as* or *s-aw.*

Seven, it is obvious that to make an intelligent guess about a single word in a sentence, one must be able to recognize practically all the other words that surround it. While the statement *Bill was the dog* is grammatically correct, it is logically improbable, since few dogs are named *Bill.* The improbability of *was* would require the child to make a check of the letters in *was* and *saw* and to make the necessary correction to *saw.*

Eight, the value of context cues for beginning readers depends on the spelling-sound similarity of the words being taught. As Hartley (1971) has shown, if a list of words with minimal spelling-sound differences are taught (*hen-ten-pen-men*), the use of the words *plus* a context cue "seemed to have a depressing effect" on the learning of such words. However, "a graphic stimulus word plus a context cue was most successful when presented with a maximal contrast list" (p. 118) such as *rake-show-king-ten.* This evidence suggests that when minimal contrast words (ones in which only one grapheme difference is apparent, as in *hen-ten*), are taught in phonics, the pupil may not attempt to employ context cues.

Nine, sometimes written words (words without intonation to aid their meaning) fail to give the intended meanings of their authors. For the full meanings of the following sentences to emerge, one would have to read them aloud, giving them the emphases indicated by the italics:

The *dog* bit the man.
The dog *bit* the man.
The dog bit the *man.*

Then, to help children correctly assign the part-of-speech category that is needed before a word can be given its proper sounding, have children read such sentences as:

Will you *permit* me to burn these papers?
Do you have a *permit* to burn these papers?

Other words to be used: *conflict, contract, address, rebel, import, setup (set up), greenhouse (green house).*

In the sentence, Cooking apples can be enjoyable, does *cooking apples* refer to the type of apples or to the process of cooking them? At other times, only the punctuation or capitalization settles the meaning:

I'd like to eat Mother. I'd like to eat, Mother.
Professor Rakes leaves at noon. Professor rakes leaves at noon.

The ambiguity of some sentences cannot be resolved. Unless the word order is changed or additional words or sentences are given, their meaning is unclear. For example:

The chicken was too hot to eat.
The shooting of the hunters was terrible.

Ten, if a sentence is in the passive voice rather than the active voice (or, as described in transformational grammar, a passive transformation rather than a kernel sentence), the effectiveness of context cues may be reduced:

1. The dog was *chasing* a cat. (active voice, or kernel sentence)
2. The dog was *chased* by a cat. (passive voice, or passive transformation)

It has been corroborated "that transformations take more time to understand than the underlying kernel sentences" even for mature readers (Schlesinger 1968, p. 45). This suggests that the teacher use kernel sentences rather than transformations, at least at the early levels of word recognition.

Eleven, it may seem at first that the child can always use context to decide on whether a sentence is a question. That would be a handy use of context. Notice how the beginning words of these sentences signal that they will be questions:

Is the girl taking her doll?
Did the girl take her doll?
Who took the doll?
What did the girl take?
Which girl took the doll?
When did the girl take the doll?

This context cue does not always work, however. For example:

When he left he took his coat.
What helped him most was his strength.

Children's Use of Context Cues

Discussions of children's use of context cues usually present sentences like *Pick up the* _____ as examples of the kind of tasks children should be given when one teaches them how to employ context cues to recognize words. The obvious implication here is that context cues are invitations to the child to infer or guess the identity of unrecognized words, such as the missing word in *Pick up the* _____, without paying any attention to its letters. This filling in of deleted words in a sentence is called the *cloze procedure* or *cloze technique.* Such exercises avoid directing children to use essential letter cues to word recognition.

There seems to be no defensible reason, however, for using partial sentences like *Pick up the* _____ for teaching children to utilize context cues. Children looking at a sentence context for help in reaching the identity or connotation of a word do not see a sentence with a missing word; they see a full sentence: *Pick up the paper.* However, teachers have often been advised to use cloze procedure activities for teaching children how to employ context cues. There has been no evidence presented, though, that says these activities are better for this purpose than are activities that use complete, normally-appearing sentences.

Those who believe that word recognition is essentially a "guessing game" rather than a precise and accurate procedure tend to defend the use of the cloze procedure in word recognition teaching. It is noticeable, however, that such defenders of the cloze procedure do not cite any convincing research evidence as support for this assumption (Rye, 1982). There appears to be a good reason for this avoidance of research findings: such findings give little support to the advocates of the use of cloze procedure for developing children's powers of word recognition. The research as a whole indicates that the cloze procedure "is no more or less effective than many other widely used instructional methods" (Jongsma, 1980, p. 20). Specifically, the cloze procedure "is least effective in improving word knowledge or vocabulary" (p. 20).

As noted, the cloze procedure intentionally obscures words in a sentence. It is highly important, however, that when context cues are relied on for help in identifying unrecognized words the boundaries of these words be clearly defined. It is advisable, therefore, that the unrecognized word in question not only be seen by the reader but that it be underlined before an appeal for help from context cues is made. The child has the best chance of identifying a word when its image is made as distinctive as possible.

With the reasonable conviction in mind that complete sentences are the best material with which to find uses for context cues, how might the child actually go about using context to decode a word? For this purpose let's take a word that research has shown may be difficult for children to decode, *paper,* and examine the process a child might go through to decode it with context.

We (Groff, 1983) found that after children had reached an approximate pronunciation of paper as /paper/, 20 percent still could not infer and reproduce its correct pronunciation. Let's assume that a child who is one of that 20 percent has tried unsuccessfully to decide *paper* in the sentence, *Pick up the paper*, using phonics rules and a search for little words (*pa*) and for phonograms (*ap* and *er*), and that the approximate pronunciations of *paper*, /paper/ or /poper/, that were reached were not close enough to the word's real pronunciation for this child to infer the word. Identifying *paper* is especially difficult in this case since it is the last word in the sentence. It is thought that the words that *follow* an unrecognized word offer more cues to its identity than do words that precede it (Spache and Spache, 1977).

We have here a child who has applied correctly all he or she knows about word recognition, but to no avail. What is the utility of the sentence context, *Pick up the*, to the child who cannot recognize *paper*? How can an analysis of the sentence in which *paper* is found help the child recognize this word? How can the child be taught to search for and exploit context cues of use in its recognition?

There is some help in the context of the sentence *Pick up the paper* that can be pointed out to the child. Children can be led to understand that *the* in the sentence signals the advent of the name of something, a noun. Further, it can be deduced from the sentence that the thing this noun stands for is not so heavy that it cannot be lifted or moved. In addition, the command function of this sentence implies that picking up the noun-object is a socially desirable action and that this object is something that may not be normally found or desired at the place where it now is.

It is apparent, however, that the employment of these context cues may still not result in the decoding of *paper*, unless by chance they cause the child to think of *paper* and then to realize that it is indeed the identity of the mystery word. The unpredictability of this result illustrates well the fact that placing one's reliance on context cues will not always resolve the problem of how to decode exceptional words (words whose unpredictable spellings make it difficult for the child to use phonics to gain approximate pronunciations of these words, from which inferences can be made of their correct pronunciations). The case of *Pick up the paper* underlines the truism that at times in word recognition, nothing will take the place of having on hand someone who is able to tell the child the identity of an unrecognized written word.

Suppose, however, that *Pick up the paper* were part of an ongoing series of sentences: *Clean up your room. Pick up the paper. Put it in the trash can.*

Now the possibility that context cues can come to the assistance of our puzzled pupil is improved. Children who find themselves baffled by *paper* in a sentence could thus be told to read the next sentence in a passage, and/or reread the preceding one, to determine if these sentences give cues as to how to correct the approximate pronunciation, /paper/ or /poper/, to /pāpər/.

The teacher can also show pupils that there are other sentence structures in which the chances for decoding *paper* are greater than was the case for *Pick up the paper.* Children can be taught that if they encounter such sentences a search for context cues might be helpful. Ames (1966) has suggested a list of such sentences:

> *The paper that he wrote today was lost.*
> *Paper is something to write on.*
> *Kites, boxes, and books are made of paper.*
> *To make a book you need ink, paste, and paper.*
> *This is not heavy. It's made of paper.*
> *Paper, like leaves, can blow away.*
> *He tore the paper into little pieces.*
> *Paper is used a lot in school.*
> *I want something to made a mask. I need some paper.*
> *It will take a lot of paper to cover this box.*
> *I found a use for this paper. It makes a good mask.*
> *"What are you doing with that paper?" "Making a mask."*
> *When he wrote his paper his pencil broke.*
> *He wrote too hard and tore his paper.*
> *By writing hard you will tear your paper.*

In each of these sentences *paper* has a unique relationship with the rest of the words in the sentence. After each of these sentences is presented by the teacher, a discussion could be conducted aimed at predicting how the structure of these various sentences might act as context cues for decoding the word *paper.* In effect, the teacher tells pupils: "This is what some try to do when they try to read a word they cannot recognize. I want you to try to do these same things when you see a word that you cannot read."

Context Cues and Decoding Skills

It is apparent from the preceding discussion that teaching context cue usage will take considerable time and effort by the teacher. Since there is only so much time that can be alloted for the development of word recognition skills, it must be asked if extensive context cue instruction is a wise use of this scarce classroom commodity. To answer this question, keep in mind that the word recognition program as described in Chapter 7 is designed to teach children to successfully decode the vowel letters in these words: *bed, came, seat, boil, cloud, down, smooth, wood, arm, care, cord, fire, her, cold, might, find,* and *all.*

Accordingly, if the child who encounters *paper* as an unrecognized word had successfully progressed through this word recognition program, he or she would simply have given the *a* in *paper* its "long" sound, and in this way would have gained a satisfactorily approximate pronunciation of this word. The word recognition program that this book describes teaches the child that if the application of "short" vowel sounds to closed syllables, like *ap* in *paper,* does not work, the pertinent "long" vowel sound should be applied. If the word recognition skills described in Chapters 7 and 8 are acquired by children, they would have little if any need for using context cues to decode *paper.*

Nonetheless, teachers are often advised that they should teach children to use context cues in close conjunction with their phonics skills. This instruction should adopt the following pattern, Durkin (1983) says: First the child is presented with a written sentence—*It takes practice to be a swimmer,* for example. There is thought to be one word, *practice,* in this sentence that the child is likely not to recognize. Then the child is asked to read all the words in the sentence except *practice.* At this point the child is directed to guess or infer the identity of *practice.* Only after this does the child apply phonics rules to decode *practice.* (Smith and Johnson [1980] would have the child at this juncture decode only the first letter of *practice* and guess again at its identity.) Now the entire sentence is read by the child. He or she then asks, "Does this reading make sense?"

We agree that phonics skills and context cues can be used in conjunction. We disagree, however, with the above recommendations for carrying them out. For one thing, these recommendations fail to reveal how a teacher can tell whether pupils are likely to be unable to recognize words like *practice.* For a child with decoding skills, this word is predictably spelled. Using the word recognition rules we have described in Chapters 7 and 8 children would decode it as /praktĭs/, a pronunciation of this word that is approximate enough to its true pronunciation that the latter can be inferred. If *practice* is in the child's speaking-listening vocabulary there may be no need here for context cues to be invoked.

If context cues were employed in this situation—that is, to verify whether *practice* is a suitable word for the slot in the sentence it occupies—it would be better to activate them *after* the decoding of *practice*, not in advance, as Durkin (1983) recommends. This decision is in keeping with the modern research on context cues suggesting that the effects of context cues on the comprehension of sentences are more likely to take place *after* word recognition has been accomplished than before.

Context Cues and Word Meanings

We have stressed so far that it is sensible in word recognition to utilize as nearly as possible the words that are already in the speaking/listening vocabulary of children. In this case, of course, there is no need to develop children's understandings of the connotations of these words, nor to establish their grasp of the meaning (denotation) of an unknown word. Bringing children into reading inevitably will result, however, in their need to add to their vocabularies new connotations or denotations of words.

We therefore move at this point to a discussion of an aspect of context cues not as yet considered in detail: the effect that context cues have on children's gaining new word meanings.

Up to this point we have emphasized how context cues can help children determine which particular connotation of a word its author intended for it. This use of context cues by children assumes that they already know a number of connotations of a given word. Context cues can help children decide here which of these various meanings of a word its author wanted to transmit. It is a different matter for a child to learn via context cues a new connotation of a word, or to learn for the first time what a word means (its denotation).

At this point it is well to remember "that the principal contributor to reading comprehension is vocabulary knowledge" (Johnson & Pearson, 1978, p. 37). It is vital, therefore, to reveal to children that an application of context cues may contribute to the recognition of unknown words, thus furthering their comprehension of them. Unfortunately, the effectiveness of teaching children this application of context cues has not been resolved experimentally. From their review of the research on this matter Sternberg, Powell, and Kaye (1983, p. 128) conclude "that current versions of the method may well have been oversold." These reading experts are optimistic, nonetheless, that "better versions can be devised."

There are certain conditions that complicate children's use of context cues for understanding connotations and denotations of words. The utility of context cues for this purpose will likely be enhanced if an unknown word appears frequently in a passage being read. If an unknown word appears in various sentence contexts, more effective use of context cues is possible, since the child had more chances to use various contexts in deciding on its meaning. Then, if the unknown word is critical to an understanding of the material being read, context cues may have a more significant function. In this case children cannot simply skip the word in question without doing serious damage to their comprehension. When a word is critical in this sense children will also have greater incentive to study it, perhaps through the use of context cues.

The uses of context cues may be negatively influenced, however, if there is a large number of unknown words in a sentence. Here children can become overwhelmed by the immensity of the word recognition task presented them, so much so that they may be inclined to simply give up trying to comprehend. In addition, if an unknown word is not located reasonably close to the relevant context cues, its identification may be difficult to uncover. Finally, context cues lose their importance if an unknown word is "decomposable," that is, if children know how to break it down into its morphemes and then to infer its meaning from an analysis of these word parts. (See the previous discussion of morphemic analysis on pp. 105-106). Children here may find morphemic analysis to be a satisfactory substitute for the employment of context cues, one that can be easier for them to utilize to gain word meanings.

Pearson and Johnson (1978) offer a "taxonomy" of the connotations of words that provides some insight into the types of connotations that children might be able to gain through the application of context cues. First, the child might learn in this way that words have similar or opposing meanings—that they are synonyms or antonyms. Next, children might find through the study of sentences that pairs of words often occur together, like *walk-slow; run-fast.* Then sentences that relate the classification of a word (such as *animal*) to examples of its class (*dog*) could be examined. This is followed by a demonstration, through sentence structure study, of how the classification of a word like *walk* can have different levels of intensity (*stroll, stumble*). Finally, context cues may be useful for gaining the intended denotation of words that can have different meanings, although they are spelled identically (*fly, lead*). On the other hand, there seems little usefulness for context cues with words called homophones: He *threw* the ball *through* the window. The spellings of such words give more assistance in their recognition than can context cues.

Despite the unsettled nature of the use of context cues for the acquisition of connotations and denotations of words, we remain hopeful that this use of context cues can be functional for children if it is taught directly. In this direct instruction children learn how to examine sentence contexts to make inferences about the connotations of familiar words and the denotations of unfamiliar ones.

We have argued previously that the cloze procedure, wherein children fill in the words omitted from sentences, is not an acceptable kind of direct word recognition instruction. The same can be said for the use of the so-called *maze procedure*. Here children use context cues to read sentences like *Pick up the paper. parade. parking.* We know of no evidence that the use of artificial-appearing sentences like this one teach the use of context cues better than does the use of normal-appearing sentences. Indeed, maze exercises may avoid the necessity for careful examination of letter sequence.

Certain other conditions should prevail in this direct instruction. **One,** teachers should make sure that any given activity designed for this purpose actually involves unknown connotations or denotations. It has been suggested, for example, that children read the following sentences for this purpose:

Wind the clock before bedtime.
The *wind* blew hard.

To give *wind* its proper pronunciation in each of these sentences does require the use of context cues. It does not teach children connotations and denotations of words, however. The same criticism can be made for having children read and rearrange scrambled sentences like *Door the open,* or read and delete the extraneous word in a sentence like *The new girl apple moved here.*

Two, the activity designed to teach directly the use of context cues for gaining connotations and denotations of words should be instruction and should not simply test what children already know. Having children give the conventional and slang denotations of *fuzz,* for example, is simply a test of what they already know. Having them complete analogies like *Good is to bad as light is to bright, naughty, dark, happy,* has the same shortcoming. (This is an exercise in logic, not context.) To teach the use of context for learning word connotations and denotations, it is better to have a group of children first attempt to read a passage and then underline words they could not recognize. (Make sure that there is no penalty or embarrassment to children for making such admissions.) Once this underlining is done, the children can meet to discuss the uses of context cues as an aid to the solution of their word recognition problems. The unknown word can be studied in a variety of sentences such as those given on page 125.

Tests of children's knowledge of the meanings of written words do have a merit, nonetheless. From the results of such tests the teacher can determine whether children know a particular word, and once this fact is established, a set of practice sentences can be constructed for the word. (See page 125.) Placing an unknown word in a variety of sentence constructs gives the child repeated opportunities to learn its meaning or meanings. Research (Harris & Sipay, 1980) suggests that the best procedure is for the teacher to first tell children the meaning of an unknown written word; then children read this target word in the context of a variety of sentence structures. This method proved to be better for helping children remember the denotations of words than did their unaided discovery of word meanings through the use of context cues.

The development of children's understanding of figurative language, euphemisms, and circumlocutions also can be done in this manner. Again, the teacher first explains the particular usage that is in question and then has children read it in a variety of sentence constructs in which it is found.

Other activities for having children use context cues for gaining the connotation or denotation of a word include the following:

1. Even an apparently simple word like *show* can be put into different contexts, which require that different meanings be brought to it.

   Did he *show* the judge the photographs that were taken?
   (put into sight)
   Perhaps the judge will *show* him some mercy.   (grant)
   The evidence will *show* that Mr. Brown was guilty.   (prove)
   The DA will *show* how the accident happened.   (explain)

2. Somewhat different contexts can be given from which pupils are asked to read a difficult word, concentrating on the context for this purpose.

   a. The unknown word is *defined* by the passage:
      Level lands between mountains are called <u>valleys</u>.
      The name that is given for animals with warm blood is <u>mammal</u>.

b. A passage uses a word and its *synonym:*
He is the meanest, most <u>cruel</u> man in town.
The careless boy did the work in a <u>sloppy</u> manner.

c. A *familiar expression* is used:
That pan leaks like a <u>sieve</u>.

d. A passage uses a word and its *antonym:*
The boy awoke from a deep <u>slumber</u>.

e. An *immediate experience* helps.
The baby lions were <u>gamboling</u> with the ball just as kittens do.

f. The missing word can *conclude* or *summarize* the passage:
Each time he walked through the graveyard he became more <u>apprehensive</u>.

g. The passage has a *figure of speech:*
The dam will be built to <u>harness</u> the river.
The cat's eyes <u>sparkled</u> like little lights.

h. An *appositive* is a context cue:
The minutes, a <u>record</u> of the meeting, were kept by Jane.

i. The appearance of a *series of items* can classify an unfamiliar word:
He likes to write many different kinds of things—poems, <u>essays</u>, plays, and stories.

3. Use a paragraph in which the word to be determined by context cues is imbedded:

   The boys walked by the red circus tent. "Why are all the people going in there?" said Bob.
   "The *menagerie* is in there," explained his older brother. "Let's go in and find out what animals they have."

4. Part of the use of context cues involves the knowledge that certain words (pronouns) can stand in the place of (fill the sentence slot for) certain kinds of nouns. It is useful, therefore, to go through passages making sure that children are conscious of this, showing them how anaphora works, and testing their ability to find the word the pronoun stands in the place of.

5. Have children replace words in slots. For example, have them think of words that would fit the slot occupied by *few* in *Few men were*

working. (*Many, more, most of the, only a few of the*, etc.) This can be done with many adjectives and adverbs.

6. Say: "What word like the one in the slot is the word that makes the sentences a good one?" Write:

The man was an *act.* (actor)
She is very *music.* (musical)
Did he use good *judge?* (judgment)
Obey the *safe* rules. (safety)
Always be *social* with strangers. (sociable)

7. Discuss with children the special meanings of idioms. For example:

The man *had a run* of luck.
The man *ran out* of luck.

Unresolved Issues about Context Cues

Issues regarding the usefulness of context cues still need resolution. Until they are decided upon, teachers will remain unsure as to the degree that context cues aid children in word recognition. Some of these issues are discussed below.

• Modern research suggests that many reading experts now give context cues too prominent a place in word recognition instruction. These experts accordingly hold some unauthenticated views as to the ways context cues apply to word recognition and how the use of context should be taught to children. The exact extent to which these traditional views on context cues need change will depend on future research into this subject.

• Teachers need more experimental evidence as to how children actually apply context cues in normal reading conditions. Most of the commentary on this topic at present is subjective, or of an anecdotal nature. Research on context cues has also been done in large part with college students, not with young children.

• Teachers have been advised to teach the uses of context cues to children in reading conditions they never face. It remains an empirical question whether teaching children to guess the identity of missing words in sentences, for example, can develop faulty word recognition habits. The loyalty of many of today's reading experts to methods of teaching context cues that use only partial sentence structures, particularly sentences with omitted words, causes them to be forgetful of the principle that instruction in reading skills should be given in the context into which these skills are to be transferred later.

• Teachers need experimental evidence as to the extent to which pupils who are becoming increasingly well-grounded in phonics skills are aided in word recognition by the application of context cues. The degree to which phonics skills and context cues complement each other at the various stages of children's development of word recognition ability is yet to be determined.

• The processes of recognizing words and gaining word meanings through the application of context cues are often confused in discussions of these matters. The difference between using context cues as an aid to the identification of written words that are *not* in the child's speaking/listening vocabulary and using context cues to gain the connotation of a written word that is in the child's speaking/listening vocabulary is often not clearly delineated.

• It is often implied in discussions of the utility of context cues that they have a generalized usefulness. The modern research (Perfetti, 1985) suggests, however, that words that occur with high frequency, for example, are less difficult to recognize, and thus that the child has less need for context cues to identify them. So far, not enough is known about such matters to give teachers reliable advice as to their importance in instruction.

SUMMARY

Because the context of a word affects its meaning in the sentence, context has potential for aiding children in reading. But context cues are evidently not as helpful to children as once thought by reading experts; they can become a crutch to be used as a substitute for applying phonics techniques. Guessing a word's identity on the basis of the sentence's grammar or meaning can be useless, and it may become a bad habit.

The use of context clues in early reading instruction has some drawbacks and limitations. Context cues have greater possibilities for developing word connotations than they have for arriving at an approximate pronunciation of a word (from which the child can reach its real pronunciation), or for making other judgments about the word. For word recognition, therefore, context cues may be more helpful as confirmation to phonemic and morphemic judgements about an unrecognized word than for anything else.

REFERENCES

Ames, W.S. (1966). The development of a classification scheme of contextual aids. *Reading Research Quarterly*, 2, 57–82.

Biemiller, A. (1970). The development of the use of graphic and contextual information as children learn to read. *Reading Research Quarterly*, 6, 75–96.

Chester, R.D. (1972). Differences in learnability of content and function words presented in isolation and oral context when taught to high and low socioeconomic level students. *Dissertation Abstracts International*, 32, 3833A.

Durkin, D. (1983). *Teaching them to read.* Boston, MA: Allyn and Bacon

Goodman, K.S. (1965). A linguistic study of cues and miscues in reading. *Elementary English*, 42, 639–643.

Gough, P.B. (1981). A comment on Goodman. In M. Kamil (Ed.), *Directions in reading: Research and instruction.* Washington, DC: National Reading Conference.

Gough, P.B. (1983). Context, form, and interaction. In K. Raymer (Ed.). *Eye movements in reading: Perceptual and language processes.* New York, NY: Academic.

Gough, P.B. (1984). Word recognition. In P.D. Pearson (Ed.), *Handbook of reading research.* New York, NY: Longman.

Groff, P. (1979). Children's recognition of words in isolation and in context. *Reading Horizons*, 19, 134–138.

Groff, P. (1983). A test of the utility of phonics rules. *Reading Psychology*, 4, 217–225.

Harris, A.J., & Sipay, E.R. (1980). *How to increase reading ability.* New York, NY: Longman.

Hartley, R.M. (1971). A method of increasing the ability of first grade pupils to use phonetic generalizations. *California Journal of Educational Research*, 22, 9–16.

Henderson, L. (1982). *Orthography and word recognition in reading.* New York, NY: Academic.

Johnson, D.D., & Baumann, J.F. (1984). Word identification. In P.D. Pearson (Ed.), *Handbook of reading research.* New York, NY: Longman.

Johnson, D.D., & Pearson, P.D. (1978). *Teaching reading vocabulary.* New York, NY: Holt, Rinehart and Winston.

Jongsma, E.A. (1980). *Cloze instruction research: A second look.* Newark, DE: International Reading Association.

Lesgold, A.M., & Resnick, L.B. (1982). How reading disabilities develop: Perspectives from a longitudinal study. In J.P. Das, R. Mulcahy, & A.E. Wall (Eds.), *Theory and research in learning disability.* New York, NY: Plenum.

Nicholson, T., & Hill, D. (1985). Good readers don't guess—taking another look at the issue of whether children read words better in context or in isolation. *Reading Psychology*, 6, 181–198.

Pearson, P.D. (1978). On bridging gaps and spanning chasms. *Curriculum Inquiry*, 8, 353–362.

Pearson, P.D., & Johnson, D.D. (1978). *Teaching reading comprehension.* New York, NY: Holt, Rinehart and Winston.

Perfetti, C.A. (1985). *Reading ability.* New York, NY: Oxford.

Richek, M.A., List, L.K. & Learner, J.W. (1983). *Reading problems: Diagnosis and remediation.* Englewood Cliffs, NJ: Prentice-Hall.

Rye, J. (1982). *Cloze procedure and the teaching of reading.* London: Heinemann.

Samuels, S.J., & Kamil, M.L. (1984). Models of the reading process. In P.D. Pearson (Ed.), *Handbook of reading research.* New York, NY: Longman.

Schlesinger, I.M. (1968). *Sentence structure and the reading process.* The Hague: Mouton.

Singer, H., et al. (1973–74). The effects of pictures and contextual conditions on learning responses to printed words. *Reading Research Quarterly,* 9, 555–567.

Smith, F. (1971). *Understanding reading.* New York, NY: Holt, Rinehart and Winston.

Smith, N.B., & Robinson, H.A. (1980). *Reading instruction for today's children.* Englewood Cliffs, NJ: Prentice-Hall.

Smith, R.J. & Johnson, D.D. (1980). *Teaching children to read.* Reading, MA: Addison-Wesley.

Spache, G.D., & Spache, E.B. (1977). *Reading in the elementary school.* Boston, MA: Allyn and Bacon.

Stanovich, K.E. (1980). Toward an interactive-compensatory model of individual differences in the development of reading fluency. *Reading Research Quarterly,* 16, 32–71.

Sternberg, R.J., Powell, J.S., & Kaye, D.B. (1983). Teaching vocabulary-building skills: A contextual approach. In A.C. Wilkinson (Ed.), *Classroom computers and cognitive science.* New York, NY: Academic.

10

TEACHING WORD RECOGNITION TO LINGUISTICALLY DIVERSE CHILDREN

Children who speak no English or very little English, or a nonstandard dialect of English, bring special challenges to the reading classroom. The teacher of word recognition needs to be aware of these issues and the way they may affect children's ability to learn to read.

Teachers today may find themselves sharing a classroom with children who speak several different foreign languages. This situation may be complicated by the fact that today's immigrants differ from those of previous decades in that more of them bring Asian languages to the classroom. Since they also may have economically disadvantaged backgrounds, attitudes of some people toward these children and their languages or dialects may be negative (Ebel, 1980). These non-English-speaking children are not achieving well in reading, it is clear. The recent survey of their reading and writing by the National Assessment of Educational Progress found them scoring substantially below the average child who speaks standard English (Editors, *Phi Delta Kappan*, 1986).

Foreign Language Speakers

The characteristics of children who speak a foreign language that may affect their ability to learn to read English include the following:

- a limited vocabulary in English
- a vocabulary in their native language that does not translate into equivalent English words
- a different phonological system
- a different grammatical system
- a different writing system
- different linguistic behavior—for example, refusal to make eye contact as a sign of politeness and respect for the teacher.

When one learns a new language, one at first expects it to be constructed the same as one's first language. The tendency when speaking is thus to mentally translate from one's first language into the new one, using parallel words, the same grammatical structure, and the same phonology. For this reason a Chinese learning English is likely to use verb forms and plurals that are incorrect in English, like *He go to see a movie today, He go to see a movie yesterday, There are three book on the table, It don't really matter to me, He like to do it*—not because of carelessness but because in Chinese these would be correct forms (Cheong, 1970). Similarly, in Japanese singular and plural are not distinguished: *book* can be either singular or plural in that language, and Japanese speakers leave it up to the rest of the sentence to show the number meant. To do otherwise in Japanese would be redundant. Unlike English the Japanese language has a plural pronoun for *you*, one that can only be translated as *you-all* (Martin 1954). Standard Russian omits the copula *is* in such expressions as *He is sick*, so it is correct in Russian to say *He sick* (Carroll, 1971). In Navaho *he* and *she* are interchangeable, and the Navaho language has more complicated verb forms than does English (Kluckhohn & Leighton, 1946). In Spanish, negation is accomplished by attaching a negative form to everything that can be negated, so it would be correct in Spanish to say *I didn't hurt nobody* (Stockwell, et al, 1965). Turkish is devoid of grammatical gender, so the sex of persons spoken about does not affect the form of words. In Turkish there is only one pronoun, and it means *he, she* or *it* (Whitely, 1972).

If a child learning English is already literate in a language whose orthography is different from that of English, such as in Vietnamese, this child has the added problem of adapting to an entirely new writing system. If the child is literate in Arabic, for example, he or she is used to reading and writing from right to left (Barnitz, 1982).

The cultural system the foreign language child brings to the classroom may also mean that he or she has different attitudes toward language, toward the teacher, and toward learning, attitudes that may not intersect with English language classroom practices. Mexican and Mexican-American children, for example, like many American Indian children, are family- and social group- oriented. They may thus achieve better in a situation where the task set for them is cooperative rather than competitive (Kagan & Madsen, 1971). Spelling bees and other "me-against-you" activities may embarrass and even appall them. Teachers of inner-city black children often misinterpret their linguistic behavior like a refusal to make eye contact; in the black culture this is politeness, not furtiveness.

Children of Mediterranean cultures often stand much closer to the persons they are conversing with than is customary in America, where such shortened distances may make listeners uncomfortable.

It is interference from the phonological system of the foreign child's first language that may pose the most difficulty in teaching him or her English word recognition. If a child cannot hear the phonemes of English he or she obviously will not be able to learn phonics very well. Take, for example, the sound system of Spanish, some varieties of which have no /sh/ sound and no /th/ or /th/, but which has another sound that English is lacking, one that is a cross between /h/ and /k/. In addition, the Spanish way of pronouncing /p/, /t/, and /k/ is different from ours; these phonemes may sound to the teacher like /b/, /d/, and /g/. Children literate in Spanish may decode /r/ as something like /d/ or /t/, so *berry* may sound like *Betty* (Seymour, 1969). One specialist in Spanish-to-English instruction estimates that English phonic generalizations apply to Spanish only 85 percent of the time (Thonis, 1976).

Spanish is not the only language that has no /th/ or /th/; these phonemes are often the most difficult for many foreigners to learn (Barnett, 1964). The only Germans who use these sounds are the ones who lisp. Japanese has no /l/ sound, so a Japanese child trying to pronounce an English word ending in /l/ may say it with a vowel sound, like /oo/, since most syllables in Japanese, as in Italian, end in vowels (Seymour, 1969). In Tamil /k/ and /g/ are not separate phonemes (Quirk, 1964). Hawaiian has no /d/; Iroquoian and Tlingit have no /l/ (Ioup & Weinberger, in press). Teaching English as a Second Language (ESL) thus is no simple matter.

Getting ESL Children Ready to Recognize Written Words

To prepare children who do not speak English well to recognize English written words, the teacher should:

1. **Become familiar with the target language.**

There is no substitute for exact knowledge of the ESL child's language situation. By "exact knowledge" of the target language we mean understanding of its grammatical system, its phonology, its basic vocabulary, and its requirements for appropriate linguistic behavior (when and how to speak politely to adults, for example).

Many sources of detailed information on the grammar, phonology, lexicon, and language behavior of speakers of various tongues are now available; for example, Peñalosa (1980), Frey (1976), Saville-Troike (1976, 1977), Ching (1976), Rodriguez (1981), Trager & Henderson (1977), and Stockwell, et al. (1965). From such sources the teacher can compile a checklist of differences in the native language that may interfere with ESL children's grasp of English phonology, grammar, and vocabulary, and compare each item with the program of phonics instruction being used, so that when each of these differences arises the teacher is ready to give special aid to children on that point.

A sample checklist of difficulties in English for Spanish-speaking children could look like the following (Ching, 1976; and Peñalosa, 1980):

a. Phonology
   (1) Difficult vowel sounds: /i/, /a/, /ə/, /ōo/.
   (2) Difficult consonant sounds: /v/, /th/, /z/, /zh/, /j/.
   (3) Words that end in /r/ plus the consonants /d, t, l, p, s/ are pronounced in Spanish without that final consonant.
   (4) No Spanish words begin with an /s/-cluster. No clusters of /s/ with /t, p, k, f, m, n, or l/ occur in any Spanish words. The Spanish child tends to begin such /s/-cluster words with a vowel sound.
   (5) Final consonant clusters /sp/, /sk/, and /st/ are difficult.
   (6) Mexican Spanish has no /sh/.

b. Grammar
   (1) Spanish has different subject-predicate agreement (*The cars runs*).
   (2) Spanish has different verb tense formation (*I need help yesterday*).
   (3) Spanish has different negative forms (*He no go home, He not catch the bird*).
   (4) Spanish omits *the* or *a* in some contexts (*He is farmer*).
   (5) Spanish omits some pronouns (*Is hot today*).
   (6) Spanish adjective order is different (*The cap red is pretty*).
   (7) Spanish has different comparatives (*Is more big*).

A rather complete checklist of Haitian Creole speakers learning English is found in Hall and Hall (1971). One for Chinese speakers learning English is provided by Ching (1976).

2. **Fit Instruction to Local Requirements.** The teacher must learn about local regulations concerning the stage of ESL children's learning at which they are expected to learn to read English. For example, does the state or the school system mandate that children learn to speak English before learning to read English? Is the child expected to learn to speak

and read English at the same time? Is there a program in effect for teaching reading in a foreign language first? Instruction must be adapted to such constraints.

There is much controversy over the kind of instruction that the foreign language (FL)-speaking child should receive. Proposals for this purpose range from *immersion* to *transitional* to *maintenance*. In the immersion approach the FL child from school entry onward reads only in the second language, English. Transition programs teach FL children in their native language along with English for about two or three years and then immerse them in English. A plan somewhere between these two uses bilingual teachers who accept FL pupils' oral language but respond to this foreign language only in English. Pupils here are introduced to English from school entry onward. Maintenance programs are ones in which students receive "instruction in both languages *equally* throughout their school careers." (Ovando & Collier, 1985, p. 39).

The transitional approach, or a variation of it, is the most widely used one for teaching English as a second language. The deliberate use of both the native language of the FL child and English interchangeably by both pupils and teachers also is "probably the most common pattern of language use in bilingual classrooms" say Ovando and Collier (1985, p. 82). In this pattern, called "code switching," English is usually spoken more often than the foreign language in question. A less frequently used pattern is the alternative language approach wherein for equal portions of the school day the FL child is totally immersed in either his or her native language, or in English.

There remains much disagreement as to which of these approaches is the best one. For English-speaking children learning a foreign language "immersion bilingual education works very well" (Ovando & Collier, 1985, p. 43). On the other hand, it is said that the immersion approach will not work for the FL child learning English. Some experts in bilingual education thus advise that FL children remain in maintenance programs all the way through high school. To this effect Ovando and Collier (1985, p. 38) claim that "all research findings in studies that have been methodologically well done show that the longer students remain in a quality bilingual program the more successful they are in school achievement in both first and second languages." The "quality bilingual program" in their judgment is the maintenance approach. It does not appear at present, however, that most schools have the money needed to implement this approach.

3. **Assess the ESL Child's Language.** Two techniques will help the teacher find out the individual ESL child's knowledge of English and this child's difficulties with English grammar and phonology. One technique is to learn about them incidentally while giving language instruction. The other is to give informal but direct individual diagnosis. The teacher may want to try both of these techniques.

a. **Incidental Assessment Through Instruction.** ESL teachers often recommend the Language Experience Approach as a way to begin work on word recognition (for example, Feeley, 1977; Wiesendanger & Berlem, 1979). In this approach the class first has an educational experience together, perhaps a visit to a zoo, and then dictates to the teacher an account of the experience, which is edited by the teacher. While going through this process the teacher is able to gain a general idea of the children's ability to use English vocabulary, grammar, and phonology. This process also helps develop some English listening-speaking vocabulary on the part of the ESL learner.

b. **Direct Individual Assessment.** A direct method is to check each ESL child's understanding of English by giving him or her a series of commands, like *Put the pencil on top of the book*, by asking questions, like *What color is your sweater?* and by asking for descriptions, as in *Tell me about your family* (Allen, 1977). One specialist in teaching the Spanish-speaking child has devised a set of ten commands as a test of comprehension, a set of ten others as a test of speaking, and two sets of words, phrases, and sentences as a test of reading (Thonis, 1976).

To assess children's phonology, the teacher can ask each child to repeat the following sentences, in which the boldfaced letters stand for sounds often difficult for foreign speakers to say:

Victor Williams walked slowly through the house.
Charles said, "Shame on you! Are you too young to walk fast?" It is easy to jump over the shovel. (Allen, 1977, p. 506)

4. **Make Assistance Specific.** The teacher should use prearranged lists of foreign language speakers' specific problems with grammar and phonology in order to give the best help on these items. If, for example, Spanish-speaking children tend to pronounce and read *ship* as *chip*, give them help with the formation of the /sh/ sound: Have them attend while you pronounce the sound, and ask them to make the sound as you listen. Show children whose language has no /th/ or /th/ sound how to make each of these sounds by letting breath out while sticking the tongue

between the teeth. If necessary, explain that in English we do not say, "Hunger is killing me" but "I am hungry". Devise sentences for practicing English forms that give children diverse opportunities for reinforcing them.

5. **Take Advantage of ESL Organizations and State and Local Materials Centers.** In ESL teaching there is great need for classroom materials that bring children's language problems to the forefront and give teachers opportunities for teaching standard English speech and for reinforcing its use. To learn how to stock the classroom with language-stimulating materials, investigate the offerings of national, regional, and local organizations and materials centers that offer such aids as filmstrips, picture books, conferences, and other ideas. One successful ESL teacher recommends the use of bilingual teacher aides, parent help, and peer teaching (Perez, 1979).

6. **Use ESL Techniques Proved to be Effective.** Modeling and contrastive drills are often used successfully in teaching English to ESL children. The words, phrases, sentences, and dialogue practiced orally in such drills can be used by the reading teacher as material for use in word recognition.

These ESL language drills generally work in the following ways. For children who speak no English at all, for example, the teacher can begin by naming classroom objects (chalk, blackboard, eraser) and modeling such sentences as "This is an eraser," which the children repeat. The teacher then moves to questions, like "Is this chalk?" indicating that the children's reply is "Yes, this is chalk" (Rodriguez, 1981). Pattern practice is similar. Using a picture, the teacher may ask, "Is this a bird?" indicating that the correct reply is either "Yes, this is a bird" or "No, this is not a bird" (Frey, 1976). In substitution drills, children learn to substitute pronouns, for example: "Peter's going to school. *He's* going to school" (Ching, 1976). Transformation or conversion drills work like this: After learning the names of occupations, children point to pictures and say:

He's a dentist; he's not a musician.
 "   " musician; "   "   " farmer. (etc.)
(Kreidler, 1977)

A set of handy pictures for such work is provided in the Bowmar/Noble (1985) ESL kit. Such drills and materials can be adapted for reading use by the teacher of word recognition.

7. **Become Aware of Cultural Aspects of the Given Foreign Language That**

May Condition the Way One Teaches Children Who Speak It. In a project at the Rough Rock Demonstration School in Arizona, teachers found that students' main difficulty, despite the great differences between English and Navaho, was not grammar and phonology but ethnicity: The children rejected reading materials describing English culture and learned best with materials that pictured Navaho life. In this project the children were taught to read bilingually, with stories both in English and in Navaho (Hoffman, 1969).

Peer teaching has proved an effective supplementary procedure with Mexican-American children. Such children are used to having other children act as substitute parents (Dixon, 1976) so they respond well to their peers as tutors.

Speakers of Nonstandard English

The situation of the child born in the United States, or other English-speaking countries, who speaks English with a nonstandard dialect is different from that of the English as a Second Language (ESL) pupil. As it will be shown in the pages to follow, the latest research evidence indicates that the use of a nonstandard dialect by native American children need not interfere with these children's learning to read. In the past some reading experts (Stewart, 1969) held that the dialect was a definite handicap to children's acquisition of reading skills. That conclusion no longer prevails.

There are several regional or geographical dialects in the United States, as noted in Chapter 2. Some are quite distinctive. Examples of the folk speech of western North Carolina include *it* pronounced as *hit, his* pronounced *his'n, contrary* used as a verb, and forms like *I ain't never seen no sech thing, nohow.* Although the advent of radio, television, and increased travel have had a leveling effect on Appalachian speech, such forms can still be heard (Fink, 1974).

Today's teacher will more likely encounter a nonstandard socioeconomic or ethnic dialect known as Black English (BE). BE is different from Standard English (SE) in at least four ways. It has:

(1) a variant vocabulary
(2) a different grammatical system
(3) a different phonological system, and

(4) some different kinds of linguistic behavior, such as refusal to make eye contact during dialogues.

It will be shown that the cause of BE children's relatively low achievement in reading cannot be attributed to their use of this dialect. It is important, nonetheless, that for purposes of communication with BE children that the teacher understand this dialect. To this effect, it is well to know that BE and SE vocabulary overlap. Although Black English speakers may use the word *we-all* instead of the possessive *our* (Stewart, 1969), like many SE speakers they may use *spigot* instead of *faucet, skillet* instead of *frying pan,* or *kin* instead of *family* (Burke, 1973). The use of *tote* for *carry* and *carry* for *conduct* are common in some SE dialects as well as in BE (Dillard, 1972). And Black ethnic slang like *rap* is so colorful that it has rapidly been entering Standard English.

It is phonological and grammatical differences that especially make BE sound different from SE. Although many of these differences can be found in other English dialects, especially those spoken in economically depressed areas, certain of these differences are found much more frequently in BE (Shuy, 1971). Extensive lists of such differences have been recorded.

Briefly stated, BE substitutes certain consonants and vowels for others so that *mouth* is pronounced *mouf, brother* is *bruvver,* and *time* sounds like *Tom.* It deletes some final consonant clusters so that *tool* is pronounced like *too* and *six* is pronounced the same as *sick.* It also constructs some of its tenses differently, with resulting sentences like *He working, He be working,* and *He work yesterday* (Seymour, 1971).

Perhaps even more striking are the grammatical differences between SE and BE, particularly the way tenses with *be* are formed in BE, where *be* is usually an anxiliary, as *have* is in SE. *Done* is also an auxiliary; *done did* in BE means *have done* in SE (Johnson, 1970b). A BE tense called the habitual, one that is lacking in SE, has forms like *He be doing it.* The BE way of forming the present tense, on the other hand, is without any form of *be: He running: My Momma working.* Another sharp difference is that no changes in grammar are used to indicate the past tense: If you ask a BE speaker, "How did you get here?" he or she may reply, "I walk." Plurals, too, are expressed more as they are in Chinese, Japanese, and French—without plural markers in nouns, as in *those man.* Other inflectional differences can be heard.

The only true classroom problem concerning BE and the teaching of reading, however, probably lies in the BE speaker's and teacher's under-standing of it. The BE child may have no inkling that his or her speech is, in the teacher's view, nonstandard English. On the other hand, the teacher may not be aware that the BE child's speech is a typical, regularized, organized, and precise dialect. The teacher who does not know that differences in BE are regular ones may believe that the child is omitting speech sounds and inflections because of carelessness, not realizing that such omissions are part of the BE dialect. Because many BE differences parallel those in immature SE speech (*bruvver*) and in some nonstandard white speech (*dese, dem*), the teacher may view this speech, and therefore the BE child, negatively. Reinforcing such problems are cultural differ-ences like the BE speaker's laughing behind one's hand—as Japanese women do (it's considered impolite to do otherwise), and refusing eye contact.

Getting BE Speakers Ready for Word Recognition

We recommend the following practices and principles to the teacher of word recognition working with BE speakers:

1. **The Extent to Which the Speaking of BE Interferes With Children's Acquisition of Word Recognition Skills Has Been a Controversial Issue.** In this regard Padek (1981) interprets the research to say that the BE child does not need to speak SE in order to understand it. Dummett (1984, p. 32) contends that there is "no research evidence to prove that Black English . . . actually interferes with the reading process." Trautman and Falk (1982) and Ekwall and Shanker (1985) agree. In any event, Schwartz (1982) observes, the research on this issue has so many weaknesses in its design and implementation that no conclusive decisions should be drawn from it.

The teacher thus should not approach the teaching of word recogni-tion to BE children under the assumption that until these children learn to speak SE they will be unable to learn to read it. This conclusion does not imply that teaching BE children to speak SE is an undesirable goal. To the contrary, the penalties for the BE child for speaking this dialect "are almost universal—miseducation, negative self-concepts, negative attitudes on the part of significant others, inappropriate educational and psychological assessments and placement" (Taylor, 1983, p. 1). It is clear that full access to the high social status and financial rewards of the upper levels of social, political, and economic life currently is unavailable to those who do not have a command of SE.

While the attainment of SE by the BE child should thus be the longterm goal of the school for the obvious reasons, word recognition teaching should not await this accomplishment. To the contrary, until research says otherwise the teacher should assume that BE children can learn to recognize words written in SE contexts—that their BE will not interfere with their reading development—and should proceed energetically to demonstrate this belief.

2. **Whether Children Should Read Any Written BE is a Controversial Issue.** A survey of the research brings to light no convincing research evidence that attempting to change pupils' BE dialect results in improved ability to read. In fact, there is some evidence that trying to change these pupils' dialect before teaching them to read has a negative effect on decoding skills (Rystrom, 1970).

Some reading experts interpret this finding to suggest that the earliest writing that BE children see in school, such as language experience charts, include some phrases written in BE, in order to "give the children the feeling that their own language is part of the formal classroom setting" (Labov, 1980, p. 63). There is some evidence that the Language Experience Approach, which utilizes experience charts dictated by children, may contribute to success in beginning reading for BE speakers (Bougere, 1981), and that this approach can create a reading environment more consonant with the nonstandard-speaking child's background (Knapp, 1974).

If BE expressions are written the teacher may want to also write the language experience story in SE in order to show the child what that looks like (Loban, 1968). It is traditional for teachers to edit children's experience charts and other dictation, explaining, "This is another way to say it." Such editing of BE must be done sensitively so that BE children will not be confused by it. There is no research evidence, however, to guide the teacher as to how long BE renderings, if used, should be permitted. This must be up to the teacher's discretion.

Shuy (1979, p. 189) contends, however, that "there has been little research to support" the idea that materials of *any* kind written in BE especially help BE children learn to read. The critical judgment of this eminent linguist convinces us that it is unnecessary to have children read BE. Thus we recommend the following practices.

3. **Word Recognition Instruction For BE Children Should Be Conducted in**

SE and Not in BE. There has been strong opposition to this conclusion from those who contend that BE children should be taught to read in their nonstandard dialect (Smitherman, 1983). In this regard the National Council of Teachers of English went on record in 1974 in support of the idea that BE speakers have the right to use their dialect in school work (O'Donnell, 1978). The "bidialectal" approach to reading instruction, using BE phonology and written versions of BE, has fallen out of favor since the 1970's, however (Taylor, Payne, & Cole, 1983). As Toohey (1986, p. 132) rightly observes, at present there is "little parental, institutional, or finally, academic support for minority bidialectal programs and they are not common in . . . schools today."

Therefore, in teaching phonics to the BE child the teacher should not use BE phonology. However, as we have noted, teachers do have the responsibility to understand the relationships between BE and SE phonology. The BE child will also have to gain this understanding. For example, in teaching the /r/-*r* correspondence in *for* teachers will not expect the BE child to decode *for* as /fôr/. They will be satisfied, instead, when this child decodes *for* as /fō/. In this instance the teacher understands that the BE child has recognized *for* but has translated its pronunciation into his or her BE dialect.

Studies have shown that teachers of reading confuse differences between SE and BE dialect with deficiencies in the latter (Adler, 1973; Gottesman, 1972). Even professionals in the American Speech and Hearing Association have had difficulties along these lines (Taylor, 1986). A BE speaker who says *bruvver* for *brother* may not be using immature speech but a regular dialect substitution. That child may need to learn that SE has the sound /th/ represented by the letters *th.* Even if children are speaking BE most "can learn to discriminate sounds in words if they are taught to do so independent of their articulation" (Cohen & Cooper, 1972, p. 43). This means that whether a BE child actually pronounces the word *ask* as /ask/ or not, that child can be taught to understand that the sequence of letters *a, s, k* stands for the sounds /ask/ in the word *ask.*

4. **Use Printed Materials Written in SE.** Experiments with basal readers written in BE have had contradictory results, in part probably because of differences in the children's ages, the goals of the research, the tasks presented to the children, the features of the studies, and the children's own dialects (Harber, 1978). We agree with the conclusions of Fasold (1969) and Shuy (1979) that written SE is as adequate for BE speakers as it

is for SE speakers, and so with Melmed (1973, p. 81) that "Standard English texts can adequately be used to teach BE speakers to read."

5. **Spend Much Time on Phoneme-grapheme Work.** Research evidence shows that low socioeconomic children do less well in decoding than they might "because of inadequate early instruction and experience with decoding skill" (Hart, et al., 1980, p. 644). The studies summarized by Harber (1978) indicate the crucial importance for BE speakers to learn certain word recognition skills. This research indicates that an important factor in the development of reading achievement for BE children is "heavy emphasis on reading with phonics instruction" (p. 37). Almost all the BE children in one study could readily hear differences between phonemes; they had difficulty in saying whether given phonemes occurred in spoken words. The researchers in this study (Wallach, et al., 1977) recommended that this phonemic analysis skill be taught at the start of BE children's school careers.

Learning to use letters to recognize words has even more value for linguistically diverse children than for SE children. For the linguistically diverse child there are speech sounds in SE that are nonobvious or ambiguous. Paying attention to letters in words helps this child clarify whether to or how to conceptualize letters as separate speech sounds. Ehri (1984, p. 146) has found that "if children's pronunciations are nonstandard and if spellings symbolize standard pronunciations, print may teach children how to say these words." After written language is established in children's memories as a visual representation for speech the spelling of words can improve children's memory for the SE sounds to be given written words. Paying close attention to the spelling of words may thus help the linguistically diverse child speak Standard English.

6. **Utilize Materials That Reflect BE Children's Ethnic Backgrounds.** Studies indicate that the relationship of reading materials to BE children's backgrounds has "a profound effect on reading performance (Joag-dev, 1980). We agree that "reading materials and reading instruction must draw, as much as possible, on experiences and settings appropriate to the children" (Strickland, 1972, pp. 222–223). Including in the classroom library books about black children and using texts in SE with a few BE expressions have been found motivational (Yellin, 1980). It is not always easy for middle-class white teachers to identify children's literature that is culturally relevant, but librarians can help.

7. **Avoid Telling Children That Their BE Speech is "Wrong" or "Bad."** Black English is not an inferior mode of linguistic expression; it is a

different and less universally-accepted system of speaking the language than is SE. It is essential that the teacher of word recognition accept this idea because the teacher's attitude toward BE children's language probably has an effect on their ability to learn to read. Their poor self-concept is often caused in part by real or perceived disparagement of their language (Harber, 1978).

The difficulties that BE children have in learning to recognize words are thus attributable to an extent to the negative attitudes of teachers toward BE. The way teachers interact with pupils obviously has a significant influence on their development of reading skills. If teachers believe, for example, that BE is a dialect greatly deficient in grammar and vocabulary—that is, that BE is a highly inferior mode of linguistic expression—they doubtless will communicate this negative bias to the BE child. The harmful effects of this bias can be described: say that the BE child reads aloud, satisfactorily translating the written SE of the text into BE, displaying no loss of the author's intended meaning, and that despite this adequate interpretation of the meaning of the text the BE child is repeatedly interrupted by the teacher and criticized for reading aloud poorly. The insensitivity of this teacher to the child's competent rendering of the author's text, and the teacher's consequent unwarranted criticism, is unfortunately not uncommon in today's classrooms. It has been shown that "teachers may evaluate students' reading ability and potential based on the students' culturally based communicative/interactional style rather than on other criteria more directly related to reading" (Bloome & Green, 1984, p. 407). The courts have taken this fact into consideration in ruling that teachers may not ridicule or harshly disparage the use of BE by children (Frieman, 1983).

It is both legally and educationally important, then, that teachers understand that BE children may use a style of communication that differs from that expected in traditional school situations. These children may answer test questions in terms of their own experiences and creative impulses rather than in the way the test-maker intended. It has been observed, also, that BE children may engage in sophisticated verbal exchanges on the playground that they do not display in formal classroom settings. Moreover, "there is now widespread acceptance among language specialists that the linguistic style common among various cultural groups is a viable communicative system" (Terrell, 1984, p. 122). This viewpoint was accepted in 1983 as the official policy on social dialects by the American Speech-Language-Hearing Association. A teacher unwilling to take these circumstances into consideration in word recognition instruction may hamper the growth of BE children's reading development. In short, teachers' reactions to the way BE children use language should not be allowed to become an impediment to their development of word recognition skills.

8. **Part of the Difficulty the BE Child Has in Learning to Recognize Words Appears to be Beyond the Power of the Teacher to Remedy.** It "has been relatively well accepted," as Wigfield & Asher (1984, p. 427) note, that home factors outweigh school factors in the determination of the level of children's reading achievement. This conclusion appears especially true in regard to BE children. The out-of-school influences on these children may be a greater determinant of their relatively low reading achievement than are the linguistic factors related to their use of BE. For example, BE children's home life often does not develop in them the motivation necessary for high achievement in reading. Parents of BE children may make inadequate plans for their children to attain this goal. These parents can be ineffective in conducting learning situations and experiences in the home that foster reading achievement. BE children also may develop more loyalty to their peer group—that is, conform more to its expectations and standards—than to those of their parents. Unfortunately, these peer groups often are unaware of, or will not accept, the fact that SE is the prestige dialect in education, business, literature, science, and technology.

SUMMARY

This chapter has discussed the preparation that needs to be provided by teachers for linguistically diverse children if they are to acquire word recognition skills in the most effective manner. We have noted that one crucial thing the teacher must remember is that ESL children have needs in this respect that are different from those of native-born American children who speak a nonstandard English dialect. Getting ESL children ready to recognize written words in English can be a more complicated and lengthy process than is the case for BE children. Hence the large number of bilingual education programs across the country. On the other hand, the research says the fact that children speak BE can no longer be offered as a reason these children fail to learn to read.

A second critical thing for the teacher to remember is that research tells us that the cultural, sociological, and psychological factors associated with ESL and BE must be carefully taken into account in word recognition instruction. Teachers who do not understand and/or reject the significance of these factors will hinder the success of their word recognition instruction with ESL and BE children.

Finally, it is important for teachers to remember that once ESL and BE children begin to learn written word recognition, they will acquire this skill in much the same way as does the SE child. The advice we have given in this book for teaching children to recognize monosyllabic and multisyllabic words thus is useful for teaching ESL and BE children as well for children in general.

REFERENCES

Adler, S. (1973). Articulation deviances and social class membership. *Journal of Learning Disabilities*, 6, 650–654.

Allen, V. (1977). The non-English speaking child in your classroom. *Reading Teacher*, 30, 504–508.

Barnett, L. (1964). *The treasure of our tongue*. New York, NY: Mentor.

Barnitz, J.G. (1982). Orthographies, bilingualism and learning to read English as a second language. *Reading Teacher*, 35, 560–567.

Bloome, D., & Green, J. (1984). Directions in the sociolinguistic study of reading. In P.D. Pearson (Ed.), *Handbook of reading research*. New York, NY: Longman.

Bougere, M.G. (1981). Dialect and reading disabilities. *Research and Development in Education*, 14, 67–73.

Bowmar/Noble. (1985). *Bowmar/Noble's experiences in English [kit]: An ESL program*. Oklahoma City, OK: Bowmar/Noble.

Burke, C. (1973). Dialect and the reading process In Roger Shuy (Ed.), *Language differences, Do they interfere?* Newark, DE: International Reading Association.

Carroll, J.W. (1971). Speech at Preconvention Institute, International Reading Association Annual Convention.

Cheong, G. (1970). Does the English language overtax our human energy? *Elementary English*, 47, 56–58.

Ching, D. (1976). *Reading and the bilingual child*. Newark, DE: International Reading Association.

Cohen, S.A., and Cooper, T. (1972). Seven fallacies: reading retardation and the urban disadvantaged beginning reader. *Reading Teacher*, 26, 38–45.

Dillard, J.L. (1972). *Black English*. New York, NY: Random House.

Dixon, C.N. (1976). Teaching strategies for the Mexican-American child. *Reading Teacher*, 30, 141–145.

Dummett, L. (1984). The enigma—The persistent failure of black children in learning to read. *Reading World*, 24, 31–37.

Ebel, C. (1980). An update: Teaching reading to students of English as a second language. *Reading Teacher*, 33, 403–407.

Editors, *Phi Delta Kappan.* (1986). Non-English-speaking students need help in reading: NAEP. *Phi Delta Kappan,* 67, 543.

Ehri, L.C. (1984). How orthography alters spoken language competencies in children learning to read and spell. In J. Downing & R. Valtin (Eds.), *Language awareness and learning to read.* New York, NY: Springer-Verlag.

Ekwall, E.E., & Shanker, J.L. (1985). *Teaching reading in the elementary school.* Columbus, OH: Charles E. Merrill.

Fasold, R. (1969). Orthography in reading materials for black English speaking children. In J.C. Baratz and R. Shuy (eds.). *Teaching black children to read.* Washington, DC: CAI, 68–91.

Fasold, R. (1971). What can an English teacher do about nonstandard dialect? *English Record,* 21, 82–90.

Feeley, J.T. (1977). Bilingual instruction: Puerto Rico and the mainland. *Reading Teacher,* 30, 741–744.

Fink, P. (1974). *Bits of mountain speech.* Boone, NC: Appalachian Consortium Press.

Frey, B.J. (1976). *Basic helps for teaching English as a second language.* Tucson, AZ: CBS.

Frieman, E.B. (1983). The Ann Arbor decision: The importance of teachers' attitudes toward language. *Elementary School Journal,* 83, 41–47.

Gottesman, R. (1972). Auditory discriminational ability in Negro dialect-speaking children. *Journal of Learning Disabilities,* 5, 94–101.

Hall, R.M.R., & Hall, B.L. (1971). A contrastive Creole-English checklist. *The English Record,* 21, 136–147.

Harber, J.R. (1978). *Reading and the black English-speaking child; An annotated bibliography.* Newark, DE: International Reading Association.

Hart, J.T., et al. (1980). Black English phonology and learning to read. *Journal of Educational Psychology,* 72, 636–646.

Hoffman, V. (1969). Language learning at Rough Rock. *Childhood Education,* 46, 139–145.

Ioup, G., and Weinberger, S. (In press). *Interlanguage phonology.* Cambridge, MA: Newbury House.

Joag-dev, C. (1980). Studies of the bicultural reader, *Reading Education Report No. 12.* Champaign, IL: University of Illinois and Cambridge, MA: Bolt, Beranek, and Newman.

Johnson, K. (1971). Black children's reading of standard and dialect texts. Unpublished manuscript.

Johnson, K. (1970a). Influence of nonstandard Negro dialect. *Florida Foreign Language Reporter,* 8, 148–150.

Johnson, K. (1970b). Unpublished speech at TESOL meeting, Washington, DC.

Kagen, S., and Madsen, M.C. (1971). Cooperation and competition of Mexican, Mexican-American and Anglo-American children of two ages under four instructional sets. *Developmental Psychology,* 5, 32–39.

Kluckhohn, C., and D. Leighton. (1946). *The Navaho.* Cambridge, MA: Harvard University Press.

Knapp, M. (1979). Black dialect and reading: What teachers need to know. Unpublished paper read at the IRA Annual Convention.

Kreidler, C.J. (1977). Pictures for practice. In M. Saville-Troike (Ed.), *Classroom practices in ESL and bilingual education.* Washington, DC: TESOL.

Labov, W. (1980). Pro and con: Allow "Black English" in schools? Yes. *U.S. News & World Report,* 88, 63–64.

Loban, W. (1968). Teaching children who speak social class dialects. *Elementary English,* 45, 592–618.

Martin, S.E. (1954). *Essential Japanese.* Rutland, VT: Tuttle.

Melmed, P. (1973). Black English phonology: The question of reading interference. In J. Laffey and R. Shuy (Eds.), *Language differences: Do they interfere?* Newark, DE: International Reading Association.

O'Donnell, R.C. (1978). Rights, responsibilities, and standards of English usage. *High School Journal,* 61, 221–227.

Ovando, C.J., & Collier, V.P. (1985). *Bilingual and ESL classrooms.* New York, NY: McGraw-Hill.

Padek, N. (1981). The language and educational needs of children who speak Black English. *Reading Teacher,* 34, 144–151.

Peñalosa, F. (1980). *Chicano sociolinguistics: A brief introduction.* Rowley, MA: Newbury House.

Perez, S.A. (1979). How to effectively teach Spanish-speaking children, even if you're not bilingual. *Language Arts,* 56, 159–62.

Quirk, R. (1964). English language and the structural approach. In Quirk, R. (Ed.), *The teaching of English.* London: OUP.

Rodriguez, R.J. (1981). *Mainstreaming the non-English speaking student.* Urbana, IL: ERIC clearinghouse on Reading and Communication Skills, National Council of Teachers of English.

Rystrom, R. (1970). Dialect training and reading: A further look. *Reading Research Quarterly,* 5, 581–599.

Saville-Troike, M. (1976). *Foundations for teaching English as a second language.* Englewood Cliffs, NJ: Prentice-Hall.

Saville-Troike, M. (Ed.) (1977). *Classroom practices in ESL and bilingual education.* Washington, DC: TESOL.

Schwartz, J.I. (1982). Dialect interference in the attainment of literacy. *Journal of Reading,* 25, 440–446.

Seymour, D.Z. (1971). Black children, black speech. *Commonwealth,* 95, 175–178.

Seymour, D.Z. (1969). Summary of possible problems in reading English for those already literate in Spanish. Unpublished manuscript.

Shuy, R. (1973). Nonstandard dialect problems: An overview. In R. Shuy and J. Laffey (Eds.), *Language differences:* Do they interfere? Newark, DE: International Reading Association.

Shuy, R.W. (1979). The mismatch of child language and school language: Implications of beginning reading instruction. In L.B. Resnick & P.A. Weaver (Eds.), *Theory and practice of early reading,* volume 1, Hillsdale, NJ: Lawrence Erlbaum.

Smitherman, G. (1983). Language and liberation. *Journal of Negro Education,* 52, 15–23.

Stewart, W. (1969). On the use of Negro dialect in the teaching of reading. In

J. Baratz and R. Shuy (Eds.), *Teaching black children to read.* Washington, DC: Center for Applied Linguistics.

Stockwell, R.P., J.D. Bower, & John W. Martin. (1965). *The grammatical structures of English and Spanish.* Chicago, IL: University of Chicago Press.

Strickland, D. (1972). Black is beautiful vs. white is right. *Elementary English,* 49, 220–3.

Taylor, O.L. (1983). Preface. *Journal of Negro Education,* 52, 1–2.

Taylor, O.L., Payne, K.T., and Cole, P. (1983). A survey of bidialectal language arts programs in the United States. *Journal of Negro Education.* 52, 35–45.

Taylor, O.L. (1986). *Treatment of communication disorders in culturally and linguistically diverse populations.* San Diego, CA: College Hill.

Terrell, S.L. (1984). Issues in layperson bias toward the cultural difference view. In S. Adler (Ed.), *Cultural language differences.* Springfield, IL: Charles C Thomas.

Thonis, E.W. (1976). *Literacy for America's Spanish speaking children.* Newark, DE: International Reading Association.

Toohey, K. (1986). Minority educational failure: Is dialect a factor? *Curriculum Inquiry,* 16, 127–145.

Trager, E.C., and Henderson, S.C. (1977). *The PD's: Pronunciation drills for learners of English.* Portland, OR: English Language Services.

Trautman, D.E., & Falk, J.S. (1982). Speaking BE and reading—Is there a problem of interference? *Journal of Negro Education,* 51, 123–133.

Wallach, L.; Wallach, M., Dozier, M., & Kaplan, N. (1977). Poor children learning to read do not have trouble with auditory discrimination, but do have trouble with phoneme recognition. *Journal of Educational Psychology,* 69, 36–39.

Whitely, S. (1972). Letter to the *New York Times Magazine,* May 7.

Wiesendanger, K., & Berlem, E. (1979). Adapting language experience to reading for bilingual pupils, *Reading Teacher,* 32, 671–673.

Wigfield, A., & Asher, S.R. (1984). Social and motivational influences on reading. In P.D. Pearson (Ed.), *Handbook of reading research.* New York, NY: Longman.

Yellin, D. (1980). Black English controversy; Implications from the Ann Arbor case. *Journal of Reading,* 24, 150–154.

GLOSSARY

Affixes. A collective term for prefixes and suffixes.

Allograph. One of the variety of graphic forms a letter may be given. For example, *A* and *a* are allographs of this letter.

Allophone. A sound that is part of a bundle of sounds that makes up a *phoneme*. The difference in sound among allophones is not enough to affect any meaning difference, e.g., *law—lit*. Since meaning is unaffected, an allophone is not classified as a separate phoneme.

Alphabetic principle. Refers to the use of a set of letters, an alphabet, to represent the *phonemes* of a language. Chinese writing, as an example, is not based on the alphabetic principle.

Auditory blending. A procedure of *word recognition* in which the individual *phonemes* of a word are first isolated and then blended together one after the other to form the sound of the word.

Auditory perception. The ability to hear sounds, including individual *phonemes*.

Basal readers. A series of books, written for each grade level in the elementary school, that purport to provide the basic instruction in reading.

Blends. See consonant-letter cluster or vowel-letter cluster.

Checked vowels. *Vowel phonemes* heard in *closed syllables,* /i, a, o͞o, u, e/.

Closed syllable. A *syllable* that ends in a *consonant phoneme*. Also called *phonogram* in this book.

Code-emphasis method or **approach.** The method used in beginning reading instruction in which there is a direct, intensive, systematic, and early teaching of *phonics.*

Compound words. Words of two *syllables* in which each syllable is an autonomous word. For example, *outside, into.*

Computer-assisted instruction. Instruction that utilizes computer-directed material that is projected on a TV screen and is designed to teach, drill, and evaluate children's word recognition skills.

Consonant. A *phoneme* made by an obstruction or blocking or some other restriction of the free passage of breath through the speech cavities as one speaks. We describe consonants as *plosives, fricatives, nasals, laterals,* and *semivowels.*

Consonant blend. See consonant-letter cluster.

Consonant letter. A letter used to represent a *consonant phoneme* in writing.

Consonant-letter cluster. Cluster of adjacent *consonant letters* in words, like *st* in *step.* Often called consonant blends.

Context cues. The cues to *word recognition* supplied by the remainder of the sentence, paragraph, or discourse in which the given word appears.

Correlation. A shortened form of *coefficient of correlation (r),* a statistical index that reveals the relationship between two sets of numerical scores. A 1.00 *r* indicates a perfect relationship; an *r* of .00 no relationship.

Critical reading. Reading done to judge the quality, truthfulness, usefulness, timeliness, etc., of reading material.

Cursive handwriting. A writing style in which the letters are connected, e.g., *cursive.*

Decode. To decode a word is to discover the *phonemes* its letters represent. Decoding is one part of *word recognition;* the use of *context cues* is another part.

Diacritical marking. A special mark added to conventional letters in dictionaries to indicate the *phoneme* the marked letter represents, e.g., ē (be), or th (*the*). This system is used in this book to record phonemes in writing.

Dialect. One form of a given language, e.g., English, spoken in a certain locality or geographical area, or by a racial or social group. A dialect has different pronunciations from other dialects, and yet is not sufficiently distinct from other dialects in a language to be regarded as a different language. While dialects correspond roughly to speech regions, any speech region can have at least two dialects represented by the *standard* and *nonstandard speech* of the region.

Dictionary syllabication. The set of rules dictionaries have used to explain how they divide *multisyllabic words,* e.g., *chok-ing.* This can be contrasted with the way many dictionaries syllabicate words in their *phonemic spellings* of these words, e.g., *cho-king.*

Digraph. A pair of letters (in a word) that represents a single *phoneme.* For example, *th* in *path* and *ee* in *meet.*

Diphthong. A blend or fusion of two adjacent *vowel phonemes* in a single *syllable*. Diphthongs begin with the first vowel phoneme and then glide or gradually change into the second vowel phoneme. Some phoneticians say all vowel sounds are diphthongized to some extent. It is easy, however, to hear diphthongs in the words *pay, hide, owl, cold,* and *boil.*

Distribution of phonemes. Refers to the permissible sequences of *speech sounds* that are found in English words. See **spelling patterns.** There are some sequences of sounds that English speakers do not make, e.g., /*shp*ild/.

Encode. To encode a word is to spell it. Encode is the opposite of *decode.*

Exceptional words. In this book this term is used to refer to any word at a given level whose *spelling patterns* have not been taught to that point.

Eye-voice span. The extent of time in oral reading that the voice trails behind where the eye is fixated on the print. In oral reading the fixation of the reader's eye on the print of a text always is ahead of any word that has been read aloud in the text.

Free vowels. All vowel sounds other than *checked vowels.* Free vowels can occur in any place in syllables.

Fricatives. *Consonants* made with a continuously flowing but partly constricted breath stream. Notice this when you say words with the phonemes /s, z, sh, zh, f, v, th, th, h/.

Function words. Words other than verbs, adverbs, nouns, or adjectives. Also called *marker words* or *structure words.* In the following sentence the function words are in italics: *Who* were *the* man *and* woman *in the* big car?

Glide. A *phoneme* characterized by a rapid change in resonance that is produced by a gradually changing movement of the speech organs involved. Glides are often said to be /w, y, r, hw/.

Grapheme. The written representation of a *phoneme.* Graphemes can be single letters, e.g., *hit* has three graphemes: *h-i-t.* This is not always so. For example, *though* has two graphemes: *th-ough.*

Graphemics. The scientific study of the manner in which graphemes are used to represent *phonemes.*

Graphonemes. Another word for *phonograms.*

High-frequency words. The most commonly spoken and written words in English. A small number of these words accounts for a relatively large percentage of all the running words one speaks or reads.

Homophone. A word that has the same *phonemes* as another word but has a different meaning, as in *bare — bear.*

Implicit speech. See silent speech.

Incidental or **indirect phonics.** A *phonics* program in which phonics is taught only when it is deemed the child needs it to recognize a word. This approach contrasts with *systematic phonics*.

Inflections. See intonation.

Informal reading inventory. A process of evaluation of oral reading that counts all omissions, mispronunciations, substitutions, additions, and repetitions of words, as well as the times the reader is inattentive to punctuation. From the scores thus obtained the reader is said to be reading at a frustration level, an instructional level, or an independent level.

Intonation. The pattern of changes in pitch that occur when one speaks or reads a word aloud.

Juncture. Points between two adjacent *syllables* or *phonemes* are called junctures. *Close juncture* is the normal transition between *phonemes* or between syllables, as in *fry* or *funny*. *Open juncture* is a more obvious pause or break heard between certain syllables. Two strongly stressed syllables do not exist next to each other without an obvious pause or break, an open juncture, between them. Sometimes this is the only means of establishing meanings for words, e.g., *nitrate* vs. *night-rate, I scream* vs. *ice cream*.

Language Experience Approach. An approach to beginning reading in which the children aided by the teacher compose stories, about their experiences, and learn to read them.

Lateral phoneme. A *phoneme* spoken when the voiced breath stream escapes laterally over the side of the tongue. Notice this in /l/.

Less-accented vowel. See schwa.

Linguistics. The scientific study of language. This includes *phonetics, phonemics*, grammar, *semantics*, and *morphology*.

Linguistic transcription symbol. A symbol especially designed by linguists to write spoken language. For example, the word *myth* could be written /MIΘ/.

Long vowels. The *phonemes* /ā, ē, ī, ō, ū/ are often called "long" vowels.

Manuscript handwriting. The style in which letters are not connected, e.g., manuscript.

Marker letter e. An *e* is called a marker letter when it occurs in words like *hate*. It is said to be part of the vowel *grapheme* for this word. It signals that the *a* in *hate* will be read with a given sound.

Marker words. See function words.

Meaning-emphasis method or **approach.** A method of teaching reading in which it is held if children are given "meaningful" material to read, this, in itself, will develop most of their *word recognition* skills. This method is the opposite of the *code-emphasis method*.

Metacognition. The ability to consciously reflect on the thinking processes one uses when reading, to actively use these processes, and to take cognitive remedial action when these processes prove unsuccessful or unsatisfactory.

Miscues. The deviations from the actual printed text a child makes when reading a passage aloud.

Monosyllabic words. Words that have one syllable.

Morpheme. The smallest meaningful unit in our language. A morpheme can be a single letter, *s* in *cats*. The word *cats* is two morphemes, since *cat* means one thing and *s* (pluralness) means another. Thus it can be seen that the term *word* is insufficient to explain what is meant by "smallest meaningful unit" in language. Some morphemes like *dog*, *jump*, or *good* can occur without being attached to any other morpheme. They are *free* forms. Other morphemes like *re, ex, ed, er* cannot occur alone. These are *bound* forms. Roughly, then, morphemes are the free form words plus bound forms represented by inflections (e.g., *s, ed, ing*) and derivations (words using prefixes and suffixes). The *syllable* is not the same as a morpheme. For example, *Mississippi* is one morpheme and four syllables; *goes* is two morphemes and one syllable. It is difficult at times to generalize about morphemes, however. "How do you do?" is considered one morpheme, since it is a formalistic greeting and not a question. *Dancer* is two morphemes: *danc-er*, but *finger* and *father*, which have *er*, have one morpheme each. *Reread* is two morphemes; *remote* is one.

Morphemic analysis. Breaking up multisyllabic words into their different units of meaning (morphemes) for the purpose of identifying their meanings.

Morphophonemic spelling. The relationship between the morphemes of a word and its sound-spelling correspondences. Often this involves the spelling in a derivation of a word in which a spelling-sound correspondence in a base word is different than in the derivation, for example, in *bomb* versus *bombard*.

Multisyllabic words. Words with more than one syllable.

Nasal phoneme. *Phonemes* spoken so that an opening is left for the speech breath to enter the nasal passages; heard when you say /m, n, ng/.

Nonstandard speech or dialect. A variety of phonemes, intonation, grammar and vocabulary used by low-income, poorly educated people in a speech region, or by a particular ethnic group. Each speech region has both standard and nonstandard speakers.

Open syllable. A syllable that ends in a *vowel phoneme.*

Orthography. Another name for the spelling system. Sometimes referred to as the scientific study of spelling.

Phoneme. A discrete, identifiable speech sound. We say there are 41 phonemes in General American *dialect.* Other speech areas in the United States have more or different phonemes. *Speech sounds* and *phonemes* are synonymous terms.

Phonemic spelling. The spelling of a word according to some aspect of *predictable spelling.* For example, *rat* is spelled phonemically. Its *phonemic transcription* /rat/ is the same as its letter spelling, *rat.* To the contrary, *of* is not spelled phonemically.

Phonemic transcription. The manner in which one can record a phoneme of a language with a written symbol. Phonemic transcriptions are written between slant lines, / /.

Phonetic alphabet. See **phonemic transcription.**

Phonic analysis. The use of phonics information to *decode* words.

Phonics. The information taken from *phonetics, phonemics,* and *graphemics* that children learning to read and spell can use to help them understand the *spelling-phoneme correspondences* of English.

Phonics generalization or rule. A *spelling-sound correspondence* that occurs as a *predictable spelling.* For example, one phonics rule is that the *vowel letter* in a VC spelling in *monosyllabic words* is read as a *short vowel,* as in h*a*t.

Phonogram. See **closed syllable.**

Phonology. Another term for *phonemics.*

Plosive. This is a *phoneme* spoken so that the speech breath is stopped and then subsequently released in a somewhat explosive puff of air; it is heard, for example, when you say /p, b, t, d, k, g/.

Polysyllabic words. Words that have more than two *syllables.*

Predictable spelling. A word or *syllable* spelled with letters that predict with a high degree of confidence for the reader which *phonemes* these letters represent. For example, the spelling of *rat* is predictable since *r-a-t* are letters commonly used to represent the three phonemes spoken in this pattern. Contrariwise, *of* is unpredictable since *o-f* are not commonly used to represent the phonemes /uv/. The term is also used in this book to mean any sound-spelling correspondence, at any given level, a child has been so far taught to recognize.

Prominence. A collective term that includes all the aspects of pitch, *stress, juncture,* sonority, and loudness that distinguish the dominant sound of a syllable (a *vowel phoneme*).

Pseudoword. A series of letters seen in true words but never seen in the combination displayed in a pseudoword. For example, *tr* and *ut* are seen in *try* and *hut.* These letters can therefore be used to write the pseudoword *trut.* Pseudowords are useful in testing a child's ability to apply *phonics* information.

Psycholinguistics. The scientific study of the relationships of *linguistics* and human behavior.

R-colored vowel. Any *vowel phoneme* in a *syllable* that immediately precedes the /r/ *phoneme.*

Reading. In this book reading is defined as (1) the skills of *word recognition* and (2) the ability to understand (comprehend) the meanings intended by the author of a given passage of writing.

Reading readiness. The training children supposedly need before beginning to learn to recognize written words.

Recurrent spelling patterns. See **closed syllable, predictable spelling.**

Redundancy. See **sequential redundancy.**

Schema. The knowledge stored in the reader's memory that helps him or her acquire and interpret new information found in material being read.

Schwa. A *vowel phoneme* that is less accented, that has less *prominence,* than other vowels. Usually heard in *multisyllabic words:* canal, batter, pencil, kingdom, minute.

Semantics. The scientific study of the connotations and denotations (meanings) of words.

Semivowel. A phoneme that can be either a *vowel* or a *consonant* depending on where it is heard. Linguists disagree as to what semivowels are. For the purposes of this book we call /w/ and /y/ semivowels.

Sequential redundancy. The likelihood that if a certain letter appears in a *syllable* or word, only certain other letters will follow. For example, *u* follows *q* almost always.

Short vowels. Said to be the *phonemes* /a, e, i, o, u/.

Sight words. Words said to be recognized by a beginning reader without any analysis of the letters of the word for cues to its recognition. A widespread but fallacious notion as to how beginning readers recognize words.

Silent speech. Subvocalization, or the inner, implicit speech one makes when reading. Mature readers use less silent speech in *reading* than do beginning or poor readers.

Sonority. This refers to the resonance of *phonemes.* The phonemes /m/, /n/, and /ng/ are sonorous consonants. Contrast these with /t/ or /p/. Vowels have more sonority than consonants.

Speech region. A geographical area of the United States where one hears a different *dialect* from that spoken in another speech region. The boundaries of some speech regions are blurred and difficult to define.

Speech sound. See phoneme.

Spelling patterns. Refers to the sequential ordering of letters in *syllables* allowed in writing English. For example, *rat* is a spelling pattern; *rta* is not. See **closed syllable** and **predictable spelling.**

Spelling reform. The attempts made to concoct an English alphabet large enough to have the same number of different letters as we have *phonemes.* This reform proposes also that one letter, and one letter only, be used to represent each phoneme.

Spelling-phoneme correspondences. The relationships between the *phonemes* and the *graphemes* that represent them in writing. Some of these correspondences are said to be *predictable spellings;* others are not.

Standard speech. A variety of *phonemes, intonation,* grammar, and vocabulary used by the higher-income, better-educated people in a *speech region.*

Stress. This is a combination of loudness, duration, and/or rising pitch in *phonemes.* Linguists also believe there are three or four relative levels of stress in words (not all words have all levels, of course).

Structure words. See function words.

Syllabic. The speech sound given *prominence* in a *syllable,* usually a *vowel.* Can be /m, n, l/.

Syllable. A syllable consists of a *vowel phoneme* (its prominent sound) and usually one or more *consonant phonemes* that precede or follow the vowel phoneme. *Phonemes* must be spoken in syllables to be heard as such. Thus the syllable is the irreducible unit of speech. How the boundaries of syllables are determined is a controversial matter in *linguistics.*

Systematic phonics. See code-emphasis method.

Unvoiced phoneme. See voiceless phoneme.

Visual perception or **discrimination**. The ability to see individual items in any larger visual display, or against a background. In *reading readiness* the term often refers to children's abilities to identify geometric forms, to match designs, to name parts of a picture, and to follow directions in displays where eye tracking or eye pursuit is called for.

Vocal cords. Two folds of ligament and elastic membrane located at the top of the windpipe (in the larnyx), directly behind the Adam's apple. Air pressure through the windpipe acts on the membranes, which are blocked, narrowed, or vibrated as various *phonemes* are made.

Voiced phoneme. A phoneme made when the vocal cords are in vibration. Heard when we say /b, d, g, v, th, z, zh, j, w/.

Voiceless phoneme. A phoneme made when the vocal cords are more at rest than when a *voiced phoneme* is said. Heard when we say /p, t, k, f, th, s, sh, ch, h/.

Vowel. A *phoneme* made with an unobstructed passage of breath through the speech cavities as one speaks. We have described in this book *checked, free,* and free, *less-accented* vowel *phonemes.* Vowel *phonemes* have greater *prominence* than *consonant phonemes.*

Vowel-letter cluster. Two or more adjacent letters in a *syllable* that represent a *vowel phoneme* or *diphthong.* If this is two letters, it is often called a vowel *digraph.*

Vowel letters. Letters used to represent vowel *phonemes* in writing.

Whole-word method. See sight words.

Word recognition. The ability to gain the identity of a word after seeing it in print. See **reading**. Words are recognized by a combination of *phonics* and *context cues.*

APPENDIX A: ACTIVITIES FOR DEVELOPING RECOGNITION OF MONOSYLLABIC WORDS

Activities for Level 1

Auditory

1. Read a poem to the class. Repeat the first verse, then the first line. Ask children to say the first word in the poem, the second, and so on. Select another line and do the same.

2. After the class has sung a favorite song, review the first verse and ask who can remember the first word in the song, the second, and so on. Select another verse, or the chorus, and do the same.

3. Explain that some words are short and some take longer to say. Read this word list and ask whether each word is short or long.

potato	chalk
hot	shoes
principal	newspaper
evidently	happily

4. Use this list of phrases to give children practice in counting the number of words they hear. Correct any misconceptions.

on the street	pick up your pencil
chilly day	time to go
open your eyes	eating lunch
where is mom	came outside

Visual

1. Prepare classroom experience charts that children dictate to the teacher. Through a discussion of the events written, help the children realize that the charts represent their oral language written down. Establish the fact that a word we say aloud may be written down, "and this is what it looks like."

2. From children's dictations, prepare short handwritten books about the doings of the class or individuals. Have them copied for everyone. Ask all the children to look at the first page. Show them the name of the story. Read aloud the name of the story and ask how many words are in it. Write these words on the chalkboard. Ask someone to point to the first word, the second, and so on. Ask children to locate these words on other pages of the book.

3. Put titles of favorite stories on strips of paper 11 × 14 inches long. Ask children to fold back the first word of the story, the second, and so on.

4. Tell children some words are short and some are long. Display short and long words. Use an old experience chart to have children look for short and long words.

Activities for Level 2

Step 1: Identifying and Naming Initial Consonant Letters. The objective of these activities is to teach children to identify initial consonant letters quickly by name.

1. Write two letters, for example, *t* and *s,* on the chalkboard. Children are given two cards, one with a *t,* one with an *s.* (Clip two corners of the cards, left and right, to help the child hold it right side up.) Say: "This is *t.* This is *s.* Say the names with me, *t, s.*" Point to the letters on the board.

2. Say: "Look at your cards. Hold up *t.* Hold up *s.*" Be sure all the children in the group are holding up the right card. Alternate *t* and *s* a few times.

3. Say: "Let's see if I can fool you. Is this *t?*" (Write some other letter.) "Is this *t?*" Write a *t.* Repeat for *s.*

4. Say: "If I write *t,* hold up your *t* card. Hold up your *t* card only if I write *t.*" About every third time write *t.* Repeat for *s.*

5. Say: "Now watch carefully. Does this word [write a one-vowel word such as *tag*] begin with *t?* Is *t* the first letter in this word? If it is, hold up your *t* card." Write a few words, half of which do not start with *t.* Repeat with *s.*

6. Say: "I will write an *s* word or a *t* word [a word beginning with *t*].

When I write an *s* word, hold up your *s* card. When I write a *t* word, hold up your *t* card." Write a few one-vowel words beginning with either *t* or *s*.

7. Say: "I will write a word with *s* in it." (Write *sat.*) Draw a block around the beginning letter. "What letter is this?" Do the same for *tar*. Then have children draw a block around the beginning consonant letter of several one-vowel words: ⒮ap, ⒮un, ⒮aw, and ⒮at. Stress drawing a block around the *beginning* letter. Do the same for *t*.

8. Say: "I will write a word with *t* in it." (Write *sat.*) Draw a block around the last letter. "What letter is this?" Do the same for *tar*. Then have the children draw a block around the final consonant letter of several one-vowel words: ma⒯, sa⒯, pu⒯, etc. Stress drawing a block around the final consonant. Do the same for *s*.

9. Say: "See the *r*. Circle all the letters like the first letter." Give the children work to complete in this format, presenting several rows:

s — s   s   t   s

t — t   s   t   s

Or say: "See the *r*. Circle all the letters in a row that are just like it. Let's do the first row together."

10. Say: "Circle the words that begin like the first letter in each row." Give the children work to complete in this format, presenting several rows:

s — sag   run   tag   sat

t — tag   sag   toy   top

Or say: "See the *r*. Circle all the words in the row that start just like it. Let's do the first row together."

11. Say: "Mark the letter that is different from the others." Give a format like this one:

t   t   t   s

12. Say: "Mark the word that is different from the others." Present a format such as this one:

tag   sun   tag   tag

13. Say: "Put a line under the two letters if they are alike." Use a format like this one:

s   s
s   t

14. Say: "Put a line under the two words if they are alike." Use a format like this one:

tag   tag
sag   tag

15. Say: "How many *s*'s can you find in this row? Count them. Show how many with your fingers."

s s s s
s t t s

Then repeat the process for *t*.

16. Present pairs of words that are alike except that one contains the first letter (*t*) and the other the second letter (*s*), for example, *tag-sag, so-to*, etc. Say: "What part of this word [write *tag*] is different from this word [write *rag*]?" Write one word underneath the other one.

17. Say: "Look at these numbers [1 through 9]. Some numbers have *t* by them. Some have *s* by them. What numbers have *t* by them? Which ones have *s* by them?" Make up a worksheet using this format:

1 t   6 s
2 s   7 s
3 t   8 t
4 t   9 t
5 s

(Obviously, this activity is designed also to teach the numbers 1 through 9.)

18. Say: "Draw lines from a letter in one column to one like it in the second column." Use this format:

s   t
s   s
t   s

19. Say: "Draw lines from a word in one column to the same word in the second column." Follow this format:

tag   tag
sun   sun
sun   tag

20. Say: "Draw a line from a letter in one column to the word that begins with the same letter in the second column. Let's do the first one together." Try this format:

s   tag
t   tag

21. Say: "I will write a word. If *t* is at the beginning, hold up your fist [show them]. If *t* is at the *end*, hold up your fingers [show them]." Words to use: *bat-tub-rat-dot-tap*, etc. Also do this with *s: sat-has-tis-sap-sam*, etc.

22. As each letter is taught and children have learned its name, associate the letter with a one-vowel word that begins with one consonant. Do not use clusters *br cr, sn, tr*, etc. Instead use words that have three phonemes *c-v-c*, and that are spelled with three one-letter graphemes (*cat*). (Remember, this is not possible for *q*.)

23. Cut and shape pipe cleaners into lower-case letter forms. Glue these letters on small cards with a strong adhesive. Play this game. Say: "Close your eyes. I will give you a card. On the card is a letter. Feel the letter. Don't look at it! Can you tell me what letter is on the card?" This game can also be played by pairs of pupils.

Step 2: Identifying and Naming Initial Vowel Letters. The objective of these activities is to teach children to identify initial vowel letters quickly by name.

In *Step 1* we have given 23 example of exercises useful for teaching children to identify and name *consonant* letters. The format of these 23 exercises can be used for teaching *vowel* letter identification. In *Step 2* substitute vowel letters for the consonant letters in all these exercises. For example:

1. Write two vowel letters, *o* and *i* on the chalkboard. Children are given two cards, one with an *o*, one with an *i.* Say: "This is *o*. This is *i.* Say the names with me, *o, i.*" Point to the letters on the board.

2. Say: "Look at your cards. Hold up *o*. Hold up *i.*" Be sure all the children in the group are holding up the right card. Alternate *o* and *i* a few times.

. . .

9. Say: "See the *o.* Circle all the letters like the first letter." Give the children work to complete in this format, presenting several rows:

```
o  —  o  o  i  o
i  —  i  o  i  o
```
. . .

12. Say: "Mark the word that is different from the others." Present a format such as this one:

or   it   or   or

Proceed through the exercises in *Step 2* in the order given in *Step 1*. These exercises are arranged in an ascending order of difficulty.

Activities for Level 3

1. Begin by having children listen to the sounds in a word you say and having them count the sounds. Say, "My word is *an*. It has two sounds in it, /a/ and /n/, /a/ /n/, /an/. How many sounds in *an?*"

   "Now you count the sounds in my word. My word is *ant*. It means a little insect. Ant. The sounds in *ant* are /a/ /n/ /t/. How many sounds in *ant?*" Continue with *in, tin, tan, end, net, tent*.

2. Give each child four 3 × 5 blank cards. Read aloud words with two, three, and four phonemes, such as:

in	tin	tent
on	tag	band
no	top	stop
up	pet	pest
an	got	pond

   Have the children put the four blank cards in a row at the tops of their desks. After you read a word aloud, say its speech sounds separately, then say the word as a whole again. Children are to repeat this three-step process. They then select the number of cards needed to match the number of the word's speech sounds. Have them select a card for each speech sound they make so that they will associate one sound with each card. Repeat the sounds of a word as often as needed to establish them.

3. Say a word and make a mark on the chalkboard for every sound in a word. Use the word list of a previous lesson. When the children have caught on to the technique, let volunteers try making the chalkboard marks for the sounds in words as you say them. Those at their seats may make pencil marks on a paper for each sound in

a word, then be ready to say how many marks they made for a word.

4. Once the children are familiar with the letter-phoneme concept, read the words from an earlier lesson and have the children tell how many sounds there are in each word. They must prove their answer by making the separate sounds of each word. See how many children can do this without having the separate sounds made for them by the teacher.

5. Read the words of previous lessons and have the children demonstrate the separate sounds in words. ("Who can make the separate sounds in *ten?*") Then graduate to words they have not worked with before.

6. Say the separate sounds of some words. Have children tell which word those sounds make: "My first word has /t/ /o/ /p/. What's my word? Who can guess it first?"

Activities for Level 4

1. Present pictures of a *toe, tire, tent,* etc. Have the class listen carefully as the teacher reads each word and shows the picture. Have the class say the words as the pictures are shown. Have the class think of other words that begin like *toe, tire, tent.* Ask the pupils to name all the objects in a picture that begin like *toe, tire, tent.*

2. Present pictures of a *toe, tire, saw, tent, six.* Have the class listen as the teacher reads each word while showing the picture. Then have the class pick out the two pictures whose beginning sounds are not the same as the other three.

3. Say: "Look at these pictures." Present pictures of a *tail,* a *tack,* something or someone *tall,* a *team,* *ten* things, *two* things, a *tire,* a piece of *toast,* a *toe,* a *tongue,* a *tooth,* something with a *torn top,* a *tub* or *tank,* etc. Say: "Let's say the names of these things. I'll write their names on the board. What letter do you see at the beginnings of these words?"

4. Say: "Listen to these words: *tag, toy, take.*" Ask a pupil to repeat each word after the teacher says it. Write the words on the board, directly under each other. Say: "What letter do they begin with?"

5. Say: "What are these?" (*teeth*) (Point to teeth. Child says, "teeth.")

"How many fingers?" (*two*) (*ten*)

"Your shoelaces are tied . . . " (*tight*)

"Bread we eat for breakfast is . . . " (*toast*)

"This is the bottom. This is the . . . " (*top*)

As children are able to give the *t-word* responses for these questions, write the words on the board one directly under another. Ask: "What letter do these words begin with?"

6. Say: "Can you think of some other words that begin like these words?" (words gained in item 5). Write these words that begin with *t.*

7. Say: "Hold up your *t* card (previously given to each child) if you hear a word that begins with the *t* sound: *teeth, ten, sun, time.*" Use a list of *t* words to make up lists of words to use for this activity. Choose some other words besides *t* words from the lists to include in this activity.

8. Say: "Hold up your *t* card if you hear a word that begins like *tag.*" Use the lists of words made up for item 5.

9. Read a sentence that has several *t* words. Children hold up hands when they hear a *t* word.

10. Say: "Let's look around the classroom and name everything we can see that we think begins like *toe, tire,* or *tack.*" As children name things, write them on the board. Have them check each time to be sure that the names begin with *t.* The teacher also can arrange to have several small objects such as a tool, a tack, a top, and so on available for this procedure.

11. Fold newsprint or a length of brown paper into two parts. On one part children paste pictures whose names begin with *t* and on the other half names that begin with *s.*

12. Say: "How many words can we think of to put in this slot?"

    Susan will play with her t_____."

    Write the t_____ on the board. Write each word the class gives on the board. Check to make sure it begins with *t.*

13. Say: "Can you think of a word that would fit this slot? There is more than one word that will fit."

    Mike likes to play with his _____t. (cat, bat, jet, pet)

    Karen has a new t_____. (toy, top, doll)

14. Have children write either *s* or *t* if they hear the sound in a word. Give the children a page with the numbers 1, 2, 3, etc., written on it. The children write the letter, if they hear it, by the numbered word.

15. Say: "Hold up one finger if you hear the sound of *t* at the beginning of a word I say. Hold up two fingers if you hear the sound at the end. Listen: *top*. Is the *t* sound at the beginning or the end? Listen: *pot*. Is the *t* sound at the beginning or the end? Listen: *tot*. Beginning or end?" Continue with other one-vowel words that begin and end with the phoneme /t/.

16. Say: "Listen to this word: *top*. In which square does the *t* go?" Write on the board three squares.

☐ ☐ ☐

17. Say: "Listen to this word: *hat*. In which square does the *t* go?" Write on the board three squares.

☐ ☐ ☐

18. Play beginning or end phoneme-grapheme bingo. Give children cards on which words have been written in squares that begin or end with *t*. For example:

at	tap	take
it	Free	fit
sit	tell	tip

First, write ＿＿＿*t* or *t*＿＿＿ on the board. Children put a counter on the word with this form on their card. After this, write the entire word and have children play as before.

19. Say: "Let's write the letter that will make a word." Write on the board *at*. Say: "This is *at*. "Say it. Can we add this (write *t* and *s*) to at to make a word?" Continue with other phonograms (see Chapter 8).

Play letter-sound bingo. Give children cards on which letters have been written in squares. For example:

t	s	s
t	Free	t
s	t	s

Say: "Listen to this word. If it begins (or ends) with a *t* (or *s*) put a counter on a *t* (or *s*)."

20. Say: "Can you think of an animal whose name begins with the first sound you hear in *top* (or *sit*)?" Write the names they offer on the board. Ask: "Does this word have the same first letter as *top?*"

21. After children have learned five to ten consonant phoneme-grapheme correspondences, the teacher can present a picture-letter game. Here each child has a small pocket chart that holds five or six cards. These cards have a letter on one side and a picture on the other. One child holds up a card holder so that another child sees

On the other side of each of these cards is drawn a picture whose name begins with the letter shown. If the child shown the card can guess the name of the picture, he or she scores a point.

22. Another useful game is "Portholes." Make holes through which a pencil will pass at regular spaces in a piece of heavy construction paper. Over each hole place a picture and its name. On the reverse side of this perforated sheet put a letter above each hole. The game is played as one child sticks a pencil through a hole on the picture side. The child on the other side notes the letter above this hole and proceeds to guess the name of the picture. The pupil scores a point for each correct guess.

23. "Half-Moons" is another letter-sound game. Letters to be learned are printed on cards that have a jigsaw puzzle form:

Then this beginning or end letter is fitted onto other cards:

⊃ in⏽   ⎸an ⊂

24. "Brick Wall" is even more challenging. Here children are given a basic left-side "wall" on which they "build" words. For example, after they have learned a few consonant phoneme-grapheme correspondences, they can build a wall like this:

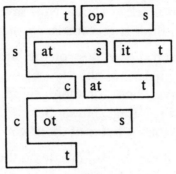

25. Say: "Can we trade the first letters in these words?" Write $\frac{tip}{sip}$ on the board. "Can we trade these first letters?" Write:

take	top	tell
sack	sack	sail

26. Toward the end of this level, alternate spellings for the same sound should be taught in this way. The phoneme /k/, for example, is spelled *k* and *c.* Say: "Let's read these words: *king, kite, keep.* Now say these words: *can, cup, cap.*" Write the words in this way:

k	ing
k	ite
k	eep
c	an
c	up
c	ap

Say: "Do these words begin with the same sound? What two letters can you use to spell this sound?"

27. After several correspondences have been learned, this activity is useful. Say: "Jim had a dog. (Write *dog* on the board.) Jim had a large dog. (Write *large dog* on the board.) Who can think of some other thing about Jim's dog that begins like *large?*"

28. Say: "What word in the first sentence helps you know the word in the second sentence?" Write on the board:

> The dog was fat.   The toy fell on the floor.
> I lost my h_____.   Can you t_____ a story?

29. Say: "Where in these three words do you hear the same sound?" Write these words on the board and say them: *rip, sap, top*. Draw a square around the final letter in each word. Now say: "Where in these three words do you hear the same sound: *dog, tag, rag?*" Write, say, and mark as above. Now say: "Where do you hear the same sound in these three words: *cat, mat, fat?*"

To develop children's awareness of the single consonant phoneme-grapheme correspondences at the *ends* of one-syllable words, use the kinds of activities given here for the development of this awareness of *beginning* sounds and spellings. Now, offer children examples that direct them to the final consonant letter of these words.

30. Say: "Look at these words." (Write on the board in this fashion.)

> lack
> link
> rake
> tall
> ring

Read these words over and add *b* to each word. What is the one word you cannot add *b* to? Why can't we add *b* to *tall?*" Elicit the idea that *bt* never go together at the beginning of a word.

31. Say: "Make a different word out of each of these words by adding s to it:

> led
> pot
> tub
> pin

32. Say: "Listen to this word *stop*. Say it." Write on the board *top* and *stop*, one word under the other. Say: "What letter is added to *top* to make *stop?* Listen again to the differences in *top* and *stop*. Look at this word. (Write *pin*.) Let's say it. What happens when I add *s* to *pin?* Can you say the word?" Repeat this for several other words of this kind.

33. Say: "Listen to the *th* sound at the beginning of these words." Say these words and write them on the board one under the other:

> thin
> thank
> third

"Hold up your hand if you hear the *th* sound at the beginning of these words. Hold up your fist if you hear it at the end." Say and write these words:

bath	teeth
cloth	thump
thick	thief
fifth	thorn
thing	truth

Say: "Hold up your hand when you hear a *th* in this story:

The *third* boy in line had some*th*ing in his mou*th*. Was it a too*th*?

34. To reinforce visual learning of letter names and short words while teaching the concept of the phoneme, give children a sheet with these letters: *a, n, t, e, t, n.* Let them cut the sheets apart so that each letter is on a separate piece; they can store the six letters in an old envelope. Have them spread the letters across the top of their desks.

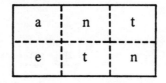

Tell them they are going to build real words with these six letters. Begin with *an.* Say the word and ask how many sounds are in it; say them separately, too. Explain that the word *an* begins with the letter *a;* hold one up. Have them select the *a* and place it in front of them. Say the *a* stands for the first sound in *an,* the sound /a/. Ask who will say the second sound in *an* (/n/). Help them select the *n* and say it stands for the sound /n/. Say it goes right after the *a;* check to see if all understand that this means on the right. Write the word *an* on the board; run your hand under it from left to right as you say it as a word, say it sound by sound, and say it as a word again, as the children do the same with the cards at their desks. Say, "You have made the word *an*."

Then let the children build the words *ant, ten, net,* and *tent* in the same way. Work slowly, helping children associate each sound with each letter.

Activities for Level 5

1. Write two phonograms on the chalkboard, e.g., *an* and *in.* (See Chapter 5 for a list of high-frequency phonograms that can be used.) Children are given two cards, one with *an* and the other with *in.* Clip the upper corners of the cards to aid children in holding them up the right way.

2. Say: "This is *a-n, an.*" (By saying the word as well as the name of the letters some incidental perception of the whole phonogram is encouraged.) "This is *i-n, in.* Say the letter names with me: *a-n, i-n.*" Do not require the naming of the word at this step.

3. Say: "Look at your cards. Hold up *a-n.*" Alternate a few times. Be sure that the children are holding up the correct card.

4. Say: "If I write what is on your card, hold it up." Alternate writing *an* or *in* with *ab, ad, ag, it, ib, ig,* or any other consonant phonogram the letters of which the children have previously learned to identify.

5. Say: "Can you find *a-n* in this word?" Write $\boxed{\text{t}}\,\boxed{\text{an}}$. "In these?" Write

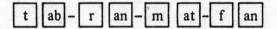

$$\boxed{\text{t}}\,\boxed{\text{ab}}-\boxed{\text{r}}\,\boxed{\text{an}}-\boxed{\text{m}}\,\boxed{\text{at}}-\boxed{\text{f}}\,\boxed{\text{an}}$$

6. Say: "If you see *a-n* in a word, hold up your *a-n* card. If you see *i-n* in a word, hold up your *i-n* card." Alternate writing *tan, tin, fan, fin,* etc.

7. Say: "What are the names of the two letters on this card?" Have children do this several times during the teaching of any two phonograms.

8. Say: "How many *a-n*'s can you find in this row? Count them. Show how many with your fingers." (Repeat for *i-n, in.*)

an	it	an	an
it	it	it	an
an	it	it	an
an	an	an	an

9. Present pairs of words that are alike except that one contains the first phonogram (*an*) and the other contains the second (*in*), for example, *tan-tin, fan-fin, dan-din.* Say: "What part of this word (write *tan*) is different from this word (write *tin*)?" Write the words one under the other.

10. Give children work to complete in this format, presenting several rows:

    an—an   in   an   in
    in—in   in   in   an

    Say: "See *a-n*, circle all the words in the row that are just like it. Let's do the first row together."

11. Say: "Mark the one in each row that is different from the others."

    it   it   it   an
    an   it   an   an
    it   it   an   it
    an   an   it   an

12. Say: "Put a line under the two in each row if they are alike."

    it   it
    an   an
    an   it
    an   an
    it   an

13. Say: "Look at these numbers (1 through 9). Some numbers have *a-n* by them. Some have *i-t* by them. What numbers have *a-n* by them? Which have *i-t* by them?"

    1.   it   6.   an
    2.   an   7.   an
    3.   it   8.   it
    4.   it   9.   it
    5.   an

Begin now having the child hear the phonograms in words.

1. Write the word *sat* on the board. Say: "What is a word that rhymes with *sat*?" As the first word is mentioned, erase the *s* from *sat* and substitute the new consonant letter, *b*, for example. Have the class read the new word, *bat.* Now say, "What is a word that rhymes with *bat*?" Continue as with *sat.*

2. Say: "Listen to this. I have an old cat who is very fat. Who can tell me the two words that rhyme?" Write these on the board. Erase *c* and *f* to show *at*. Add *c* to *at* and ask, "What is this word?" Do the same with *f*.

3. Say: "Listen to this. The man hit the fly with a pan. What words rhyme? What do I need to do to change this (write *man* on board) to *pan?*" Elicit the idea. Erase *m*, add *p*.

4. Say: "Listen to this. The kitten was fat. Which of these words (write *rat* and *run*) rhymes with *fat?* Why is *run* not like *fat?* Does it look like *fat?*"

5. Say: "Fill in this blank." Write on the board: The cat was _____at.

6. Say: "Raise your hand if you hear two rhyming words." Read pairs of one-vowel words that either rhyme or do not.

7. Read sentences as these aloud. Write the rhyming words one under the other on the board.

> It's fun to eat a bun.
>
> Which do you want—a rake or a cake?
>
> My cat sat on the pillow.
>
> He threw his cap into my lap.

8. Say: "Choose the word that rhymes and fits." Write on the board:

> He has my tack.
>
> Please give it _____. (Offer *pack, lack, rack, back.*)

9. Say: "Can you think of words that rhyme with *can?*" Children may think of *man, ran, fan, pan, tan, van*. Write these on the board, one under the other. "What two letters are the same in these words? We will call *an* a phonogram since it makes these words rhyme." (It is necessary at some point to introduce the term *phonogram* and give many examples of it. Later when this term is used, children will know to what it refers, saving much time in teaching.)

10. Say: "What is a color that rhymes with *sled?* What is a toy that rhymes with *tall?*" Write *sled* on the board and all the rhyming words given for it. Do the same with *tall*.

11. Say: "Listen to this phonogram: *un*. Let's see how many words we can make with the letters we know." Write some consonant letters

on the board. Point to each letter and say, "Put it on the front of *un*. Now say the word."

12. Say: "If these words have the same phonograms, put a line under them. Put a mark only if they have the same phonogram."

mark-bark	tall-bell	tell-tan
tell-bell	tin-tan	bell-bark

13. Set up phonogram charts such as the following:

First sound	*Phonogram*
/b/	ed
	ig
	an
	op
	ib
	us

First have the class put the sound /b/ with these phonograms. Then try other beginning sounds. Always write the words.

14. Say: "Listen to this phonogram: *an*. Do you hear *an* at the beginning or end of this word: *ant*? (Write on the board to verify.) Do you hear *an* at the beginning or end of this word: *plan?*" Verify by writing on the board.

15. Say: "Listen to this phonogram: *ed*. Find *ed* in these words and underline it." (Write *sled, bed, fed,* etc.)

16. Say: "What is this phonogram?" Say *"ed"* and write it on the board. "Let's add *b* to it. What word do we have? Now let's add *f*. Now *r*," etc.

17. Say: "Find the phonograms in these words: *pan, pin, pun, pen*." Write the words on the board as the pupils say them. Write the phonograms one under the other:

an
in
un
en

Then say: "What letter makes these phonograms different?"

18. Say: "Hold up your phonogram card when you hear your phonogram in a word I say aloud." Give each child two cards on which are written *og* and *ag*. Read aloud a list such as *dog, log, sag, bag, bog, lag, rag, fog*. Make sure that the response of each child is correct

after each word. (The teacher can type or ditto copies of each story in the basal reader, stories dictated by pupils, or other reading materials that are being used with the class. Have the children underline all the phonograms indicated by the teacher. After almost all the common phonograms are learned, have the class mark any phonogram in the duplicated story that they think they see.)

19. Write *t* and *s* on the board. Say: "Put these letters in front of these phonograms to make new words":

__an   __en   __in   __on   __un

20. Write these words on the right side of the board:

hat
tin
fin
bat
bin
cat

Give children *at* and *in* phonogram cards. Have them match the phonogram with the word.

21. Play phonogram bingo. Say: "Listen to these words as I read them." Write the words on the board at first. Then play the game without writing them on the board. Say, "Put a counter on the square that has a phonogram you hear."

at	an	at
in	free	an
in	it	in

22. Say: "Each of these phonograms has a number." Write:

1. at
2. in

"Put the number of the phonogram for these words."

_____ bat
_____ din
_____ sit
_____ fat, etc.

23. Generate a list of one-vowel words using a selected phonogram as a base. Ask children to attach letters to the phonograms to make words:

     un   and
     run   land
     fun, etc.   sand, etc.

24. Give the class two phonogram cards, one with *in* and one with *at.* Say: "This is *in.* This is *at.* Hold up your *in* card if you see it in a word I write on the board. Do the same for *at.*"

25. Say: "I will write a letter on the board. Bring up your *in* card or your *at* card to see if we can make a new word." Write:

     c   at
     r   in
     t   (on one side of the board and)   in   (on the other).
     b   at
     f   at

26. Say: "Draw a line from one to the other to make a word." (See item 25.)

27. Say: "What are these letters?" (Write *f* and *p.*) "If this is *pit*" (write it), "this must be _____" (write *fit*). Follow these steps with several other combinations with other phonograms.

28. Use some context-cue activities involving the phonogram words taught in the above activities. Try to include a context-cue activity within as many of the above activities as is possible.

Activities for Level 6

The teacher is encouraged to adapt the activities given for Level 5 for use with the marker *e* words of Level 6:

1. Since marker *e* words should be taught as phonograms (*ake* for *bake*), it is appropriate to have many exercises using phonograms as parts of words that rhyme. Rhyming activities are relatively easy for children to understand and participate in.

2. Activities involving the addition of single consonant letters and consonant clusters to marker *e* phonograms can be used.

3. Phonograms can be chosen from a list or recalled from memory to complete exercises where an initial consonant or consonant cluster is given, as in s_____ (*side*), sp_____ (*spoke*).

4. Marker *e* phonogram cards can be used for many activities. These cards are used by children to signal which phonogram they hear or see written.

5. Children can identify words that have indicated marker *e* phonograms and put these into categories or lists. Children find it intriguing to be allowed to select their own special marker *e* phonogram and then go on a search to find words in which it is found.

6. As children practice with marker *e* phonograms, the teacher can evaluate their abilities to detect marker *e* phonograms in two ways. One is to have children read to the teacher words or sentences in which certain selected marker *e* phonograms are involved. This is a time-consuming activity, so it is often necessary, two, to have children underline all the marker *e* phonograms of a certain kind in copy prepared for this purpose. The latter practice has the possible danger, of course, that the child will be able to mark a phonogram correctly without being able to actually read the word in which it is embedded. This emphasizes the need to have someone listen to the child read words involving these phonograms and to give immediate feedback as to the child's accuracy with them. Older children, teacher aides, or helping parents can be utilized for this.

7. Playing games with marker *e* phonograms is conducive to heightened interest for pupils and probably a corresponding higher degree of learning than nongame activities. (See Appendix B for descriptions of several of these games.)

8. The plural forms of the marker *e* phonograms should be demonstrated for pupils. The general ways to do this are given in Level 4. This activity should be the one with which the teacher concludes, at any particular time, the work to be done with marker *e* phonograms.

9. Finally, we want to emphasize the special value of teaching marker *e* words as "contrastive spelling patterns." One of the best ways for the child to learn to respond habitually to *hat* as /hat/ and *hate* as /hāt/ is to see these spelling patterns repeatedly in frames such as

hat, __at
hate, __ate,

I hate my hat, I _____ him,　　or,　　hat　rate　　(connect
　　　　　　　　　　　　　　　　　　mat　gate　　the

I lost my _____.   rat   mate
                                   gat   hate   words).

Activities for Level 7

The teacher is directed to the activities described in earlier levels, especially 5 and 6, and is encouraged to adapt them for use with these new phonograms. These activities involve the following:

1. Using phonograms as rhyming words
2. Adding single letters to phonograms
3. Adding consonant clusters to phonograms
4. Filling in phonograms when the initial consonant or consonant cluster is given: s_____ (*seat*), sp_____ (*spoil*)
5. Using phonogram cards, cards on which the phonograms of Level 6 are written, for children to signal which phonogram is heard in words read or written by the teacher
6. Identifying words that have an indicated phonogram and putting these into lists
7. Marking phonograms in prepared copy that has many words spelled with vowel-cluster phonograms
8. Playing phonogram bingo

(Also see Appendix B for descriptions of games that can be played with phonogram cards.) The plural forms and the possessive forms of the phonograms of Level 7 should also be demonstrated with pupils.

Activities for Level 8

The activities for developing this perception of vowel-*r* phonograms can precede much as was described for other phonograms in Level 5. These activities can be seen to involve the following:

1. Using phonograms as rhyming words
2. Adding single letters to phonograms
3. Adding consonant clusters to phonograms
4. Filling in phonograms when the initial consonant or consonant cluster is given: f_____ (*farm*), sp_____ (*spark, spare*)

5. Using phonogram cards on which the phonograms of Level 7 are written, for children to signal which phonogram is heard in words read or written by the teacher

6. Identifying words that have the indicated phonogram, and putting these into lists

7. Marking phonograms in prepared copy that has many words spelled with the vowel-*r* combination

8. Playing phonogram games (see Appendix B)

Activities for Level 9

1. Say: "Listen to this word and tell me the last letter in it. *Seed.*" Children should readily come up with *d*, since they have had such activities for some time. Write *seed* on the board to prove they are right.

2. Say: "Do you think there is a *d* at the end of this word? *See.*" Children should say, "No." Write the word *see.* Under it write *seed* to show again that *d* was added to *seed.*

3. Say: "Look at these two words":

seen

see

"What are the words? What is added to *seen* that is not in *see?*"

4. "What are some words that rhyme with *see?*" Children should say *me, he, three, free, tree.* Write these. "What letter or letters do we see at the end of these words?"

5. Say: "Listen to these words. Hold up a finger if they end like *see.* Hold up a fist if they end like *seed.*"

seen, me, free, seep, seem, he

6. Say: "Fill in the blank."

I can s_____ him.
Have you s_____ him?

The remainder of the types of closed syllables can be taught the following ways:

7. Say: "Listen to this word. *My.* Does it rhyme with *sky?*" Write *my* and *sky* on the board.

8. Say: "What letter do these two words end with?" Write *dry* and *fry*.

9. Say: "Can you think of a word that rhymes with *my* and *sky?*" As children give the words, write them on the board so that *y* is lined up for each word.

10. Say: "Look at this word." Write *drop.* "Now I'll take this off." Erase *op.* "Now I'll add *y.* What word do we have?"

11. "Which consonant cluster can you add *y* to?" Write:

    sh_____   br_____   cr_____   fr_____   dr_____   bl_____

12. Say: "Listen to these three words. How many rhyme with *my?*" Write the words *dry-fry-free* on the board.

13. Say: "Listen to these words." Write the words *me-free-key-sea-row-ski* on the board. "Which one does not rhyme?"

14. Say: "Now look at these words." Write *we, key, tea, ski, low.* "Which one does not rhyme with the others?"

    Continue items 13 and 14 with combinations like these until the children readily hear and see the endings:

day, they, jaw	by, toe, guy, die, high
slow, go, oh, two, toe	grew, too, true, boy, who

15. Say: "Which are the two words that rhyme?"

    by-bay-be-blow-now-die

16. Give children cards on which the words *bay, he, snow, plow, drew, boy, draw* are written. Then say a few words with open syllables. Children hold up a card that rhymes with a word said.

Activities for Level 10

At Level 10 the main task for the pupil is to recognize some additional phonograms. The general task, then, is the same as it was for previous levels when phonograms were taught. Accordingly, the activities for developing the perception of the phonograms at Level 10 can proceed in much the same way as described for Levels 5, 6, 7, and 8.

In Level 10 the major emphasis should be placed upon impressing pupils with the need to be versatile in the reading of phonograms. In teaching Level 10 phonograms, therefore, it is desirable to have many activities in which pupils see a series of words that end with the same consonant-letter cluster, for example, *ll,* and that have the same spelling pattern, *CVCC*, but where certain selected numbers of words represent the vowel sounds /a, e, i, o, u/ and others the vowel sounds /ō, o, ĭ/. This can be seen for the following:

mast	nest	mist	most	must	bank
fall	fell	fill	roll	gull	tax

Typical activities of this nature would be done by saying: "Read this list of words." (Use Level 10 words.) "Now, let's mark the phonograms in them. Can you think of a rhyming word for each of the words?"

Say: "Put *a, e, i, o, u* in the blank and read the word." Write m_____st. Continue this with all the post-vowel consonant-letter clusters (except *ght*) in Level 9: *ld, nd, lt, ll, nk, x, xt.*

Finally, present the plural forms of all the words taught at Level 10.

APPENDIX B: READING GAMES

Most of the following games are played with decks of letter, letter cluster, phonogram, or word cards. Have children make the cards for letters, word parts, or words.

1. **Fish. Old Maid. Rummy.** All these familiar games can be played.

2. **Password.** Second child guesses the card the first child has read silently. The first child gives letter clues.

3. **Vowel or Consonant Match.** Take turns in matching or reading cards whose letters, which represent a certain sound, are in color.

4. **Bingo.** One child reads cards while others place their cards on spaces.

5. **Picture-Card Match.** Children cut out and paste pictures on cards. Then they match these with word cards.

6. **Dice.** Use 1″ by 1″ lumber. Cut off in 1″ pieces to make cubes. Print letters, words, etc., on each block. Roll out and read.

7. **Scrambled Words.** Match cards in which letters are scrambled with those that use the same letters to make a word. A form of anagrams.

8. **Phonemic Words.** Match word cards spelled "phonemically" with those spelled conventionally, e.g., *cats-kats, laughed-laft.*

9. **Word Guess.** Child chooses word card from deck. Others try to guess what it is, letter by letter.

10. **Tachistoscope Game.** Cut out some familiar shape, e.g., a football. Print words, letters, etc., on continuing strips of paper. Slip the strips into slots in the football so one word shows for a brief time.

11. **Railway.** Each word card is in the form of a different railway car. Who can make up the longest train?

12. **Reader Words.** During each reader lesson have children write several cards from the lesson. Pair up and flash the cards to each other.

13. **Carpenter.** Read a card from a deck and add a shingle to the roof of a play house or a board to its side.

14. **Checkers.** Paste word cards on checker squares. Play game as usual except child must say word for the space moved into.

15. **Picture Checkers.** Paste pictures on checkerboard square. The object is to cover pictures with word cards naming them.

16. **Categories.** Mix up many word cards that refer to several categories (home, play, etc., or parts of speech). First child to sort out the deck wins.

17. **Clothespins.** A part of a word is written on a clothespin. The other part is on a card. Pin the two together. Also use pins and pictures.

18. **Magnet.** Tape pictures on a cookie sheet. Glue small bar magnet to each card. Children attach cards to proper pictures.

19. **Fish.** Use same word cards as with 18. Here children "fish" in a bag or bowl for the cards with a fishing pole with a magnet for a "hook."

20. **Racing Game.** Make a race track divided into spaces. Use small toys or cars. Each card read from deck allows child to move down the track. (Do same to "climb" a mountain, stairway, or a beanstalk, to "slide" down a slide, to "land" a plane, to "score" a round of golf (have different par—words read—for different holes), or to "pull" feathers out of a turkey's tail.)

21. **Synonyms-Antonyms.** Make a chart with a list of words and adjoining spaces. Child puts synonym or antonym card into the spaces.

22. **Memory.** Players pick a card from the deck, look at it (or show it) momentarily, and place it face down. Players try to match it with one in their hands.

23. **Spin and Win.** Paste word cards on colored poker chips. Child uses a spinner, sees the color it indicates, and reads the matching poker chip.

24. **Ring Toss.** The number of the peg the ring lands on represents a deck of word cards. The higher the number, the more difficult the cards. Score equals number of cards read plus the number of the deck they came from.

25. **Basket Toss.** Same idea as 24. If children make a "basket" with a

bean bag they get a card to read. Vary this by tossing the bean bag onto squares with different numbers that refer to decks of cards.

26. **Riddle.** Write simple riddles on cards. Have pictures or other cards to answer them.

27. **Shoestring Match.** Use shoestrings of different colors. Attach the end of each string to a spot on a chart of the same color, and to a word, letter, etc., of the same color. Print a row of words, letters, etc., in black on the opposite side of the chart. Children insert a colored string into a hole alongside the black words. Then they turn the chart over to see if the color of the string pushed through matches the color surrounding the hole on the back side of the chart. Use for matching and contrasting.

28. **Look for Little Words.** Distribute deck of word cards face down evenly to players. Players in turn expose a word. They get a point for every little word they can read in the exposed multisyllabic word.

29. **Synonym (Antonym) Search.** Underline words in sentences written on a chart. Children find words from their decks as synonyms or antonyms.

30. **Mix and Match.** One child spreads out cards face down. Second child turns over cards one at a time, returning them face down, and tries to remember which cards are pairs.

31. **Pocketchart.** One child places cards face down in pocketchart, then shows a duplicate card for one of those so placed. Other children try to remember where the matching card is on the chart.

32. **Writing.** One child begins to print a word, pausing after each letter. Other children guess from cards in their hands what the word is.

33. **Pairs.** One child places cards face down in a pocketchart. One of the cards so placed matches another. Child who can recall the pairs wins.

34. **Thinking.** One child with a word card concealed from other children says, "I'm thinking of a word." Others guess what it is from cards they hold. They can ask questions, e.g., "Does it begin with a *b?*"

35. **Parts.** Distribute word-part cards. One child holds up one part of a

word. The child who can match it wins. Also played so that two parts make a word.

36. **Whistle or Hum.** Children begin by slowly turning over word cards from their decks. Teacher whistles or hums a familiar tune. When the music stops, each child must read the card turned over at that moment.

37. **Dominoes.** Play dominoes with words or word parts. Tape words on dominoes.

38. **Pegboard.** Cut up pegboard into 12" by 12" sizes. Each child plays with pegs of a different color. For each card read, child may place a peg. At end of game count to see who has the most pegs. Also played so that first child to finish a design wins.

39. **Tick-Tack-Toe.** Make a T–T–T design on a chart. Cover each space with a word card, face down. Begin by turning over a card. If read, place a colored chip on it. First to read three in a row wins.

40. **Scrabble.** Play with Scrabble pieces, or make these out of small ceramic tiles marked with a felt-tip pen.

41. **Word Wheels.** Staple together, at the center, two circles cut from tag paper. One circle is larger than the other. On the inner circle write letters or letter clusters. On the outer circle write phonograms. To play turn the inner wheel so that words are made.

42. **Baseball.** Construct a baseball diagram on a chart. The players move their "men" around the bases as they successfully read cards. A miss is an "out."

43. **Envelope.** Have children place pictures in envelopes or shoe boxes labeled with cards that represent the name or some part of the name of the picture.

44. **Spinner.** Construct a circle cut into colors or numbers with a spinner in the middle. (Children can also bring these from home.) Designate decks of cards as 1, 2, 3, etc., or as colors. Child spins and reads from deck indicated.

45. **Phonogram.** Deal four or more word cards to each child. First child reads a card. All other children who have that phonogram in any of their cards give those cards to the reader. Game ends when one child runs out of cards.

46. **Syllables.** Three cards are dealt out. On each a syllable is printed. Players draw and discard from a deck until they can make a two-syllable word.

47. **Syllable Racehorse.** Have three decks of cards. Each deck is made up of 1-, 2-, and 3-syllable words respectively. If children can read a word from a deck, they can move their "horses" around the track 1, 2, or 3 spaces.

48. **Affixes.** Child draws a card from a deck of root words and then from a deck of affixes. The winner is the one who can make the most words before the time runs out.

49. **Compounds.** The same game as 48 except each deck contains possible parts of a compound word.

50. **Choose.** Children pick a word card from a deck and read it if they can. Score is the number of words read in 10 tries plus the number of letters in each word read.

51. **Blankety-Blanks.** Play the same as 50 except there are blank cards in the deck. If a blank is drawn child gets to draw a card from an opponent's discard pile (one the opponent has already read).

52. **Rhymes.** Child chooses from a deck of cards, in turn with another child, until one gets two words that rhyme. A phonogram game.

53. **Challenge.** One player reads word card, for example, with five letters. If an opponent has a five-letter word, he or she reads it. Otherwise the opponent must draw and then challenge the first player.

54. **Blast-Off.** A child who reads the first ten word cards—10, 9, 8, 7 . . . 0—is the first to blast off a rocket.

55. **I Spy.** Display words. One child says, "I spy a *d* (for example)." Child wins who can guess what word this is.

56. **Lay an Egg.** Use egg cartons. First child to read 12 word cards fills up a carton and wins.

57. **Paper Clip.** Print words in a random order on a game board. Children throw two paper clips onto the board. They score a point for each word (letter, letter cluster, syllable) they can read (or spell).

58. **Change-Around.** Provide deck of cards with C–V–C spellings, e.g.,

can. By adding *e* to this word, pupils see if they can read a new word.

59. **Bowling.** Make up bowling score sheets.

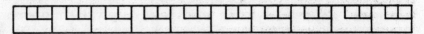

Each player reads a word card in the shape of a bowling pin and marks the number on the card onto a score sheet. Player with high score after 10 "frames" wins. Play with words of 2, 3, 4 . . . 9, or 10 letters. Depending on word, child can score 10 points.

60. **Maze.** Create a maze with several dead ends. Each time a word is read a child moves a space (or indicated spaces) through the maze. If a dead end is reached, player must retrace steps to get back on the right path.

61. **Function Words.** Write sentences on game boards in which function words are left out. From their packs of function words, children fill in the missing spaces.

62. **Who—What—When—Where.** Have four boxes labeled with these words. Players read a word card and get a point if they can put it into one of the four boxes. No points for words that will not fit.

INDEX